Actual Reviews from Amazon Readers on a previous book of Dr. Phyllis K. Walters called *The Christmas Slayings*

"...Wonderful book by Dr. Walters, she tells an amazing story that you won't want to put down. I look forward to future books from her."

"... Very interesting book and well written. My heart and prayers go out to all those involved."

"...Very well written and interesting. The author portrays how childhood abuse and family circumstance lead to a downhill cascade resulting in life in prison."

" Walters crafted the book so the reader could have the true life experience of interviewing people in jail."

"Therapists do more than evaluate clients, they help tell the whole story. It is a bonus when they can bring families together in unexpected ways. If you love true crime—try this one!"

Copyright Page

Editing and Design by: Paula F. Howard, A Howard Activity LLC
Cover Design by: Robert Hurley at TheWritersMall.com
ISBN: 9781736206126
PRINTED IN THE UNITED STATES OF AMERICA
KDP PUBLISHING

More copies may be ordered online at Amazon.com
or through https://www.TheWritersMall.com

WIVES WHO KILL

Based on True Stories
Phyllis K. Walters

DEDICATION

I dedicate this book to all survivors of rape, incest, domestic violence, human trafficking, and postpartum psychosis. My hope is for anyone who experiences these travesties not to suffer in silence but to seek out support and learn to live productive lives despite their suffering. My heart goes out to you.

ACKNOWLEDGEMENTS

First and foremost, I would like to acknowledge the love and support from my husband, Dan, as well as our large blended and extended family. Biology does not create a family. God has put us together for such a time as this, and His love unites us. No pandemic can sever our ties. I must add that we have suffered a great loss, in the untimely death of my great-niece, Heather Rapton. And more recently, our dear Christian brother, Ralph Bortone, who went to be with the Lord on November 09, 2020.

Please know whether you are simply part of my church family, The Villages neighborhood, close friends, old and new/ near and far, you matter enormously to me. I appreciate the prayers and encouragement you provide, day in and day out whether it be through personal contact, or by texts, e-mails, snail mail, social media such as Facebook and Instagram likes and comments, and phone calls. Everything is important to me.

I wish to express my sincere gratitude to my editor, Paula Howard, and my illustrator, Robert Hurley. I trust their judgment and feedback and hope the journey we have begun together will spill over into upcoming years. Thank you for partnering with me.

Additionally, I would like to recognize five of my friends who volunteered to read a significant portion of the "Wives Who Kill" unpublished manuscript. A big thanks to Christine Campbell, Sally Galliers, Penny Hyott, Debra Warner, and Carol Wren. Your time commitment, opinions, and comments meant a great deal, along with your suggestions that were implemented.

Lastly, I would like to thank my readers, those who have read my previous books and expressed the desire to read those that will follow. Your reviews on Amazon are extremely valuable. It touches my heart and utterly amazes me when you contact me for additional copies to gift to your family and friends. You are what I call my "accountability partners" . . . You give me reason to press on, tell my stories, and hopefully provide you with inspirational, spiritual, and mental challenges as well.

CAST OF CHARACTERS

(PART ONE)

The Sophie Jordan Story

Dr. Rosie Klein	Forensic Psychologist
Bucky Walker	U. Toledo Baseball Coach
Ruth Wayne	Dr. Klein's Office Manager
Judge Charles Lincoln	Friend of Bucky Walker
Sophie Washington	Defendant
Josh Greenburg	Defense Attorney- Sophie
Matthew Murphy	Prosecuting Attorney
Verna Mitchell	Corrections Officer
Trisha Small	Sophie's Neighbor
Megan Small	Daughter of Trisha
Madison Small	Daughter of Trisha
Petra Gonzalez	Sophie's Neighbor
Wes Hall	Investigative Reporter
Ron Thompson	FBI Agent
Stan Cink	School counselor

CAST OF CHARACTERS

(PART TWO)

The Hannah Fields Story

Dr. Rosie Klein	Forensic Psychologist
Bucky Walker	U. Toledo, Baseball Coach
Ruth Wayne	Dr. Klein's Office Manager
Hannah Fields	Defendant
John Chickalette	Defense Attorney-Hannah
Matthew Murphy	Prosecuting Attorney
James & Betty Michaels	Grandparents of Hannah
Ty Michaels	Uncle of Hannah
Jerry Fields	Husband of Hannah
Carly Pendleton	Best friend of Hannah
Lisa Turner	Vitim Witness Advocate and Chaplain
Dr. Argie Dyer	Prison Medic
Judge Joyce King	Presiding Judge of Panel
Wes Hall	Investigative Reporter
Ron Thompson	FBI Agent

TABLE OF CONTENTS

PART 1 - SOPHIE JORDAN STORY

TABLE OF CONTENTS

PART 2 - HANNAH FIELDS STORY

Part One

Sophie Jordan

CHAPTER ONE

THE THIRTEENTH FLOOR

Dr. Rosie Klein pushed the elevator button for the thirteenth floor. Good thing she was a brave soul. Most buildings skipped numbering a thirteenth floor for superstitious reasons. But Rosie never felt fear, just gratitude for being able to sublet Dr. Robert Seifer's suite one day a week in the downtown district to do her forensics work close to the courthouse.

"You don't care if it's on the 13th floor, Rosie?" she remembered him asking her when she signed the sublease contract.

"Not if you don't, Dr. Seifer. I'm happy you're willing to share this office space with me one day a week Will every Friday work for you?"

"Sure thing, Rosie. I'm glad to help you out when I'm not here anyway." His eyes were as kind as his words. She had always liked the man.

"My assistant, Ruth, stays at my Summerhill office. Your downtown space gives me access to meeting clients closer to the courthouse. It's a tremendous help." She smiled at the tall doctor who had become her friend over the years, even a mentor at times.

Since that day, she was occasionally startled when looking up from her notes, to see men hanging outside her windows so high up on the LaSalle Building, cleaning the glass.

I guess someone must do it, she thought. But these window washers sure have courage.

As soon as she entered her office, Rosie started a small pot of coffee to share with both her nine and ten o'clock clients. The narrow, waiting area was somewhat cluttered with a variety of reading material strewn on side tables, and no receptionist to keep things tidy.

Both her clients this morning were the "garden variety," or Park Avenue-type, as some would say. This type of woman was usually referred to Rosie by their own family practice doctor or gynecologist for one reason or another. Each one had a situation that needed encouragement or approval to help them move from being immobilized, to seeing their way clear to act. What she did was help guide their thinking to figure things out for themselves.

If actual therapy was needed, it might begin at an intense pace, but would eventually transition from acute care to strategic planning of how to cope.

Life is a process of becoming, Rosie thought. *Some people just need a little more help along the way.*

After seeing both her clients and faxing their information to Ruth at the Summerhill office, Rosie cleaned the pot, turned off the lights, and made her way back down to the lobby. Surprisingly, the elevator stopped only once . . . on the seventh floor where the largest criminal law firm in Lucas County was located.

"Good morning, Dr. Klein. How are you doing now that Angel Morgan is out of your care and concern?" Attorney John Chickalette greeted her as he entered the small enclosure and saw the "down" button was already engaged.

"I'm fine. And you, Mr. Chickalette?"

Since collaborating on her last case, the two were friendly after he represented Song Lee. Song, a trusted friend of Angel Morgan, her most recent client. Both young women had been affiliated with a gang who had murdered several people before Christmas last year. The slayings had resulted in life sentences for both women even although neither had touched a weapon. Song, the daughter of prosperous South Korean parents, had been on a music scholarship at the University of Toledo. Angel, on the other hand, had been homeless, a helpless young woman searching for acceptance. Yet they both ended up in the same place – prison.

"By the way, Rosie, I don't think I ever expressed my condolences on the loss of your husband. I don't often bump into you. Today must be the first time that I've seen you one-on-one, outside the halls of justice, in a while."

"Thank you. I appreciate your sentiments." The

elevator arrived on the ground floor and both Rosie and Attorney Chickalette stepped into the foyer.

"I'm heading to the Lucas County office building to meet with Joshua Greenberg. How about you?"

"I am heading to Judge Tucker's Court for a motion to suppress hearing. Mind if I walk along with you? If my case goes forward, I might need your expertise on a matter of competency and sanity. My young client was arrested on suspicion of attempting to murder her eight-month-old son. She's also being investigated for having previously murdered her young daughter. You and I both know that no mother's state of mind can be functioning correctly under those circumstances. The question becomes: why or why not."

" How awful. Of course, you can walk with me. I'm not sure that kind of case is one to have a happy ending. But I'll be happy to help in any way I can. Just give me a call when you decide when I can help." She looked at the ground. "I enjoy being downtown now that there's no sleet and snow left. The two-block walk to the County jail and office buildings was a bit hazardous this winter."

"By the way, mind if I call you Dr. Rosie?"

"I prefer just 'Rosie', as a matter of fact."

"Most people call me 'Chick.' One last question, Rosie. Where is your big, black, threatening dog? I've seen you walking with him upon occasion."

"Threatening, Chick? Ha! That's for appearances only. He's really a sweet, gentle companion. Sometimes he's with Ruth at my Summerhill office, but I don't expect to go back there this afternoon, so I left him home today. I'm consulting with Attorney Greenberg. Then heading home, most likely to review discovery materials on a case he hopes I will agree to take on as a new case.."

They reached the County office building and walked up the steps in unison. Once they passed through the security set-up just inside the doors, they bid each other good-bye.

At the last minute, Rosie decided not to mention that one of her dearest friends was married to Judge D.P. Tucker who would be hearing Chickalette's case. If she were to take on his case and evaluate his client, would that pose a conflict of interest? She pondered the thought briefly.

I'll cross that bridge when I come to it, she decided.

CHAPTER 2

A NEW CASE

"I know your last case upset you, Boss," Ruth said, bringing a hot cup of coffee over to Dr. Klein. She loved working for this forensic psychologist in Dayton, Ohio, and had been with her for years.

"Yes, it did, Ruth, but what can I say? Angel Morgan has been transported in handcuffs wearing her orange jumpsuit and paper-thin slippers, to the Ohio Reformatory for Women. It's likely she'll spend the remainder of her life behind bars with little contact from others outside those walls. Angel slipped through the cracks of the juvenile detention system and fell into a tragic, naive life of deception and crime. But all she ever wanted was to be loved. Don't we all?"

Ruth placed the steaming cup on the side table beside Rosie's chair and quietly left the office, returning to her desk in the outer office.

Rosie liked her coffee bold, but her main man gentle and kind and decided to call Bucky to see how his morning was developing. The sound of her boyfriend's voice would thrust her into a different mindset, one of hopefulness for their future. As she waited for him to answer, she scratched Jocko's head behind each ear. The big, dark gray labradoodle had given purpose to her life after her husband died, prior to her relationship with Bucky Walker.

"Top of the morning," Bucky answered in greeting. She couldn't see his face but pictured the happiness of his smile.

"Good morning to you, too, Sunshine. Checking to see if you can spring free for lunch. I can drive over to campus before my afternoon 'Marriage and Family' class. Did I thank you for getting me appointed by the Chairman of the Psychology Department to teach a couple of courses each term?"

"Yes, Rosie. You have thanked me half a dozen times. I know you will be extremely popular, particularly since you are the only psychologist in the department who sees couples and families for counseling. And yes, I will meet you in the faculty dining room for a quick bite to eat. Does 12:30 work?"

"I can make it work. My last morning client leaves my Summerhill office at noon. I will leave Jocko here with Ruth and pick him up after my class. See you soon."

***

"Hey, boss, Joshua Greenberg is on the line. I told him you were probably available for a brief conversation before your nine o'clock client. He was pleasant but sounded eager to talk to you."

"Okay, put him on the line. He is a nice guy."

"Hello, Doctor Rosie? This is Josh Greenberg. Can I have ten minutes of your precious time?"

"Absolutely. What's on your mind?"

"You can probably guess. I need your expertise on a battered woman's syndrome case, since you're a recognized expert in BWS. If you have the time and are interested, I would like to meet to discuss the case, and if you agree, then have you appointed by the Court for the case.I represent the defendant charged with the alleged murder of her husband."

"Fine, Josh. I'm in my downtown office tomorrow and have only two clients in the morning. I can come to your office at 11:15 or so."

"That works great with my schedule, Dr. Rosie. If you find the case to your liking, I can have the discovery packet duplicated for you. If Judge Brown approves, which I am sure she will since you are on her hit parade, you'll have access to the county jail. You can probably guess that's where my client is currently housed."

"Sounds like it'll undoubtedly be a complex case, as BWS cases are. See you tomorrow."

***

Rosie buzzed Ruth. "Ruth, you can bring Ash'Lee back and top off my coffee, if you don't mind. Do I hear her playing the piano in the waiting room? She is a breath of fresh air and you, my dear office manager, are a dedicated servant of God."

Ruth smiled to herself. She enjoyed her boss' praise. It always helped to be appreciated.

"I would be delighted. It is so nice to have you back in the office without constant interruptions. Between the phone ringing off the hook, the newspaper reporters with pen and pads in hand, and the television cameras perched on the blacktop driveway, like in your last case, I thought I would go insane. And we cannot have that, now, can we? It wouldn't be rational for a crazy office manager to be scheduling appointments for a renowned forensic psychologist, would it?

"That Angel Morgan case took all your energy, my energy, and created Jocko's confusion as to who were the good guys, and who he should protect you from. That was a crazy case. I'm hoping this next one will be more along the lines of normal – if normal is what we do."

CHAPTER 3

BUCKY WALKER

Driving to campus by way of Golden Gate Boulevard, Rosie was listening to praise music which always lifted her spirits, while anticipating lunch with Bucky. She couldn't believe she had become so enamored with someone after six simple dates. Not that she had not been looking for love, and she was definitely not starving for attention. Her career was fulfilling, and her friends offered ample support and socializing opportunities.

But, when Judge Lincoln had introduced her to Albert "Bucky" Walker, he had expected them to enjoy each other's company, not really become serious or engaged to be married. He and Bucky were childhood friends, mischievous like boys at times. Rosie had appeared in Judge Lincoln's Family Court on multiple cases of custody. They experienced a cordial but professional relationship. He knew she had been widowed for several years as had his friend Bucky.

That was one thing that had drawn them together: understanding what each had gone through by losing a mate. Bucky's affection seemed authentic, based on who she was and not on what he expected from a woman. Not being needy on her part was the best time to form a new friendship. It meant one was unlikely to settle for less than a mutually respectful and satisfying relationship. It meant not settling for crumbs, so to speak.

She pulled into the parking lot. Bucky was waiting at the entrance of the faculty dining room. Rosie could see his broad smile as she walked toward him. Quickening her pace, she could see his twinkling blue eyes smiling as she drew near. They acted more like professional colleagues rather than intimately involved, middle-aged adults. At least that's what it seemed like on the outside. Inside, she felt like a schoolgirl at times, enjoying the rush of new love.

"I see you made it without a problem. Did you get caught by the long light on the highway?"

"I drove the Boulevard instead. The flowers are in bloom and the color on the trees is magnificent. You can only see a little from the highway, but close up is better, don't you think?"

"Absolutely! That's one of the things I enjoy about you, your willingness to smell the roses. Or should I say tulips and daffodils?" They laughed together. It felt good.

They ordered soup and salad and chatted about nothing particularly important. The time passed too quickly. As they left the building for their respective offices on campus, they discreetly blew each other a kiss. Rosie smiled to herself. He really loves me.

"I'll call you tonight to solidify our weekend plans," Bucky whispered, "If that fits your agenda for the evening." Rosie answered that her date with Jocko would be over by dark. Jocko enjoyed trotting briskly in the evening air. Once around the condominium grounds resulted in a half mile walk beside his dedicated mistress.

Later that evening, Rosie realized she did some of her most creative thinking when she walked Jocko. The sounds of his nails clicking on the pavement seemed to be in rhythm with her rapid breathing. It reminded her of how out-of-shape she had become after losing her husband, and spending twelve-hour days sitting in her wingback chair while reading dockets. Sometimes, she paced in her cramped office space, or stretched while trying to unclutter her mind.

As she unleashed Jocko. and refilled his bowl with cool, fresh water, the telephone rang. "Oh, hi, Mom. How are you doing? I'm so glad you called. Would you like me to bring my boyfriend, Bucky, to Oakwood for Mother's Day weekend?" An image of her mother opened in her mind's eye: soft features, full head of gray hair always stylishly cut, late eighties, and healthy.

"I was wondering if your schedule was going to allow you to visit me this year. It's been such a lovely ritual. And, yes, I can hardly wait to meet your friend, Bucky," Mom sounded excited.

"Well, I must say, Mom, he's more than just a friend. We have a future planned, God willing. And yes, we will certainly come down next month. Are you doing okay? It's hard to believe we both became widowed in the same year. Three years have passed quickly though."

"I'm fine. My lady friends and I play Mahjong once a week. I play bridge at the Washington Township Rec Center each Thursday evening after swimming ten lengths of the pool. Oh, and I'm leading Bible study on Friday mornings at Washington Heights Church. Everyone there asks about you. Sounds like you are quite busy yourself, my dear."

"That's true, Mom. The young woman charged with murder was, in fact, found guilty and sentenced to life in prison. It was the most exhausting case of my entire career, physically, mentally, and emotionally. I explored so many facets of her life, even interviewed her siblings and the staff at the Juvenile Detention Center where she spent five years for grand theft auto. I read tons of material related to her school and criminal history. No one quite knows the whereabouts of her mother or the step-father who raped and impregnated her."

"Oh, my dear, Rosie. My heart goes out to you! It's hard to know you're working with such difficult cases. But you are strong and resilient. I should know, I'm your mother!"

Rose smiled, thinking of her childhood when her mother looked after all her needs.

"Not to change the subject too quickly, Rosie, but I wanted to thank you for the beautiful cut flower arrangement of exquisite white lilies, you sent for Easter. I knew you were in the middle of that awful case, so I did not want to call and bother you. For our Good Friday service, my friend, Barbara, and I washed each other's feet just like Christ did for his disciples. On Easter, I went to an outdoor sunrise service at Carillon Park. Pastor Dave gave a touching message, and the choir led by Dr. Page was magnificent."

"I'm so glad it was enjoyable, Mom. I should have called but will make it up to you on Mother's Day. We'll make reservations at the Oakdale Club for an early dinner. Right now, I've got to go. My other phone is ringing. Love you."

"Bye, Rosie. Be safe. Love you too."

***

"Hi, Bucky. Sorry I took so long to answer. My Mom was on the house phone. I haven't spoken to her since my Dad's birthday on February first. I always call her on that day to cheer her."

"No problem, Rosie. Is she doing okay?"

"Busy as a bee. Her friends and church activities are just what the doctor ordered by her beloved Dr. Bill, that is. I would really like for you to meet her. What about Mother's Day? Would you be able to take a drive with me to see her?"

"That would be really nice. I lost my mother and father in an automobile accident when I was thirty. You are blessed to have had your parents see your kids grow up, and now to have your mom still in your life."

"I guess we never got around to talking about our parents. I'm so sorry you lost them when you were so young and at the same time. Do you want to talk about it?"

"Let us talk this week-end if that's okay with you. There's a movie I would like to see on Friday night, then our church is having an outdoor music festival with performances of praise and worship groups along with food. That's unless you have any other ideas; that would be fine with me.

"What movie?"

"It's a Tom Hanks movie called 'Forrest Gump.' Have you heard about it, or seen the previews? They say Tom Hanks and Gary Sinise are amazing in their roles as soldiers."

"I have heard about it. Touching. Inspiring, I believe. I love movie popcorn with butter. How about you?"

"Absolutely. Good, then, I'll pick you up tomorrow at five-thirty so we can see the early showing. Our hot, fresh movie popcorn with butter can be an appetizer for a light supper after."

.   "Bucky, as far as the church festival goes, I would love to go. Is it in the afternoon on Saturday or evening?   I may have to review some materials this weekend. A lawyer called me about a new murder case. I'm meeting with him in the morning. If I agree to evaluate the defendant, I'll read what I need to complete before seeing the client in the county jail on Monday."

"That's what I like about you, Rosie, things just work out like an easy puzzle. Being with you is the best part of my day. See you at five-thirty. Get some rest now."

CHAPTER 4

SOPHIE'S STORY

"Good morning. May I help you?" The plump, blue-eyed, receptionist questioned. Her bronze name plate in the Public Defender's office displayed, "Receptionist", but not her name.

"Yes, thank you. I'm Dr. Rosie Klein and have an appointment with Joshua Greenberg."

"Of course, Dr. Klein. Mr. Greenberg said to show you right in. Do you care for some water or a late morning coffee and sweet roll, perhaps, as a picker-upper?"

"So, nice of you to offer. But, no, I'm fine," Rosie replied politely. She followed Attorney Greenberg's kind receptionist into his small, but unusually tidy office.

"Good morning Dr. Rosie. I really appreciate you making time for me on such short notice." Joshua Greenberg, tall and somewhat portly, stood up from his desk chair and came around to shake Rosie's hand. He beckoned for her to take a seat at a round, mahogany table with file folders stacked neatly in the center.

"Good morning to you as well. Thank you for inviting me in on your case. I understand it's a tragic one. Please tell me about it."

"Yes, a sad case. My client, Sophie Jordan, is a forty-eight-year-old, African American woman who was charmed by a thirty-five-year-old Muslim man. She's accused of shooting him, but whether it was justified, or not, is what I need you to help me determine."

"Well, a lot will depend on her frame of mind and details of the crime," Rosie said.

"Why don't you tell me about her background story?"

"Gladly. Well, she grew up in Oberlin, Ohio, and went to the school of hard knocks. Her mother was a house maid for Professor Peter Michaels, dean of students at Oberlin College. She never knew her father who was incarcerated for the rape of a college co-ed and died in prison from unknown causes.

"After the eighth grade, Sophie quit school to babysat full-time for Professor Michaels and his wife's children. She and her mother met the Professor at church where he was the acting music director. Sophie sang in the children's choir, and her mother played the organ. Eventually, the Professor turned Sophie in for stealing his wife's pearls.

"Can I interrupt a moment? Was that ethical for him to allow a young girl to quit school to work for him?"

"I don't know if he understood that she was not sixteen. Certainly, if he did know, it clearly would not be ethical to hire her."

"Getting back to the story: Sophie did steal the

pearls but explained to me that she wanted her poor mother to have something nice. They each had one simple dress to wear to church and wore farmer jeans from a thrift store for the rest of the week. Her mother was not aware Sophie had stolen the pearls, nor that they were real. She wore them to church that next Sunday, whereby Mrs. Michaels saw them, then realized her own pearls were missing.

"Sophie's mother was mortified. But soon after that, Professor Michaels dropped the charges against Sophie because his wife decided to forgive her. Sophie and her mother quickly moved to Mt. Vernon, Ohio.

"There, her mother married for a second time. This time, it was a widowed, Amish minister. They moved to his community just outside of town. Sophie baked pies with her mother and worked the fields for her stepfather, along with his large extended family.

"One day, in the corn fields, her oldest stepbrother pushed her down, and raped her. Soon after, she emptied her little stepbrother's piggy bank. She bought a bus ticket to Columbus, Ohio. There she met up with a boy she knew from church camp who seemed to like her. Brad and his family lived what appeared to be a happy life in the city.

"What Sophie didn't know was that this boy and his older brothers were thieves. They broke into houses of wealthy people to steal. The houses were always vacant for the winter while owners were staying in Florida. The boys stole checkbooks and wrote a multitude of small, bad checks that went mostly unnoticed by the owners for quite some time.

"But Sophie was not as lucky as they were. Brad, by now her boyfriend, told her to go into Walmart, one day, and buy an expensive camera with one of the bad checks. He planned to pawn it within an hour of the purchase. Now, she had no identification, and the clerk suspected the check was fraudulent. So, as she exited the store, a security guard arrested her while her boyfriend drove away and left her there."

"I'm beginning to see a pattern for this young woman's life," Rosie said. "Please go on."

"Sophie served time until she turned eighteen. And, when she was released, the friends she had made in the Columbus Juvenile Detention Center were out on the streets by then, easy to find. They remembered her and welcomed her into their gang.

"That's when her life of crime began in earnest. At first, it consisted of stealing food to survive. But ultimately, she turned to prostitution which led to pimps who pumped her with drugs to comply with their demands. This life of prostitution and drugs went on for years. Even though she spent some of those years clean and sober while in prison for some minor thing or another. She also spent numerous stints in residential drug rehabilitation programs and halfway houses for women. But she always relapsed.

"The only program that ever gave her hope was Ana's House. It was a Christian treatment program for alcohol and drug addiction. She participated in Bible studies, a Christian twelve step addiction program, anger management, and financial management. She lived there for two years and for the first time, Sophie believed in herself."

"Too bad her story doesn't end there," Rosie interrupted. "I know how good such a Christian program can have on influencing a change in one's life. But I also know that because I'm here talking to you, this time in her life didn't last. Right?"

"Exactly," Chickalette said. "A Christian couple, Mr., and Mrs. Lambert mentored her while she was in Ana's house. They bought her clothes and invited her for holiday dinners. They gave her a Bible with her name inscribed in it and to this day she has kept it. As she was about to turn forty, they invited her to live with them in nearby Gambier, Ohio, until she could get back on her feet.

"One night, after a local church Bible study, a well-dressed, well-groomed man pulled up to the curb in a late model Mercedes. He asked her if she needed a job to which she responded, 'yes'. He told her he could provide her with a fresh start, if she would come with him to Toledo and take care of his small boys. He described himself as a businessman and widower. Sophie jumped at the chance for a new beginning, and off they went.

"But her fresh start didn't take long to reveal itself. Within two and a half-hours, she discovered herself in bondage to a wicked, mean-spirited human being. Now, she clutched her Bible and prayed for what her future would hold. By the way, Rosie, do you need a break or something to drink?"

"Thank you, Josh, but no, I'm fine. Keep going.

What a tragic story."

"Right, well, when I first met Sophie, she told me how much she longed for her mother. But, by then, she didn't know how to locate her. The widower, Farid Jordan, did have two little boys, Ali and Omar, and Sophie became fond of them. He drove them to school in the morning and she would walk to the school every afternoon and hike back home with them. She was expected to cook whatever food Farid made available to them, clean the shabby little house, and keep the boys clean too. Her bed was a mattress on the floor in the corner of the pantry. After the boys went to sleep, Farid would shove her upstairs to his bedroom and force her to have sex. He never kissed her or took his own clothes off. She would then retreat to her mattress and weep. Not exactly sure what kind of life she was living, Sophie knew, at least, this was not love.

"Then came the day, Farid told her she had to begin carrying her own weight. He told her to get a job where she could work while the kids were in school. She walked up the street and got a job as a nurse's aide at Crystal Manor nursing home. A good thing that came out of this was that the social worker, Doris Simpson, allowed her to study for her GED during her lunch hour. Farid never knew. But Farid controlled all money received. He, also, encouraged her to work overtime and on weekends, even though she received no benefits. As soon as he could manage, he stopped going to work himself, making Sophie the sole bread winner. She suspected he was conducting illegal business from their home but could never prove it.

"Then the cycle of violence began. First, there was emotional abuse such as name calling and labeling. He called her 'ugly', 'fat', and 'stupid.' He labeled her a 'slut', 'whore', 'nigger', and a useless wife. He began getting in her face and punching her in the sternum with his fist. At times he had her lie down on her mattress and he would beat her across the back, hips, and thighs with his belt. None of these wounds or bruises were visible to those with whom she worked. Her uniforms covered them as planned by this vicious, brutal man. His sons never heard or saw any of the violence. After supper, he made them play outside until bedtime."

"This man could be a case study by himself," Rosie said. "It would be interesting to know where his own abuse began. Unless it was simply within his personality.'"

"Right. Well, one day, the kind, concerned social worker, Miss Simpson, asked her: 'Sophie how are you doing?' By now, she looked awful with circles under her eyes, dirty stringy hair and nails bitten down to the quick. She often had to scrub her own hands and nails prior to assisting any resident with their hygiene routines. But Sophie answered, 'I'm okay, Miss Simpson,' even though it wasn't true.

"But because of the tenderness expressed by this caring woman, Sophie then broke down and sobbed. She couldn't tell everything for fear of being seriously injured at home if Farid heard she had talked to anybody about his treatment of her. But this one kindness and concern made the walls gradually start coming down. Miss

Simpson eventually referred her for counseling at a nearby agency. She arranged for Sophie to see Maria Lopez on her Wednesday's lunch breaks, then return to work with no one else knowing.

"Then, Farid began going out in the evenings. He was Muslim but did not practice his religion or daily religious rites. One night, on his way out the door, he casually asked Sophie, 'Where do you have lunch on Wednesdays?'

"She replied, 'What do you mean?' This infuriated him, but he said they would discuss it later when he got home that night, which they did. He made her get into a filthy tub of ice-cold water. Then, he held her head under water with his hands around her throat. When he finally released her, he demanded again: 'Where do you have lunch on Wednesdays!'

"That was the end of counseling. But this time, there were marks showing on her neck, and she was ashamed to tell Miss Simpson, so she simply walked away from her job.

"Now, because she was paid every other week, she figured it would be two weeks before Farid would know she had quit. So, every morning, she continued to walk out the door and go sit in the park or at the library, then return home as expected each evening.

"Sometime during the second week, Farid told her he was going to bring home a second wife. He told her that nothing would change except the new wife would share his bed. Sophie felt relieved, in some ways, but hatred swelled and her fear to speak out became overwhelming.

"That night, she came home and noticed a gun placed on the coffee table in front of where Farid sat. She assumed he had figured out she was not going to work. He saw her enter and demanded she get upstairs immediately. Nothing was said about her job. He shoved her onto his bed, turned her over with her face in the pillow, and savagely raped her.

"The pillow muffled her cries of anguish. Blood splattered on the sheets and his pants. He rose from the bed, changed into a pair of sweatpants, and ordered her to get downstairs and fix some food. Sophie wiped tears from her face, pulled her blood-stained pants up, and went downstairs to do as she was told.

"The next afternoon, as she approached the house with the boys, she saw a black Nissan pull out of her driveway. The windows were tinted so she couldn't see who was inside. The boys stayed outside as usual, but she entered the home. As she began to boil water for rice, Sophie noticed the gun still on the coffee table in the living room. She wondered why Farid had a weapon like that in plain sight. Was he attempting to intimidate her? Farid entered the room and casually sat down in his chair, flipping on the evening news.

"Most Muslims do not drink, but he popped the tab on his Budweiser and hollered for her to take away three other empty cans. He then put his bare feet up on the coffee table with his legs crossed at the ankles. Apparently, he soon dozed off with the can still in his hand and TV blaring.

"At that point, Sophie's mind flashed back to the

agonizing pain of the rape and the terrifying feeling of being nearly drowned in the tub. She walked around to stand in front of him and looked into the sleeping face of this man who had caused her so much anguish.

"Then, Sophie picked up the gun and shot him point blank in the chest three times. Gasping, she paused a second before tossing the gun onto the table, as she realized what she had done. She backed away and immediately, dialed 911, then called her own son, Adam, with whom she had recently reconnected, even though they had not talked in weeks. Farid had allowed no phone calls from home and her son's job prevented them from talking during work hours.

Adam knew from the sound of her muffled voice that he should get to her as soon as possible. Years before, he had been adopted at birth and only recently had found her while searching for his birth mother who was Sophie. Now, she was calling him in her desperation.

"Since it was still light outside, Farid's boys were hanging out with some neighbor friends in the yard. They neither saw nor heard any noises from the house. Sophie threw the bolt and locked them out but stood just inside the door waiting for the cops and Adam to arrive.

"Everyone pulled up to the house simultaneously. And that's her story, Rosie, at least to the best of her ability to remember. I, for one, believe it's true. I, also think she's still in shock."

"This leaves me speechless, Josh. I suppose there are no school records for me to review. What's her maiden name? What about medical records before she met him and during their marriage? Did Sophie ever end up in the emergency room, or falsify the cause of her injuries?"

"Incredibly good questions, Rosie, very astute. I don't recall medical records in the discovery packet. But unless they were requested, there would be none. One of us should ask Sophie about that."

"If I have Court approval, I will review the material this week-end and go see her on Monday afternoon. I can rearrange my schedule with no problem. You probably won't see her before Monday, will you?" Rosie asked.

"No. I have no plans to go over. I will provide you with anything you need. Because she moved around the State of Ohio, some records might take more time."

"Josh let's try to find her elementary school records. We can learn a lot from her attendance, behavior, standardized test scores, and grades. You said she went to school in Oberlin?"

"Yes, and they lived there for a while after she quit school, too."

"I wonder if Professor Michaels is still alive, and around. I would also like to track down the pastor from her church, the administrator of Ana's House, and Mr. and Mrs. Lambert, for sure. Then we have the social worker at Crystal Manor, Doris Simpson, and the counselor, Maria Lopez, whom she saw secretly. Collateral interviews are immensely helpful in developing a complete picture of a defendant. Is her son,

Adam, available to be interviewed?"

"I believe so. Well, you certainly are known for your thoroughness, Rosie, now I see why. My colleagues have expressed real admiration about your conscientiousness and professionalism. I look forward to your findings. Let me know when you have seen her."

Rosie thanked him and rose to leave. "This is quite an interesting background story. Let's see where it all takes us. Thank you for your time. I'll get to work immediately."

Chickalette handed her the discovery packet and escorted her to the door.

"I look forward to hearing what you find."

CHAPTER 5

A PROPOSAL

Meeting Bucky for the movie date made Rosie happy. It took her mind off Sophie's tragic story. After the movie, rated five stars and requiring five hankies for her, they meandered silently back to the car arm in arm.

She was lost in thought about the movie and what rating she would give it based on a system she and her friend, Linda, had developed. They had begun rating movies by their content and emotional appeal a while ago. Then Bucky broke the silence.

"Rosie, your mind has wandered. Is your stomach still hungry after all the popcorn and coffee you drank?"

"Absolutely. I could go for a cheeseburger and a chocolate shake. You?"

"I will treat you to exactly what you crave at the Burger Bistro, okay? It' a campus hot spot but should not be too busy this early on a Friday evening."

Seated across from one another at a window booth with red leather upholstery and a miniature juke box; it was comfortable and seemed like a perfect spot to relax and chat. The server, one of Bucky's university baseball players, took their order and vowed to bring the shakes back ASAP.

Bucky talked about the film, but Rosie noticed he was a little distracted as if something else was on his mind. Nevertheless, he plunged ahead and inquired about the ratings.

"First things first, Rosie. Why did you and Linda ever decide to rate movies?"

"Well, we figured it would add value to the fact that we were skipping out of work to go see Wednesday matinees. At just three dollars, it was cheap and it broke up our work week. At least by giving the movie a rating, we felt we were getting something accomplished and not just wasting an afternoon."

"That's innocent fun. Now may I tell you what else is on my mind?"

"Of course, Bucky, please go ahead."

Bucky cupped Rosie's face with both hands and looked deeply into her brown eyes. He didn't seem nervous exactly, but she could tell his next words were going to hold a lot of meaning.

"You recall inviting me to go to St. Maarten in November, right? And since you won the villa at the charity golf outing, I offered to spring for the airline tickets, right? Well, there is one more little matter that needs to be discussed. I realize this is not exactly the most romantic setting to talk about it, but... let's get married there... on the beach. How do you feel about that?"

Married, she thought. Her eyes widened as she turned the volume down on the little jukebox that was playing Elvis' song, "Can't Help Falling in Love with You" at that exact moment.

"Why, Bucky Walker, I knew you were extremely romantic, but this takes the cake. Yes. I would be delighted to marry you on the beach in St. Maarten."

A broad smile take over his face as he squeezed her hands and gently kissed her on the lips.

"You have just made me a very happy man, Rosie Klein."

"And you have made me a happy woman, Bucky Walter."

The French side of St. Maarten Island is known for delectable restaurants and sparkling, blue-water beaches, and an idea came to her.

"You know, Bucky, we can walk barefoot on the beach, then head over to the Dutch side for some fun at the gambling casinos and even open-air shopping."

"You know, Rosie, the Island has some quaint, little jewelry shops too. We can pick out your diamond ring there if you don't mind waiting."

"That's a great idea. We can select your wedding band there, too, Bucky. Would you like to have a small reception when we get back? We have lots of time to decide who to invite and where to hold it, right? Oh, and there is one more thing . . . and this is important to me: will you take ballroom dance lessons so our first dance can be a sweet little waltz? I really like Anne Murray's song, "Can I have this dance for the rest of my life?"

"I will be thrilled to take dance lessons for you. Don't forget, I need golf lessons this summer, too, so next time there is a charity golf tournament, I won't be selling tickets. No, sir, I will be a participant."

The rest of the meal was pleasant and memorable as the feeling of belonging to each other took hold. Rosie began realizing that she would be spending the rest of her life with this wonderful man. As they were ready to leave, Bucky motioned to the young waiter.

"Let me re-introduce you to our server on the way out. Sean, can we have our check now.? Remember meeting Sean Simmons and his parents at the Meet and Greet, Rosie?"

"Why yes, I'm sorry. I didn't recognize you with that white server's hat instead of a University of Toledo baseball cap. You're that great pitcher. How are you?"

"I'm fine, thanks. Coach, the guys are all happy for your promotion, but we'll miss your support and leadership. We just wanted you to know."

"I won't miss a game with you guys, Sean. Being Athletic Director means I will be there at home and on the road."

"Well, have a nice evening, Coach, and Dr. Rosie. Ahh, Coach Walker, what should I call you??"

"That is up to you, Sean. My friends call me 'Bucky' and I won't be offended if you do, too."

"Oh, and one last thing, Dr. Rosie. I'm taking your Marriage class in the fall. Isn't that cool?"

"It is, but are you trying to tell us something, Sean?" she asked with curiosity.

"No. . . No marriage for me until I'm established in a career and own a home. I just need one more elective and thought your course would be interesting."

"Good thinking, Sean. Well, thank you for your service tonight. See you soon."

The ride to Rosie's condo was peaceful.

"Even though this is a most happy occasion, I need to share some sad news with you about my new case. Would you mind coming in for a night cap and listening to my tale of woe?"

***

Pulling up to her condo, they could see two little black eyes peeking out of the front window between the blinds. His nose was pressed against the windowpane. No sound could be heard. But once they were inside, Jocko's tail began wagging, and he began to whimper.

"I think before we have our drink, my companion needs to go for a walk."

"Let me go with you. We have something to tell Jocko, don't you think?"

They walked out through the patio doors and for the first time, Jocko barked. The night was still young, the moon was full, and the North star sparkled brightly. It occurred to Rosie how lucky she was to have her two main squeezes together on this beautiful night.

They kissed in the moonlight. When Jocko pulled on the leash, they smiled at each other.

"So now what kind of nightcap do you prefer? Irish cream and decaf coffee or a cold drink?"

"Whatever is easier for you, Rosie."

"In that case, Bailey's on the rocks and no coffee. I need to tell you about the case of Sophie Jordan vs. State of Ohio. I plan to use the time we are not together this weekend to review materials and then see her at the County Jail on Monday afternoon."

"Okay," said Bucky as he took his Baileys from her hand and sat down on the loveseat. He patted the seat beside him for Rosie to join him. Jocko assumed his position at Bucky's feet.

"I don't want you to think I get emotionally involved with every murder case. This year has been exceptional. First, Angel Morgan was convicted when she never shot anyone, and now Sophie has to defend herself after shooting a man who raped and brutalized her for years."

"I understand. I don't see you as less objective or professional just because you feel compassion and want justice to be served."

"Thank you for understanding me."

Then, she proceeded to share the details as she had heard them from Attorney Greenberg. She told Bucky of her plan to solicit childhood school records and medical records and explained the importance of speaking with people who had known this defendant from childhood until her arrest.

"Wow. I can't imagine how you do your job, Rosie. How do you keep from being depressed or outraged at the outcomes of the trials?"

" I must admit. It is already a lot easier to separate my private life from my professional life now that you are such an important part of my future."

"I vow to do whatever I can in my power to keep the love of my life, relaxed and content."

As Bucky rose to leave, he took her face again in his hands, kissed her gently on the lips, and reminded her of the church festival tomorrow afternoon. As they walked to the front door, Jocko was not far behind. She watched him walk down the pathway.

There goes my soon-to-be-husband, she thought as a happy flutter stirred inside.

Walking back to the loveseat, she clicked on the eleven o'clock local news. There was the replay of the arrest of Sophie Jordan. The photographer caught Officer Kearns guiding a handcuffed Sophie to the patrol car. There had to be fifteen witnesses standing at the foot of the driveway, including the little boys, Ali and Omar, staring wide-eyed at everything.

She considered drinking some caffeine and staying up to begin reviewing case materials, but instead, shut off the TV and went to the bedroom to read something inspirational and write in her gratitude journal. She would write at least five things to be grateful for on this day that would be forever marked in her heart.

"I am truly grateful this day is over. And yet what a absolutely remarkable day it was!"

CHAPTER 6

ARREST DETAILS

Rosie grabbed a coffee and seated herself at the dining room table where she could spread out materials of Sophie's case. She positioned a notebook, pen, and yellow highlighter to her right and began reviewing the arrest reports and witness statements.

Along with the arresting officers' names, she jotted down contact information of Sophie's son, Adam, and the minor children of the deceased. Collateral interviews were going to be extremely important in establishing motive, mental state at the time of the shooting, and purpose for killing the man she stated was her batterer.

Rosie highlighted the names of neighbors who lived on either side of the Jordan house and read their written statements. In addition to Petra Gonzalez, who took the boys on the night of the murder to shelter them until Children's Protective Services arrived, there was a neighbor lady on the other side, a widow by the name of Trisha Small. Rosie also noted their phone numbers as well as identifying information of Sophie's son, Adam.

As she worked, a thought of her friend Wes Hall came to Rosie's mind. He was a great investigative reporter. On the day they first met, she had noticed him sitting in the Courtroom taking notes from her testimony. When the Judge called a fifteen-minute recess, she tracked Wes down in the corridor and introduced herself. He explained his role and said how pleased he was to meet her personally.

In the years following, she felt no hesitancy in calling on Wes to check out something or someone for her. In most cases, he would return with more information than she needed, or desired. In the case of Sophie Jordan, she planned to ask him to travel to Oberlin, Mount Vernon, Columbus, Toledo, and Gambier, to validate facts provided by Sophie regarding her life. Rosie would be willing to accompany him as her schedule allowed. This verification process was necessary, and she was glad Wes was there to help her.

Eventually, Rosie stood and stretched. She fixed a raisin bagel with cream cheese, refilled her coffee, picked up the phone and called Wes.

"Hi, Wes. Are you somewhere you can chat a few minutes?"

"Yes, Rosie. I always have time for you. My wife is at a soccer game with our daughter and I'm reading the Toledo Blade. What prompts you to call on a Saturday morning?"

"Joshua Greenberg filed a motion for me to evaluate Sophie Jordan. Judge Kate Brown approved it on the spot. I believe Sophie was a battered wife and suffered from Battered Women's Syndrome at the time of the shooting. Have you heard of her case?"

"Of course, it was all over the eleven o'clock news the night she was arrested. The media portrayed her as a cold-blooded killer. If that's true, what exactly do you need me to do?"

"She moved around the state from the eighth grade on. As you may suspect, I want to locate character witnesses. Can we have lunch on Tuesday, so I can fill you in? I'm reading the discovery material this morning and seeing her for the first time on Monday afternoon."

"Tuesday works fine. How about if we meet somewhere between your Summerhill office and the downtown newspaper office? Mancy's is quiet and gives us space to spread out. I assume you have paperwork to show me."

"I love Mancy's. How about 11:30 to beat the crowd? It's a popular place."

"Okay, see you there, Rosie. Good luck with your first contact with Sophie. She seems a bit rough and tumble."

"Where does that opinion come from?"

"Just my own since I observed her in the courtroom in front of Judge Brown who's known to be the compassionate judge. I thought she acted kind of rude. When asked how she would like to plead, she kept her head down, avoided eye contact, and pleaded 'not guilty.' But her demeanor was less than humble, you might say. Her attorney, Greenberg, seems very caring."

"I agree on both accounts. Judge Brown sentenced

my last defendant, Angel Morgan, to life sentences now being served concurrently, which means she may get out after thirty years. So, the judge tried to be as lenient as possible. And Joshua Greenberg seemed to be really taking an interest in Sophie's case. So, we'll see how it goes. Well, that's it for now, I'll see you on Tuesday, Wes."

***

Rosie turned on a selection of soft jazz and dove into the arrest reports:

The officers' names were Sgt. Jimmy Zee and Officer Suzanne Kearns. Each wrote a version of the arrest that basically confirmed the story put forth by the other. According to Sgt. Zee, the 911 operator told them there was a "domestic situation" at 7552 Georgetown Avenue. Officer Kearns' report stated the operator said there was "a shooting" reported at that address, a minor discrepancy.

Upon arrival, both officers agreed Sophie was standing just inside the door and turned the lock to allow them in. Officer Kearns stated that Sophie crumbled to the floor at her feet. Sgt. Zee described Sophie as pointing to the body of Farid Jordan. He was reclined in his chair with his head down, appearing unconscious with a chest wound.

Officer Kearns called for the EMT's while Sgt. Zee checked the victim for a pulse. He reported there was none. They did not touch the weapon, visible on the coffee table. The evidence crew would be coming to the crime scene and never wanted anything touched or moved prior to their arrival. Officer Kearns handed Sophie a tissue and led her by the arm to a chair at the dining room table.

At that point, no one knew, yet, who the perpetrator was. Sgt. Zee asked Sophie to tell them what happened. Sophie said she shot him for raping and beating her because she just "couldn't take it anymore." Officer Kearns then told Sophie she would read her Miranda rights in case she wanted a lawyer present. But Sophie signed a waiver and agreed to talk without one.

Soon after the paramedics arrived, they pronounced Farid dead at the scene. Sophie was then handcuffed and led out to the patrol car by Sgt. Zee. Officer Kearns noticed a crowd had formed and was surrounding the Jordan children. She asked the next-door neighbor, who identified herself as Petra Gonzalez, to take Ali and Omar inside her house, so they could avoid seeing their father's body removed from the house in a body bag. Officer Kearns wrote down the woman's name and contact information.

She quickly called Children's Protective Services to pick the boys up. Then, joined her partner in the patrol car, and they drove Sophie to the police station to be fingerprinted, photographed, and booked for murder.

At that point, Detective Danny Woodward joined them to interrogate the defendant. From what Dr. Rosie knew of him, Detective Woodward was a seasoned law officer, coming through the ranks from street cop to detective. In his fifteen years in the department he had seen and heard it all. Rosie perceived him to be cynical and opinionated. Probably from a hardening of the human spirit after seeing so much tragedy in his daily work.

Rosie took a break from her reading to pour a third cup of hot coffee. She hated it warm. Hot coffee should be hot, and cold coffee cold, she reasoned to herself. Up to this point, her notes had no contact phone numbers for the important follow-ups she intended to pursue.

I wonder why Detective Woodward doesn't have a partner with him, she mused. *Don't cops always work with a partner?*

She turned to the report submitted by Sgt. Jimmy Zee. Rosie had heard Sgt. Zee testify before a jury just last month. It was related to a case of less magnitude, a home invasion burglary, but she thought he was thorough and stuck to the facts as he knew them. He had impressed her.

Now she read his written report stating his version of the facts surrounding this tragic incident. Some facts were related to both his, and his partner's, responses to the 911 call. Other information was taken from the version of events provided to him by the defendant. Sgt. Zee stated he read her the Miranda rights used to inform a defendant that anything said could and would be used against them in a court of law. Also, that she had the right to an attorney present if she didn't want to talk further. She told him she had no money for an attorney. At which time, Sgt. Zee informed her that an attorney would be appointed to represent her at no cost to her once she was charged. Sophie told him she understood, he reported, but decided to sign away her rights, and agreed to talk to him without an attorney present.

After the two officers took her statement, Sophie was transported to the County jail without incident.

Next, Rosie read the report rendered by Officer Suzanne Kearns. Rosie had never met Officer Kearns but had the impression she was more open to pursuing the truth than just closing the book on this tragic case. Obviously, rendering a confession tends to create the impression of guilt. Officer Kearns mentioned the name and telephone number of the neighbor to whom she gave the children. Her version of the events was identical to her partner, Sgt. Zee's, apart from her additional statement that "…she was cooperative, but difficult to hear with her head down, and the intermittent sounds of her sobs."

Detective Danny Woodward's report stated that he arrived at the crime scene along with the crime scene investigators. He saw a weapon on the table in front of the body of Farid Jordan but did not see the defendant. He presumed it was the murder weapon used in the commission of the crime. He also reported arriving at the County Jail in time to speak with the police officers identified as Sgt. Zee and Officer Kearns.

Usually, the police officers are released at the point of a detective taking over the interrogation. But as she read, Rosie questioned whether one or both police officers sat in the same room during the interview of the defendant, or did they observe Detective Woodward's interrogation through a one-way window? She jotted down that question to ask them later if she, in fact, decided to interview them.

She also asked herself: Why was Detective Woodward without his partner? The question kept nagging at her and she intended to find out.

Sophie Jordan's version of events was consistent, as recorded in all three reports. She had added more detail based upon questions posed to her by Officer Kearns.

In her statement, she told both officers the story of the marriage, the rape, the near drowning, and the beatings leading up to her action of shooting him. She had never planned to kill him but, when she saw the gun and him asleep in the chair, something inside of her "just snapped" and she impulsively grabbed the gun for an opportunity to "escape her misery."

At the police station, when interrogated by Detective Woodward, she simply admitted to shooting "because she couldn't take it anymore." Detective Woodward didn't ask her "why?" and she didn't offer a full explanation as she had given to the two officers.

Woodward didn't press, so he never heard the full story. Maybe she just got tired of thinking about her misery.

CHAPTER 7

THE CHURCH FESTIVAL

Rosie answered the knock at the door to find "Indiana Jones"standing there – only it wasn't.

"Bucky! Ha, you look great!" she opened the door wider for him to enter the foyer.

He stood there in his Indiana Jones hat, button-down collar, light blue oxford shirt with sleeves rolled up just below his elbows, cargo pants, and brown dock-siders. She closed the door and took his arm.

"I'm looking forward to this," she smiled. They were leaving for the Spring outdoor festival at Bucky's church. Thoughts of Sophie and tragedy would soon be replaced by fresh air and laughter. Rosie had on a red boatneck shirt with navy jeans, her University of Toledo baseball cap, sunglasses, and dangling silver earrings. With a sigh of relief, she turned her thoughts and attention solely to the here-and-now.

Arriving at the church, booths displayed with handmade crafts were in neat rows. Homemade food, and freshly baked pastries were positioned around the parking lot in a horseshoe fashion. Visitors parked at an adjacent church's blacktop lot which was allowing its premises to be used. Rosie was drawn to the handmade jewelry while Bucky was drawn to the sweet-smelling Apple strudel. He meandered around with Rosie, pausing wherever she did, but kept the location of the Apple strudel booth in mind.

"Just wondering if you prefer cherry to apple strudel like my mom did," he asked.

"Oh, I'm not sure," she answered. "It'll depend on the aromas when we get there."

"Maybe you should have one of each. The more you eat, the more we'll donate to the charity our church supports," he said. "It's called the Saint Anthony's Children's Home also known as The Toledo Orphanage, Rosie."

"Really? That's where two of Angel Morgan's friends lived. Remember the case I handled with Sam and April who befriended Angel? Sam was four years older than April and looked after her when she was little. He graduated, then became a marine. When she graduated, he invited her to work on Hilton Head Island for the Summer where they met the Korean girl, Song."

"Yes, Rosie that was a sad case. But I never associated Sam and April with Saint Anthony's. I can guarantee their upbringing by the nuns was loving and caring. Too bad Sam couldn't have stayed there and attended college. He might have been one of my athletes. If he was fit enough to become a marine, you can figure he could also have been a ballplayer. But the law is the law...eighteen and out! Out of the system and into the world alone."

"Sad but true. That's when so many get into

trouble – when they're starting their lives but, make some early bad decisions. All those senseless lives lost, including Sam and April, at the hands of two troubled young men," Rosie said. "But enough of that. I say, we try to enjoy this sunshine and contribute to the cause by doing a little shopping. What do you think? Have I kept you away from the strudel booth too long?"

"Not at all. And the least I can do is buy you a little something, maybe a friendship ring or necklace until we get to St. Maarten."

"Friendship ring? Why Bucky Walters, I think we're past that, don't you?"

Even so, a sapphire pinky ring caught Rosie's eye. The stone was artificial, but she loved it and he bought it. They returned to the strudel booth to order pastries. Next to that one was a Boston Stoker coffee tent. Rosie ordered her coffee, black and Bucky ordered a soy latte. Walking across the aisle, they seated themselves at a small wrought iron table beneath a red umbrella.

"How's this spot? Are you comfortable?"

"Absolutely. Do you enjoy sitting in the sun, Bucky? There is so much we don't know about one another, our likes and dislikes."

"And desires, Rosie. Don't forget about desires."

They both laughed. "To answer your question, Rosie, I enjoy sitting in the sun if I am near water. I like to nap, read, nap, people watch, jump in the water to cool off, and did I mention 'nap'? How about you?"

"When I was a girl, I was a sun-worshipper. Our moms would take turns driving my friends and me to a stone quarry filled with cold, clean, clear spring water. The one we liked best that our parents approved was called 'Centennial.' There were concession stands and lifeguards. Usually, we walked down cement steps to ease our way into the water with time to adjust to the cold temperature. Then, we'd swim out to wooden rafts where we'd sit or stretch out and just talk. Occasionally, we took a dare and dove in from a thirty-foot ledge we called 'Suicide.'

"That sounds scary."

"Well, I didn't dive. I jumped straight down, feet first, which hurt my ankles when I landed abruptly in the water. My friends who dove said it hurt their backs."

"Are you saying you did risky stuff on a dare? I would never have pictured you as a daredevil, Rosie, even though I can see why that's a fond memory. What do you mean about it being the quarry approved by your parents? Were there others?"

"There were places with no lifeguards, no food or drink stands, and no rafts. That's where we dove into the water from small boulders along the shoreline. But we didn't begin going to those places until we were old enough to drive ourselves. Those quarries were ten miles out of town. Part of our motivation was to make new friends from other schools. I was attracted to guys who were already out of high school and once made a friend who was ten years older. He was a teacher. A couple of summers we met up there and spent time talking. Eight years later when I divorced, he ended up living down the street from my apartment. We ate dinner together a few times just to keep each other company. But it never was anything romantic."

As they finished eating, a thought came to Rosie.

"Bucky, I hate to break up our party, but I need to get home and read the discovery material. Do you mind? Would you like to come over tomorrow night for salad and pizza?"

"I don't mind, and yes, I would love to come over for dinner tomorrow. I will bring the pizza and a bottle of Chianti. Can you make us a simple salad?"

"It'll be the absolute best, you've ever known."

CHAPTER 8

SOPHIE: FIRST INTERVIEW

Rosie flashed the court order, tossed her briefcase on the conveyor belt, and stepped through the metal detector. She had already shown the deputy her ID and announced who she was there to see. As soon as she retrieved her briefcase, she headed for the locked doors.

Approaching the first one, she heard the lock release allowing her to open it. She stepped through and stood facing forward until she heard the second door release. After opening that one, she walked through and straight toward the Deputy who sets up rooms for professional visits.

"Good afternoon, Deputy Poole. How are you? I'm here to see Sophie Jordan this time."

Deputy Poole recognized Dr. Rosie from numerous previous visits and a multitude of defendant interviews for court proceedings.

"She'll be down here in a couple of minutes," he responded. "I was advised you were coming, and I believe Officer Mitchell is escorting her."

Verna Mitchell was the corrections officer who had taken such an interest in the Angel Morgan case. She had often brought Angel a tray of jail food if the interview process interfered with lunchtime.

She has a caring heart for these women, Rosie thought. "Thank you."

Soon, Officer Mitchell was directing Sophie Jordan to enter the visitation room.

Sophie walked slowly with her head down and her hands clasped together in front of her. Her short black hair showed signs of kinky, gray strands. She glanced up at Rosie with no signs of emotion on her face. Sophie gave a quick nod of acknowledgement and entered the visitation room. Officer Mitchell backed out of the room and waited to be dismissed by Dr. Rosie. Thank you, Officer Mitchell, for bringing her down so promptly."

"Please have a seat, Mrs. Jordan."

Sophie's large stiff frame seemed to relax at the tone of Dr. Rosie's command. She took a seat across from Dr. Rosie.

"I'm Dr. Rosie Klein. I've been appointed to assist you in your defense."

The room was glassed in on three sides so all interviews were visible to the deputies. The defendants were not in handcuffs for professional visits as a courtesy to the relationship. Rosie always had the defendant's back to the windows to prevent any distraction from the conversation.

Sophie sat with her head down, hands in her

lap. Dr. Rosie sat with a legal pad and pen on the table between them.

"I'm not your attorney, Sophie, so what you tell me is not privileged. That means, I cannot keep what you say private. But the more you tell me, the more likely it is that I can help your lawyer. Do you understand?"

"I understand, and I really appreciate that you want to help. What do you need from me?" Her voice was low, but strong.

"I want to hear the story from your point of view. I read the reports of the arresting officers, Zee and Kearns, and Detective Woodward. Have you read them yet?"

"Not actually. I think I told the truth to everyone. Besides, I don't read really good."

"I believe you shot your husband because of a long period of physical, mental, and emotional abuse. But, you see, it's not easy for your lawyer to prove that because Farid was not attacking you when you killed him. However, Sophie, there is a serious condition that women suffer when they've been abused repeatedly. It's known as Battered Women's Syndrome. After a while, women who suffer at the hands of a mate, respond differently than average women. We can go over your symptoms relating to that condition at another time. For now, I would like you to tell me about your relationship with Farid from beginning to end. Can you do that?"

"Yes, Dr. Klein. I first met Farid on a street corner. That sounds terrible, doesn't it? I was leaving a Bible study at church in the Village of Gambier, Ohio. He pulled up to the curb in his big, black Mercedes and rolled down the window. Since it was a small town,

I thought he was going to ask for directions. I wasn't afraid of nothing back then. But, instead, he asked me: 'Are you looking for a job? I'm desperate to find a live-in nanny for my little boys. Their mother died and I'm working twelve hours a day. I can't do it alone and I don't want them taken away from me.'

"I wasn't afraid, but I admit I was naïve. It seemed like an opportunity to make a life of my own. Since I knew Mr. and Mrs. Lambert wouldn't be home right then, I decided to go get my things and go with him. They had allowed me to live with them after my graduation from Ana's house and I knew they would be stopping for ice cream with the junior high school kids.

"That's why I knew I had enough time to grab my meager belongings at their house and leave a thank you note. So, I jumped in the car thinking he would drive me home, but he headed for the highway instead. He said I could write them from his house, and he could replace my stuff. He also mumbled something like he had to get back to Toledo and pick up his kids from the sitter. I didn't know it was so far away."

"Wow...so, you didn't intend to leave without letting the Lamberts know your plan, then. What happened next?"

"No, the Lamberts were good to me like no one else had ever been. But I realize that I've let them down." Tears flowed from her eyes and streamed down Sophie's cheeks. Dr. Rosie reached into her briefcase and handed a small packet of tissues to her.

"We got to his house after a long ride and I guess the boys were asleep upstairs. He went into the kitchen and spoke to someone real low. Then I heard the back door close. He came back and told me I could sleep on the sofa for the night. I was confused about everything, but was also very tired, so I did just that."

"What happened in the morning?"

"I woke up, and he was in the kitchen. He asked if I knew how to pour milk into a cereal bowl and make toast. His two little boys were sitting at the kitchen table.

"I said 'yes' and gave the boys their breakfast. They just stared at me. I don't think they had ever seen a black person before. After they ate, he left to take them to school and told me that I should walk three blocks to the school that afternoon and bring them home.

"That's what we did for the next few days, the same thing. He basically ignored me for about a week. I also started cooking supper with what he brought home to fix and started getting the boys to bed. He really had little to do with them. Mostly, he kept his nose in books or watching television, and he left them and me alone. No hugs. No attention to any of us."

"What happened after a week?"

"He started saying that I burned the food, and he shoved the plate across the table at me. Hot fried tomatoes and black beans landed in my lap. It was messy. It didn't hurt me, but it hurt my feelings. The boys stared at us but didn't say a word. Then, he started talking tough like he told me he was taking a drive and when he got back, they'd better be in bed and the kitchen better be clean. When he left, he slammed the door like he was mad or something."

"Is that when the abuse began?"

"Uh Huh, that very same night. By that time, I usually slept on a mattress on the floor, near the back of a small, enclosed pantry. I had a quilt but had no sheet or pillow. That night, because he was gone, I slept on the couch. He returned home and grabbed me up by my hair and shoved me up the stairs to his bedroom. He forced me to have sex with him. Then shoved me back out of the bed and told me to get my black 'you know what' downstairs."

"Did you think about running away at that point?"

"I did, but I had no money and didn't know anyone. I tried to think of a plan, but I was sort of numb for a few days. Then, as if he could read my mind, he took me out in the back yard a few nights later, after the boys were asleep, and said he has friends at the bus stations and in the highway patrol. He told me to make the most of it, take care of his boys, and keep my mouth shut. He said if I ever tried to leave, he would find me. And if he couldn't find me, he knew where to find the Lamberts. He said he would kill them."

"When did you get married?"

"That is a lie. We were never legally married. He told everyone that we were, so he would be entitled to my assets at the bank and personal information, like from hospitals. But we weren't."

"Sophie, that is new information. No one knows that. Everybody thinks you and Farid were married. You mean your last name isn't legally Jordan?"

"No. My name is Sophie Washington. I was born in Oberlin, Ohio. I never knew my father. He went to prison and died there. I quit school after the eighth grade and baby sat for a music professor's kids. I stole a pearl necklace so my mother would have something pretty to wear to church. Then, we left Oberlin and moved to Mount Vernon, Ohio. That's where my mom remarried. She married a widowed Amish farmer by the name of Levi Miller. I lost track of her after I ran away, after I was raped by Miller's teenage son, Noah. I figured it was better for all concerned if I got out of there."

"That is just terrible, Sophie. I am so sorry for what happened to you. Where did you go?"

"I took enough money from my little stepbrother's piggy bank to get a bus ticket to Columbus. I met a boy at church camp there once and figured I could find him again through his church in Columbus. It wasn't much of a plan to hike from the bus station. But it's all I had, and sure, enough, he was there."

"That was a blessing, right?"

"Not actually. I didn't know he did bad things. Brad and his brothers broke into people's houses and stole things. They would rip checks out of the middle of checkbooks they found. That way, nobody noticed the missing checks right away. When people went to Florida for the winter, the brothers stole credit cards that were left behind. Their Christian parents were good though and had no idea what their boys was up to. Brad's parents let me stay with them and go back to high school. But then, one day, Brad sent me into a store to buy an expensive camera with a stolen card. I was arrested and put into Juvenile detention until I turned 18.

"That's when I met some pretty rough girls there. They were black, too, so I felt accepted. When I got out, I walked to the closest convenience store and sort of hung out at the tables beside the store. Mostly employees took their breaks there to have a smoke. Late that day, one of my friends from Detention walked up to me and said, 'Hi Sophie. Good to see you in the fresh air.'"

"Did she live around there?" Asked Rosie.

"Yes. She lived with an older brother and I knew they didn't have jobs. I was open to just about anything at that point. Everybody had let me down, so I had nothing to lose. Her name was Sandy. She taught me how to use my body to get what I needed, mainly food and drugs."

"How long were you with Sandy?"

Well, she said I could make more money with an agent. You know, a pimp. Once I hooked up with my pimp, Nick, it was the point of no return. I was so strung out on heroine I couldn't tell night from day. Lots of times, I would be arrested for soliciting and spend time in jail. That's when I was safe and sober. But my appetite increased even though jail food leaves a lot to be desired. And sometimes, Nick would bail me out, but he always made sure I knew I owed him big time.

Used to hearing down-on-luck stories, Rosie still felt compassion for this woman, Sophie.

"To answer your question, I was with them until my thirty-eighth birthday. There had been times when the Columbus Courts ordered me to live at a rehab place. Some stints were six months, and some were up to a year. With the consent of the rehab directors, Sandy would pick me up for Sunday afternoon outings. She would buy me clothes and shoes and hand over some marijuana to sneak back into my room. She was grooming me like they do children to be sex trafficked when I left. But, because I was in those places by court order,

I had to complete the program or go back to jail. To get released, somebody would be with me in court and say I was clean, sober, and rehabilitated. Sandy would testify that she had a sewing job for me."

"Were you clean and sober, Sophie? Did Sandy have a job for you?"

"No way. I had to go back to working for Nick who married Sandy while I was in rehab. She graduated from the streets to become a big madam with high-priced call girls. That's when I decided to get into trouble on purpose so I could be rescued out. After so long, I finally learned my lesson not to trust those kinds of people anymore. It was a blessing when I was sent to Ana's House in Gambier Ohio. That's where I finally got straight and saved by the grace of God. You might say "saved by the mercy and love of Mr. and Mrs. Lambert," until the day I met Farid."

"Sophie, I appreciate your explanation of how you ended up where you are today. I think we should pick your story up later this week. I have two more questions. You mentioned a son, Adam. When did you have a child? I suspect that's another story. Also, do you know where Sandy can be found? I have a friend who will be contacting all the people who knew you as a young teen-ager, as a young woman, and while living with Farid."

"As far as Sandy goes, I can't help you. I haven't seen or heard from her in ten years. I would be a threat to her business now, "Sophie explained almost apologetically.

"I had my son, Adam, when I was in Juvenile Detention in Columbus. He resulted from the rape by Noah. They took him from me at the hospital. I don't believe in abortion but the most difficult thing I ever faced was giving up my baby. This nice Christian couple by the last name of Harris adopted him. They kept his first name. His name is Adam Robert Harris. He is light skinned because his father, Noah, was white. And he's smart. Must come from the Amish side.

"It was Mrs. Lambert who tracked Adam down. She found him in Bowling Green, Ohio, where he graduated from college and had an elementary teaching job. She took me to meet him in Lima at a McDonalds. We talked for two hours. We both cried. He understood. After that we wrote letters. Mrs. Lambert probably has kept them all with my other things."

"When did you see him next?"

"I had to tell Farid about him to have any chance of seeing him. When I first got to Toledo, I had no way to reach Adam. Then I took the job at the nursing home and Doris Simpson, the social worker, let me use her phone to contact him. The problem was Farid would not let me talk to him, so we basically wrote, and Ms. Simpson got the mail for me."

"She was an angel in disguise, wasn't she? She and Adam will make great witnesses at your trial. Don't feel ashamed, Sophie. The pregnancy was not your fault and you were in no position to raise a child. Sometimes things happen for a reason we can never understand. This was a good talk, and I will be back the end of the week. Meanwhile, get some rest."

"I feel much better and less afraid, Dr. Rosie, after meeting you and all. Thank you."

Rosie stood and beckoned the guard to let them out. Verna Mitchell stood just around the corner as if she knew precisely when the interview would end. Rosie left with her head swirling. There were so many facets to this woman's life.

She was thankful for the opportunity to do what she could on Sophie's behalf, and grateful Sophie was assigned to a decent, dedicated defense attorney like Joshua Greenberg.

Knowing how much exhaustive investigating work she was about to ask her friend, Wes Hall, to do, she wasn't sure what a fair exchange would be. She didn't think a nice dinner would suffice as an adequate token of her appreciation. As usual, she was right.

CHAPTER 9

PLEASE HELP

Parking near Mancy's Restaurant, Rosie grabbed her briefcase off the passenger seat, locked her car, and headed for the front door. In the darkened dining room, she shielded her eyes to see more clearly. Almost immediately, she spotted Wes facing her. He waved and she told the hostess her lunch date was already seated. Walking over, she slid into her side of the booth.

"Thanks again for agreeing to hear about my new client, Wes After my initial interview, I'm almost afraid to tell you how many potential witnesses I've identified."

"Let's order, then you can start from the beginning, okay?"

They each ordered unsweetened tea, cheeseburgers with fries and homemade applesauce. Then they both took out legal pads.

"Look, we're twins," she laughed. Then, she related the entire life story of Sophie while they each took notes, jotting down persons of interest in terms of their knowledge and/or relationships with Sophie. Some knew Sophie as a child, but most knew her as a grown woman. Locations spanned from Oberlin, to Columbus, to Mt. Vernon, to Gambier, and all the way up to Toledo. Current addresses were unknown.

"Rosie, tell me what exact purpose these witnesses will serve?"

"I'm hoping they'll validate Sophie's version of events from her birth until her current incarceration on the charge of murder. I need the jury to view her as a victim rather than a perpetrator with no good reason to kill. I doubt her years as a prostitute will yield much. Her friend, Sandy, who might have been useful, ended up as the wife of Nick, Sophie's pimp. Therefore, not particularly a good judge of character, I guess."

Wes smiled and nodded his head. "Where do we start"

"I'll work on getting her elementary school records from Oberlin and her records from the Columbus Juvenile Detention Center," Rosie said. "I'll also have her sign a release for me to receive copies of any medical records and talk with the mental health professionals. If I can figure out where she had her baby, Adam Washington, that would be useful."

"Sounds like they had been reunited recently," Wes offered.

"Yes, she was impregnated by the Amish kid, Noah, and gave birth while in the detention center. That means the hospital and adoption records would be in Columbus."

"Okay, Rosie, why don't I start by looking for the rehab facility, Ana's House, in Gambier, and find out how she did there, maybe locate the Lamberts. Then I'll check at Crystal Manor, where she worked here in Toledo, and talk with the social worker and counselor she saw."

They continued planning while finishing lunch.

" Let's get back in touch in a couple of weeks," Rosie said as they walked to the parking lot. Wes agreed.

"I'll call you sooner if I find anything really important," he said before driving off.

Rosie headed to the University of Toledo in time to teach her marriage class. She parked in the faculty lot and called Ruth.

"Hi, Rosie, I'm glad you checked in. I have a message from Attorney Chickalette. He wants a reply at your earliest convenience. I told him you were teaching this afternoon and wouldn't be back in the office until close to four o'clock. He said he would be waiting for your call. Hope that's okay, Boss Lady."

"That's fine, Ruth. If you need to leave before I get there, just leave the coffee pot on. I'll pick up Jocko on my way there. I hate for him to be left alone for an entire day. "

"When do you go back to see Sophie? I don't have it marked in your planner and you know how important that is, so I don't double book you."

"I'm not quite sure, Ruth. I'm using tomorrow morning to contact the crime scene witnesses, Petra Gonzalez and Trisha Small. Plus, I want to know more about the interrogation process and maybe why Detective Woodward didn't have a partner present. I find that odd."

"Any calls you want me to make?"

"Yes, please contact the members of my groups and remind them of the Women's Group tomorrow afternoon and the Post Abortion Support Group tomorrow evening. Since I'm meeting both groups this week, please tell them all to bring their homework!"

"Okay, and will you need some food for the evening group? Should I get some cheese, sausage, veggies, crackers, and dip?"

"You are the best office manager a girl could ever pray for, Ruth!"

"You, my dear, are the kindest, hardest working boss I've ever had!"

"Oh, by the way, Ruth, please clear my Friday afternoon of Mother's Day week-end. I'm taking Bucky to Oakdale to meet my mother. You know I care about you, Ruth, even though you and my mother have so much in common: BOSSY!"

"Yeah, well, somebody has to take the reins of your busy office. Besides, your mother is in for a real treat to see you glowing with happiness. You look radiant these days, you know."

"Thank you, Ruth. You know how much I appreciate your willingness to expand your job description during these past years of my sorrows and change."

"I do. Phone ringing, Rosie. Got to get back to my original job description."

***

Class discussion seemed brief and time went quickly. Rosie decided to stop by Bucky's office in the fieldhouse and catch him as a surprise. But the door was locked, and a sign indicated he would be back at 4:00 p.m. Disappointed, she left a sticky note saying she would catch him by phone later. Then she swung by her condo to pick up Jocko. He was eagerly sitting by the front door as if he knew she would be coming to take him to work.

***

As she pushed open the double doors in the front of her Summerhill office building, she noticed Ruth still working at her desk. Ruth smiled when she saw Jocko. "Hi there, Jocko. Need some water?" Jocko wagged his tail vigorously.

"Guess what, Boss? The wife of Woodward's partner was busy having a baby. That's why he wasn't with Woodward for the interrogation."

"How did you find out, Ruth?"

"Well, I happen to be close friends with Verna Mitchell, the corrections officer. We sing in 'Sweet Adelines' together. I just touched base with her since we have a rehearsal tonight for a Mother's Day performance at a country club luncheon. That's all."

"Really? Actually, I don't picture Officer Mitchell as a vocalist. Besides, I thought I knew all about your private life. How long have you been singing?"

"Oh, forty years or so. I began as a teen-ager in a youth church choir. Then, I toured the country with a Christian group. Marriage interrupted that. You know most of the rest, Rosie."

"Well, you are full of surprises, Ruth, Thanks, so much. By the way, if you have the number of Attorney Chickalette, I'll return his call now" Ruth handed Rosie the note and turned her attention to the large, black dog staring at her with big brown eyes.

Before Rosie could pick up the phone, it rang. It was Bucky calling to say how sorry he was to have missed her visit.

"That's okay. It was just impulsive on my part. I was wondering if you would like to come over and grill outside this evening. Nothing fancy."

"That would be great. I know tomorrow night you have your group. I don't know how you balance it all, Rosie." Bucky said. "Since I'll see you later, I won't talk more. There are some phone calls I must make to a few parents. They're concerned about my promotion and the future of their sons' baseball scholarships. I want to assure them nothing will change next year."

"You are very considerate, Bucky. That's one of the many qualities I love about you. Okay, so go call. I'll see you later."

Rosie dialed Chickalette, next. His office manager answered in a pleasant tone. Rosie complimented her good nature. Some office managers don't answer so politely late in the day. But it was Chickalette's request that shocked her.

"Hi Rosie. I am in serious need of your services," he greeted her. "My most recent client is being accused of murdering her two little daughters.

I'm really going to need your professional experience on this one. Ir's one of the most unusual cases I've ever had. You'd be doing me a real service. Please say you'll come onboard."

CHAPTER 10

SOPHIE: SECOND INTERVIEW

Rosie was thinking of calling Wes to finalize some plans when at that exact moment, he called her. Ruth put Wes through to Rosie.

"Hi Rosie. When did you say you are going to Oakdale? I have an idea."

"Bucky and I are going down on the Friday before Mother's Day. What do you have in mind?"

"I thought perhaps you guys could swing over to Mount Vernon and Gambier to look up the Lamberts and check out Ana's House. I will contact the Juvenile Detention facility in Columbus for Sophie's records there, and her arrest records for prostitution. What do you think?"

"Sounds like a great plan, Wes. My mother doesn't expect us till late Friday evening. Mount Vernon and Gambier are only two hours from her house in Oakdale. Meanwhile, I'm heading to the jail to see Sophie. I'll get her to sign some releases for us. Next week I plan to check in with Doris Simpson, the social worker in the nursing home where she worked, and possibly contact the counselor, Maria Lopez."

"Great Rosie."

"At some point, we may need all of them to testify as character witnesses. A lot to ask of professionals who work all week, and of the Lamberts who live so far away, I know. As a matter of fact, Columbus is a long trek for you, Wes. Are you sure you want to do that? I will definitely see you get paid for your expenses."

"No problem. I have other business to attend to at Ohio State. Working on a story of sexual abuse of female athletes by coaches. Well, glad we touched base. Bye for now."

"Bye. Don't hesitate to call if you have more questions, or need to run anything by me."

"I won't, Rosie. Feel free to do the same."

Rosie stuffed the release of information papers into a manilla envelope, slipped it into her briefcase along with the homework she wanted Sophie to complete. Then, out the door she went with a wave of her outstretched hand above her head. Ruth was on the phone conducting business as usual.

Ruth understood that Dr. Rosie's first women's group was scheduled to meet later in the afternoon. Instead of going out for lunch, she would likely stay in and help. Ruth ordered snacks and appetizers to pick up for Rosie and the members of the late afternoon and evening groups.

Rosie handed the car keys to Geoff, the valet in the La-Salle underground garage and thanked the young man. She was deep in thought as she walked to the Lucas County Jail. Other professionals appeared to be heading to the same building since she saw familiar faces. What they all had in common seemed to be the quickness and determination of their steps.

"Hi Officer Poole. I am here to interview Sophie Jordan at this time."

"Gotcha, Dr. Klein. Sign here, please, then step through the metal detector."

Rosie noticed Joshua Greenberg's signature on the visitor log. She was pleased he was showing an interest in Sophie. It appeared he had visited her for forty-five minutes yesterday.

Officers Testerman and Ambrose acknowledged Rosie with a nod and a wave as they processed an inmate and released his handcuffs. Rosie acknowledged them with a "good morning Officers" and let herself into the interview room.

Sophie entered and sat down at the table. Officer Mitchell said, "I assume you will be together until lunch. Do you want a tray, Dr. Klein?"

"No thank you, Officer Mitchell. I understand we have a common friend, my office manager and dear friend, Ruth. She is a hoot, isn't she?" Nothing more needed to be said. They laughed and Officer Mitchell left the room.

"How are you, Sophie?" Rosie asked turning her attention toward the woman sitting quietly.

"I'm okay. The chaplain stopped by on Sunday and prayed with me. I feel more positive with her prayers. Then my attorney visited yesterday morning, and now you."

"That sounds busy for you. Today, I need you to sign a few releases so we can talk to the professionals who have known you through the years. I plan to talk to Doris Simpson, and the counselor you saw. What was her name again?"

"My counselor's name is Maria Lopez. She's married to a guy from Guatemala who works as a cook in a restaurant near the campus of Owens Technical College."

"Thanks, Sophie. That helps a lot. We don't need releases signed to talk to people like the Lamberts, just to professionals who must keep your information confidential."

"I understand. I thought my counseling would be confidential, but Farid was not working and followed me to Mrs. Lopez's office one day. I trusted she would never disclose that she knew he abused me."

"I have a friend, Sophie, who is an investigative news reporter for the Toledo Blade. He will go to Columbus and look up the hospital where you gave birth to your son."

"Oh my gosh, Dr. Klein, I don't know what to say. My attorney contacted my son, Adam, and Mr. and Mrs. Lambert. He said they'll both be coming to meet with you. He's arranging for my son to visit me, too. Even though I hate for him to see me this way, I still can't wait to see him."

"That is great news, Sophie. Now that you have signed the consent forms, I want you to draw some things for me. Ok?"

"I'm not much of an artist. But I'll do my best."

"Please draw me a picture of a single person."

Sophie used a black marker and drew a stick figure of a woman with long, straight hair. The woman stood on a sidewalk, facing forward with her hands behind her back and large feet. Her eyes looked hollow, and she had no eyebrows, no expression on her face, and wore no clothing apart from a black line for a belt."

Next, Rosie asked Sophie to draw a house. It looked like a rectangular commercial building or prison. There were no doorknobs, no roof, and no chimney. There were no curtains on the windows or sidewalk leading to the building. Last, she asked Sophie to draw a tree. It had dead limbs with no sign of life and a trunk with a large, black hole in it. Although there were markers of all colors available, Sophie used only black.

"Thank you, Sophie. I would like to ask you a few questions about what we talked about the other day. Is that okay?"

"Sure. I'll do anything you say because I trust you. I don't trust most people, especially white folks. Mrs. Simpson is black you know, and so is my counselor."

"How many times did you see Mrs. Lopez?"

"I saw her three times. After I quit, I secretly kept two more appointments, but not on Wednesdays. Farid thought I was still going to work. Mrs. Lopez told me to pack an emergency bag and keep it under my bed so I could run away. Even after eight years, I was afraid he would seriously harm or kill poor Mr. and Mrs. Lambert if I left him."

"Is the bag still there?"

"I imagine it is. He would never look under my bed. He had set up a mattress for me in a pantry off the kitchen. I left something under his bed, too."

"Really, what was that?" Asked Rosie.

"The night before – you know... I shot him, he dragged me upstairs and raped me so bad...anally from behind, you know? I rolled up the bloody, messy sheet and stuffed it under his bed. Then, I changed the sheets before he would have realized it."

"Sophie, who knows about this?"

"Nobody, Dr. Rosie. I have not been asked, and it sort of slipped my mind with all this horrible confusion."

"If you don't mind, I'm going to look further into both of those matters."

"Sure, if it helps my case."

"Did the police officers talk to you about things as they brought you to jail?"

"No," Sophie answered. "They were in the front seat and I only heard them talking to each other. The woman officer said she didn't think I looked like a killer. The Sergeant said something like 'it looks like another crime of passion.' Is that a police term?"

"No. I wouldn't say so. It means it looked like you were upset with each other and somebody shot somebody else without thinking clearly. It doesn't suggest the shooting was in self-defense. Did they sit in on the interrogation with Detective Woodward?"

"No. I felt like they were probably watching through the other side of a window. He was a little gruff but sort of like Sgt. Zee. Maybe that's how men cops talk and act. I felt like a number," Sophie said, "and not like they wanted to listen to my version of what happened at all. If you ask me, they already made up their minds about what happened."

"Well, rest assured, you are an important person to Attorney Greenberg and me."

A tear had formed at the corner of Sophie's left eye and she quickly wiped it away with the heel of her hand.

"I am going to leave a paper with you," Rosie said, sliding a single sheet toward her. It had forty-four incomplete sentences to fill in. She also slid over a pencil.

"What should I do?"

"Just finish each sentence with the first thought that comes to mind. Don't take a long time to think about each one, and don't worry about spelling. I'll pick it up the next time I visit. Meanwhile, I, also, have a journal to give to you. If you could, please write down your thoughts, feelings and specific incidents or memories that happened during the eight years you spent with the Jordan family."

Just then, Verna Mitchell opened the door and said lunch was being served. She mentioned there was a tray for Sophie upstairs since Dr. Rosie had turned one down for herself.

"Officer Mitchell, I hear you're a singer! I'd really like to hear you sing, but I'll be out of town over Mother's Day weekend. Have any other performances scheduled?"

"Well, we are rehearsing a patriotic concert for

the Fourth of July. Maybe ask Ruth to give you details, Dr. Klein."

"Okay, thanks," Rosie smiled at her. Then, turning to Sophie, she said, "How about getting lunch now. Maybe you can start writing out the sentences, after that, okay?"

"Yes, Ma'am. I'm not very hungry, but I'll eat some of it. I'm thirsty, though."

Dr. Rosie reached into her briefcase and handed Sophie a small package of fruit and nuts. Officer Mitchell turned her head so as not to see the violation of policy for visitors. Sophie smiled.

"See you soon, Sophie."

Rosie exited the building and headed toward her parked car. It had been a good visit. She felt that progress was being made.

CHAPTER 11

MEETING TWO MOTHERS

Bucky called just as Rosie finished reading a collection of police reports. "Hi Rosie. You've been busy. How are you feeling tonight? Are you ready for your marriage class tomorrow? Can I sit in and learn something?"

"Hi Bucky. It's so good to hear your voice, and your humor is just what the doctor ordered. After I left the jail, I swung by and got Jocko and took him to the office with me. Everybody there enjoys a little pet therapy."

"I know your case is stressful. Anything I can do to help?"

"As a matter of fact, there is. I thought I would call Trisha Small, Sophie's next-door neighbor, and see if I can interview her on Saturday. If she agrees to see me, do you want to come along?"

"Absolutely. Breakfast before or after?"

"After. My stomach may have butterflies when we get there. I'll call Ms. Small to see if we can stop in. If I stop by your office after my class tomorrow, will you be there?"

"No, but I do want to see you. Come to the baseball diamond. Walk there and I'll drive you back to your car after practice if that's okay."

"That's right, Coach. Your season has begun. Sure, I'll gladly come over. I have no late appointments at my Summerhill office and by then, I should know if Saturday is a go."

"Get some rest, Rosie. Look forward to seeing you tomorrow."

A smile lingered on her lips after they spoke. She loved hearing his voice. Quickly, Rosie jotted down the neighbors' phone numbers, both Trisha and Petra, which she took from the witness reports.

Probably too late to call tonight, she thought, *I'll do it in the morning rather than ask Ruth to do it. I want these calls to feel personal so Trisha Small and Petra Gonzalez will feel relaxed about the interviews.*

In the event one or both declined Rosie's visit, she didn't want to subject Ruth to hearing anything demeaning or mean-spirited about Sophie, should they say it.

I wonder if they've already put up a yellow crime scene banner or no trespassing sign? Rosie thought. *I want to secure Sophie's escape bag and the soiled sheets if I can get into the house. These items could play into her plea of self-defense.*

The following morning, Rosie was able to contact both Trisha and Petra. They each agreed to be interviewed and the appointment for both was set for Saturday morning at Trisha's house.

. Rosie begged off getting a bite to eat with Bucky after his Friday baseball practice. She opted to go home and walk Jocko before dark. Saturday came quickly. Rosie and Bucky pulled up in front of the Jordan house, and took note there was no yellow crime scene tape depicting a no-trespass zone barring anyone from entering the home. She hoped to get the go-bag and sheets after the interviews next door.

She and Bucky walked up the sidewalk to the front door of Trisha's house. A lovely wreath of bright yellow sunflowers leaned against her white door. Beside the stoop was a trellis with several hundred live, tropical pink flowers. A tall, lean, pretty, blonde-haired woman in her mid-thirties opened the door before they could knock.

"You must be Trisha," Rosie ventured. She introduced herself as Dr. Klein and Mr. Walker, her fiancé. Trisha invited them in and introduced them to Petra Gonzalez, her neighbor and good friend, already seated at the kitchen table. She motioned for them to be seated at the table and offered coffee which they both accepted. Rosie noticed a bar to the right with six wine glasses hanging from a rack. The textured walls were light gray, and the home was clean and orderly. She could see through the sliding glass doors to a back patio with green wicker lawn furniture and flowering plants in decorative ceramic pots.

It was already a known fact that Trisha was a single parent of two daughters, aged ten and twelve, who worked as a beautician. Two years prior, her husband had died tragically in an accident on the interstate involving six vehicles. Since it wasn't his fault, she had received a settlement. Still, money couldn't replace her daughters' daddy.

Petra was married, worked as an occupational therapist at Crystal Manor where Sophie had worked, and was raising two sons, aged twelve and fourteen. Rosie took a sip of her coffee and decided it was time to explain the purpose of the interviews.

"I'm a forensic psychologist appointed to Sophie Jordan's case, here to research facts surrounding her relationship with Farid Jordan and her past life. I hope you can enlighten me by describing what you observed or experienced with them as your neighbors."

"I would definitely like to talk to you about Sophie and Farid," Trisha spoke first. "He would never allow my girls to walk across his yard to get to Petra's house and was quite harsh about it. He was home all day with people coming and going. I could have told him that his guests should not park in front of my yard, but I didn't. He probably would have snarled at me anyway, or worse."

"I never once saw him toss a ball with his own sons," Petra said. "Even so, he would allow my boys to come over and throw a football, but his kids could never play basketball in our driveway. I found him very controlling." She sounded aggravated, then added, "Not only that, even though Sophie and I worked at the same nursing home, she wasn't allowed to ride with me. I often wondered: what was he afraid of?"

"And who were those men in black suits who stopped over during the time Sophie was at work?" Trisha chimed in. "I bet they were involved in something illegal."

"But Trisha," Petra added, "don't forget that young, red headed, white woman who came around the week before he died. It was a day that Sophie worked but I had off for parent-teacher conferences. I found that kind of strange. I never once saw him attend any parent-teacher things, by the way. Sophie would have gone if he'd a let her. His son, Omar, was in my son, Manny's sixth grade class. Once they did a science project together, but Omar wasn't allowed to work on it at our house. The boys tried to meet in the school library during recess, but Farid found out somehow and got angry. I think Omar flunked the project."

"What can you tell me about his older son, Ali?"

"I think he was suspicious that his dad might be hurting Sophie. He told me all the boys could hear Mr. Jordan yelling at Sophie. Just one time, I saw him stand up to his father. It didn't go well, but he tried. I also found it strange that their dad, wouldn't let them come in until dinnertime, even if it was cold and dreary out. Once, I remember Ali pounding on the door. He wouldn't stop until his father opened the door. Then, he glanced inside and sort of shoved his way through the door. The door slammed leaving Omar outdoors with my boys. My older son, Miguel, came home and said Ali said he had to protect his stepmother.

"My son, Miguel, and Ali Jordan are both

graduating from the eighth grade soon. Ali has no class pictures to share with his friends and seems embarrassed when kids ask him for one, my son told me. Miguel delivers newspapers and makes spending money. He's offered to let Ali use little Manny's bike to go with him to the Dairy Queen. Ali thanked him but said he wasn't allowed."

"Wow. Farid certainly sounds like a mean-spirited man," Rosie said. "It must be very tough to grow up with a father like that. Petra, what was Sophie's job description where you both worked and how did she get along with the staff and the residents?"

"She constantly looked very tired. As a nurse's aide, she was always on her feet the entire work shift, changing bed linens, giving baths, and taking residents to the bathroom., On top of that, after her shift she had to walk to the boys' school to make sure they came directly home. After the first few years, when they didn't really need her, Farid still insisted on total supervision. In the cold, winter months, Sophie lacked a warm coat. I don't think she had any gloves, boots, or a scarf, either."

"Once, my girls went up to the door selling girl scout cookies without me knowing it," Trisha added. "If I had known, I would never have allowed them on their stoop. But no one came to the door anyway, even though everyone was in the house, I'm sure. My girls said they could hear him yelling but didn't know if it was at Sophie, the boys or the TV."

Trish offered a hot refill of coffee to everyone as Petra spoke up.

"As an occupational therapist, I specialize in rehab for hands and lower arms. There were times when I glimpsed what appeared to be swollen fingers and bruised arms on Sophie. If she saw me looking, she would quickly pull her sleeves down and walk away with her hands in her pockets. I know the swelling wasn't from arthritis. So, to put it another way, I suspected he was clever not to leave visible bruises."

"Did your husband know Farid? Was he different with men?"

"My husband, Jose, is a long-distance truck driver. We met when I worked at a diner and he drove a truck locally. When he's home, he pays attention to our boys. They go off and do stuff together like fishing or watching the Toledo Mud Hens baseball. He would get a 'hello' from Farid if they were taking out the trash at the same time. That's all."

"So, Jose and the boys like baseball. Do they play little league?" Bucky asked.

"Bucky is the baseball coach at the University of Toledo, Petra," Rosie said.

"They do play baseball, but it's just community ball. We don't have the resources for them to play on travel teams. The boys love all sports, football, basketball, and baseball. If you meet Farid's boys, you'll see how athletic they are. It's a shame they haven't played sports. Who knows? Maybe now, in foster care, they'll have the opportunity."

"Are the boys like their father?" Rosie asked as Trisha topped off her black coffee.

"No" both women said simultaneously.

"You would think Sophie was their mother," Petra said. "She was the primary caretaker, for sure. They were polite, friendly, and helpful to each other. They relied on one another. You could see it. If one fell, the other extended a hand. Ali was very protective of his little brother."

"Was Sophie well-liked at work?"

"Not really. I honestly think that's because her co-workers didn't know her. She wasn't disliked. Sophie just didn't allow anyone to reach out to her except the social worker, Doris Simpson. We all respected her privacy. She packed her lunch and ate at her desk. We think maybe she went to a counselor at lunch time on Wednesdays. But usually, she just said she needed to catch up on paperwork. In some respects, that would be true. At the end of her shift, she always left right away to get to school for the boys."

Realizing the women didn't have more to say, Rosie decided to bring the interview to a close. She could always ask them to call if they thought of new information.

"I can't thank you enough for your time and insight into this tragic situation Sophie is facing. Here is my card with my private number in case you think of anything else relevant."

As Rosie and Bucky stood to leave, both women walked them to the door. They asked Dr. Klein to say hello to Sophie and let her know they are praying for her.

"We go to a nearby church and want her to know

she has a lot of support there," Trisha said. "Once, when Farid was out of town on a Wednesday night, Sophie and the boys attended a praise and worship service with us."

"All four of our kids sing in the youth choir," Petra said. "That was the only time Ali and Omar have stepped into our church, let alone participated in singing along with everyone else."

"Sophie told me as we left that evening that she sang in a youth choir herself." Trisha said in a quiet, subdued voice. "She said her life went downhill after her mother remarried and told me when she met Farid, she was just getting back in touch with God. She didn't say it, but I believe he stole all that away from her."

"Do you think, based on how he manipulated Sophie to come with him, that he could be involved in drugs or something? Maybe all the people who come and go at the house are up to no good. The redheaded woman could be part of it, too," Petra said in an animated tone. "I was sitting in my rocking chair on the front porch that day, and she avoided eye contact with me.

"Attorney Greenberg could reveal those facts. What you have provided will assist him more than you can imagine. We can't thank you enough. Well, bye for now, and don't forget you have my card to call anytime."

CHAPTER 12

THE SEARCH

Leaving the house, Rosie looked at Bucky. "Welcome to my forensic investigative club. Consider yourself inducted as an honorary member. What did you think of that?"

"I'm in awe. Those were amazing interviews. One thing just led right into the next. They were so open with you; it was impressive."

"Frankly, I was surprised how open and forthcoming they were. I never expected such a wealth of information from the simple line of questioning I had planned. I had to write it all so quickly, my notes are like chicken-scratching. There is no way Josh Greenberg will be able to read from my notes. I need to type it all out before Monday and meet with him directly."

"What's next? Are we breaking in next door?"

"Let's walk around as though we are potential buyers. Then we can peek into the windows and look at the layout of the house. We might as well walk straight up to the front door."

They approached the front door, rang the doorbell, and as expected, no one answered. Pausing, Rosie slowly turned the knob, but it was locked, which they had assumed. The blinds were closed as neighbors reported they usually were. Trying to be discreet, they looked around and walked through the yard to the back of the house. The door to a small screened-in porch was ajar. Piles of newspapers and a bin of stacked, empty beer cans in front of the back door. They stepped in and approached the backdoor. It was unlocked.

"Uh-oh, what do we do next?" Rosie asked as she answered her own question by stepping inside.

"Well. I think we should make this short and sweet, don't you?" said Bucky.

"I agree. Let's look in the pantry where Sophie said she slept."

They walked through the kitchen and noticed a small room ahead. The small pantry was lit with a single light bulb hanging from the ceiling. A dirty, stained twin mattress was atop a low wooden platform beneath shelves containing dry goods, a can of soup, and several cans of green beans.

"It was probably meant to be a tornado shelter since it's an internal room without windows and some non-perishable food to eat. You don't suppose he locked her in there to punish her?" Rosie said without really waiting for an answer.

"Geez, we are talking about an evil man, here," she continued. "I'm looking for a small bag containing Sophie's personal necessities. She said her counselor suggested she have a bag packed in case she decided to run for her life."

Getting down on her knees, Rosie reached under Sophie's makeshift, narrow bed and felt a pair of shoes. Then Bucky dragged out a small bag just as Sophie had described.

"Here it is. She was telling you the truth. She didn't intend to kill him. She was building up the courage to leave him."

"Let's run upstairs for one quick search, Bucky."

Reaching the top step, they noticed an open door at the end of the hall. Bucky and Rosie looked at each other, then walked quickly toward the room. Time was of the essence but how could they resist the temptation to look inside.

Approaching the open door, they could see a tall dresser, a pole lamp, and a large, disheveled bed. Men's clothing was strewn all over the floor. Bucky bent down and stuck his arm under one side of the bed and felt a small, soft bundle of cloth. Pulling it out, he didn't unfold it.

"Let's look for something to put this in so we can take it to the car without being obvious." He handed Rosie a pillow. She quickly removed the case and stuffed the linens and Sophie's bag and shoes inside.

"We better get out of here. Are you taking this stuff to your condo, Rosie?"

"What choice do I have until Monday?"

"Stash them at my house," Bucky said. "It's safer. Not that I think you're in danger since he's dead. But people may think you have evidence of their illegal activity. We could be being watched right now."

"Oh my gosh. I never have thought of that. Sounds like a plan, Bucky. Thank you."

They reached the car while looking to see if anyone was peeking out from other house windows. Nothing seemed obvious. As Bucky drove them away from the scene, Rosie decided to put a call into Joshua Greenberg. "I know the Public Defender's office is closed on Saturday, but I have Greenberg's private phone number. I'll call and inform him of our evidence findings."

"Good idea, Rosie. The last thing you need is a 'tampering with evidence' charge. That could cost you big time, right?"

"You got that right. My reputation and my license. Imagine that!"

Joshua Greenberg picked up the phone on the second ring. Rosie informed him of Sophie's confession and the fact they now possessed physical evidence of extreme importance to her case.

"Tell you what, Rosie. Have your boyfriend drive you to Rudy's Hot Dog on Sylvania Avenue.

"That's fine. Do you want to chat or just pick up the goods?"

"I definitely want to hear about your interviews with the neighbor ladies and what Sophie told you about this evidence."

"We're on our way. We will wait inside. I think I owe Bucky a hotdog with Mr. Rudy Dionyssiou's special chili sauce."

As Bucky pulled away from the curb, he glanced

into his rearview mirror and noticed a late model, black Nissan sedan pulling out of a neighbor's driveway. He hesitated mentioning it to Rosie, just felt grateful they were heading to a public place, not to either of their homes.

Bucky made a turn to see if the car would follow. It did. Yep, they were being tailed. He assumed whoever was tailing them had probably secured their personal information by now. He also wondered how they knew to look for them at Farid's house? Or were they staking it out the house for whoever would stop by? Or was their own plan to search the house but foiled by Bucky and Rosie's intrusion?

Josh Greenberg was seated at a booth behind the hostess stand when they arrived. He stood and Rosie introduced him to Bucky. "Attorney Greenberg, this is my fiancé, Bucky Walker."

"Pleased to meet you. Just call me Josh."

As they placed their orders at the counter, Bucky looked over his shoulder to the parking lot. The black Nissan was parked there, strategically beneath the shadow of a tree facing the restaurant. There was a driver and a passenger but without a license plate in front, it was impossible to get the number.

"Excuse me, gentlemen. I'm going to the Ladies' Room," Rosie said as she left the two of them to get acquainted with each other.

"Josh, before Rosie return, there's something I want to tell you. Don't look out the window, but we've been followed here from Sophie's house. There are two men in a black Nissan looking this way. From what Trisha Small and Petra Gonzalez said, I believe they were involved in some business with Farid. The neighbors also identified a young, white, red headed woman who recently appeared at Farid's house while the men were there. If the men were not with her, I might have thought Farid had a mistress or potential second wife."

"Any idea as to what kind of business they were involved in?"

"The way he manipulated Sophie to get in his car and become a nanny for his kids almost sounds like a drug or trafficking problem. What do you think?"

"Here comes Rosie, Bucky. We need to clue her in so she can be super cautious when she's not with you. I'll call my friend, Ron Thompson, a former State Trooper, now F.B.I. Maybe they're on to something. Those guys in the Nissan could be undercover even. Maybe he knows something."

"Hi guys. Just in time. I see our orders on the counter with glasses for our drinks."

"Did you forgo a nutritious lunch just to fit in, Rosie? I would have guessed you would have ordered a Greek salad." They laughed and retrieved their orders.

"Rosie, don't look now, but I've just let Josh know we've been followed from Sophie's house. I suspected it but didn't want to scare you. He thinks it's possible they are FBI and could have been watching the house."

"Right, Rosie. Bucky has sharp eyes. Meanwhile, I urge you go to Bucky's house and remain there until you hear from me. I have a friend to call." Josh sounded firm about it.

"Josh, what about Jocko, my dog. I can't simply leave him at my place."

"Listen, Rosie, we can swing by and pick up Jocko and then go to my house," Bucky said. "Josh, will you touch base with us later?"

"Sure, as soon as I hear from Agent Thompson. He knows I wouldn't call him on the weekend if it wasn't really important."

"Okay, then, I suggest we enjoy our lunch and not raise any suspicion on the part of those gentlemen in the parking lot."

"I'll try, but my appetite isn't what it was when I first smelled the sweet aroma of Rudy's hot dog sauce," Rosie said looking glum. The men chuckled.

Finishing lunch, they picked up to-go orders and Greenberg discreetly slipped the stash from under the beds into a Rudy's plastic-to go bag with their take-out. Rosie and Bucky each carried food in a similar bag and casually waved as they parted, heading to their cars.

Reaching her condo, Rosie dashed inside and met Jocko face to face in the foyer. She grabbed his leash, a bag of dry food, and his special red water bowl. She quickly packed an overnight bag with essentials, a pair of pajamas, and a change of clothes and quickly locked the door behind them.

"Are we still being followed, Bucky?" She looked around as they drove out of her complex towards Bucky's place.

"I haven't seen any lights following us since we left the restaurant."

"Maybe it's time I call my reporter friend, Wes. He's usually one step ahead of me when it comes to being curious about unusual things

"You might want to wait until you're safely situated at my house. Then you can relax and bring him up to date. Just because I don't see anyone following us, doesn't mean they won't be perched down the street from my front door."

"You're right. I'll wait. Jocko is a great watch dog. He'll bark if he hears or senses the slightest strange thing. Can we walk him when we get to your place?"

"I have a fenced yard. How about if I sit outside with him while you make your call?"

"Good idea. You are definitely thinking straighter than I am. Do you mind if I invite Wes over?"

"Not at all. Any friend of yours is a friend of mine, you know."

"How about I fix a salad and use Rudy's sauce on spaghetti tonight. I have a bottle of Chianti. I remember you like Chianti when you eat Italian. I can also tell from your smile that you do."

"Tonight, just might be a night to remember," Bucky said with a wink and a smile.

CHAPTER 13

TRAFFICK RING

Wes was lounging in a backyard chair watching his children kick a soccer ball into their small net. His since-forever fiancée', Sherri, was teaching the kids how to play chess. The kids lived at the Lucas County Sheriff's Ranch and Wes visited whenever time allowed. He recognized Rosie's number when his phone rang.

"Hey, Rosie. How do I deserve the pleasure of a Saturday phone call from you? That's either good or bad."

"Hi Wes. Well, some things have come up related to Sophie's case and I really value your perspective. Do you have time to hear me out?"

"Yep, all the time in the world. Shoot."

Rosie explained the information Sophie had shared regarding evidence that could be crucial to determine her plea of self-defense. She told Wes about the soiled sheets showing abuse along with the small escape bag which Sophie's counselor had urged her to pack in case she could get away from Farid.

"But get this, Wes, when Bucky and I gathered the evidence and left to meet Attorney Greenberg at Rudy's, he noticed we were being followed! We gave Greenberg the evidence and headed to my house to pick-up my dog. I'm staying at Bucky's now until we determine who was following us. Do you have any idea if the FBI would have been watching the house?"

"Well, first, you had a day...As for the FBI, I honestly don't know. What do you want me to do?"

"For starters, find out what's so important if the FBI would be involved. I don't think they were interested in Sophie's get away bag and it's doubtful they would know about the sheets. But there must be something in the house they want, or don't want us to find. Either way, somebody knows something we don't. Now, I'm wondering exactly what Farid was doing. It's obvious he was up to something. We spoke with the neighbors Trisha and Petra, who described a lot of traffic coming and going to see Farid in past days while Sophie worked. They also said a woman began showing up the week before Sophie shot him. She could be significant."

"Rosie, I have been investigating a human trafficking ring lately. I think I told you about that. If they didn't have girls at Farid's house, maybe he was supplying drugs for such a trafficking ring. Toledo is a huge hub for transferring girls, young women, and even boys by carriers such as vans, trucks, and empty train cars. Sometimes there's a woman involved in securing victims without resistance. They trust a strange woman whereas they may have been taught to ignore or run from men."

"Gosh, Wes, that's horrible. I don't deal with such an underbelly of crime too often. There are two little girls living next to Sophie's house. Even though Farid is dead, we should warn Trisha to always supervise her daughters. Then the question remains: What evidence is in the house, and who wants it out of there?"

"Based on previous cases, my guess is there could be a camera or damaging photographs of victims and potential victims in there. I know from research I'm doing for a newspaper expose I'm writing for the Toledo Blade. Columbus is another hot spot for sex trafficking. It could explain why Farid was in the Mount Vernon/Gambier area when he lured Sophie to become his nannie. They frequently use the promise of a better life or a job when seducing women. With kids, they pretend to be a friend of their parents. This has been going on for over a decade. How long was she with him?

"For eight years; his boys were small, and she took care of them," Rosie said as a thought played in her mind. "You know, Wes, the boys living on the other side of Sophie's house are potential targets too. Should we go back to the house and look for something more, or call the authorities? Maybe we should go to the school and warn them to be on the lookout for anyone suspicious."

"For now, Rosie, I would stay put with Bucky and Jocko by your side. Just call Greenberg and let him in on the info I provided. I can meet you after church tomorrow and let you know if I find out something on the guys in the Nissan. Did you get a license number?"

"No. They were parked so we couldn't see the back plate and there wasn't one on the front either. Josh Greenberg is calling a friend in the FBI to see if he knows anything. You know, Wes, the black car could even be the good guys, you know, like undercover. Ha! For all we know, they might be thinking we're the bad guys. Wouldn't that be a twist. Well, see you tomorrow."

The phone rang just as Rosie put it down. It was Josh Greenberg.

"You won't be surprised to hear; it's not you they followed this time. A black Nissan is perched down the street from my house. Seems you and Bucky are safe for the time being. I would stay put if I were you. I'm still waiting to hear from my FBI friend, Ron Thompson, and will let you know what I find out."

"I guess you would call this good news-bad news, Josh. We're having lunch with Wes Hall tomorrow after church. He thinks it could be connected to a sex trafficking ring operating here and somebody wants incriminating evidence from Sophie's house."

"Interesting. Let me know what he tells you, and I'll call you after I have spoken to Agent Thompson. I have a feeling this surveillance has nothing to do with our case but a whole lot to do with Sophie's dead common-law husband. The question remains as to who is stalking us? Obviously, they're interested in something I have or something I know, or they wouldn't have followed me home, Rosie."

"Be careful, Josh, and keep your doors locked. Try not to worry too much."

Bucky and Rosie tried to enjoy their own evening together. But when they walked Jocko, they couldn't help being vigilant and observant of any cars in sight.

"My street is a dead-end cul-de-sac, and all the residents know one another. It could be why they chose to observe Greenberg instead of us. They could also be aware that he has the 'package' we handed to him."

"I feel very safe here with you, Bucky. Jocko is

my watch dog, but I doubt he could protect me from two armed men. I wonder what the deal is with the woman?"

"I have a hunch we'll understand more pretty quickly. After all we have Wes and Agent Thompson investigating it."

Rosie's phone rang in the darkness and she fished it out of her pocket and recognized Trisha's number.

"I hope I am not bothering you, but I had to call. My girls just told me they remembered something when they were playing on their skateboards. That red-haired woman waved them over to her car. It was a blue, four seat, BMW convertible parked at the curb in front of Sophie's house. She asked for directions to the nearest I-75 ramp."

"Really! When was this, and what did they do?"

"It was on the Saturday before Farid was shot. They weren't afraid because they had seen her there before and she seemed friendly. But they couldn't help her because they don't have a clue where the I-75 ramp would be."

"Sounds like she might have been priming them so they would go for a ride with her in the future. Please don't let them out of your sight. They are both witnesses and that means great danger."

"No problem. I will walk them to school and take them to the beauty shop after school. They love being there and watching us beautify the ladies. They also have some time scheduled with their dad for next weekend. they're looking forward to it."

"One last thing, Trisha. Please let Petra and Jose know what we've found out. Boys are victims too. Her boys need to avoid leaving the yard for the time being. They may even have some information they didn't realize means something. Let her know she can call me any time."

"Will do. Good night."

CHAPTER 14

WOMAN IN BLUE CAR

Bucky held the door open for Rosie as they entered Frisch's Big Boy. They spotted Wes seated with another gentleman at a table for four. Two upholstered seats were against the wall.

"Hi Rosie, Bucky. This is Agent Ron Thompson. I understand you've worked with him on another case. He's been promoted to the FBI. As you can tell, he was interested in meeting with us directly."

"How nice you could come." Rosie said as she slipped into the seat against the wall with Bucky sliding in next to her.

"Please, call me Ron," Agent Thompson said. The group placed their orders and enjoyed a few pleasantries before Thompson spoke seriously.

"Let me tell you how I see what's happening to the three of you. This is confidential. Those guys at Farid's house and that woman are not good people. They're part of a ring under investigation. As the autopsy showed. Farid was dead before Sophie shot him. He had been poisoned. So, while Sophie did shoot him, she did not kill him. He was not asleep in his chair. He was already dead."

"Why, that means Sophie is innocent!" Rosie said. "What happens next?"

"We think these people did it. Why they poisoned your client's husband remains to be seen. It will come out. It always does. It's likely Farid no longer served their purpose, or they thought he was too soft or too difficult. I understand there were children living on either side of the house, correct?"

"Yes. Two little girls, ten and twelve years old on one side, and two boys, twelve and fourteen, on the other. Do you think they were using Farid and his boys with a plan to kidnap those kids?" Rosie asked in a hushed, tense voice.

"We think Farid was only accustomed to identifying young kids or needy older women. He had his own boys and was extremely protective of them. How many kids, twelve and fourteen, are walked to and from school by their stepmother?" Wes asked.

"So, by killing Farid and setting Sophie up, it took care of several problems. Her testimony of abuse would not be taken seriously. In their opinion it would be one of those 'He Said-She Said' cases. It might even have looked as if Sophie shot him to shut him up about her involvement. They weren't aware she had been identified by a social worker and or had confided in a counselor." Ron added.

"Let's just sit on this info for the time being. We have a search warrant for the three and have secured the house. Men are watching discreetly to avoid them from breaking in. Tell the neighbors not to be alarmed if they see our guys lurking behind the privacy fence in their yards. If your client has any idea where the deceased could have hidden damaging evidence, inform me right away. Under no circumstances are either of you, or Sophie's attorney, to go back to the house.

"Lastly, warn her not to talk to any lady prisoners about her case. Just because they're locked up doesn't mean they're not involved in the drug and sex trafficking industry. They all have ways of getting messages out," Thompson said.

"I'll head to Columbus in the morning and check out juvenile records, adult criminal records, and birth records for Sophie," Wes said. "'Washington' was her legal name, right? And her son was born in Columbus, too? What year are we thinking? Maybe 1964 when she was about 17?"

"Your purpose may have changed, Wes," Rosie said. "We were developing mitigating factors to assist in her defense. Now we're attempting to break up a sex trafficking ring. I plan to visit Sophie again tomorrow. Maybe if I go after lunch, she will have managed to eat something, even though jail food leaves a lot to be desired. I gave her some homework to do before my next visit. I want to see if she did it and go over it with her. Should I let the cat out of the bag and inform her of her innocence?"

"I'm not her attorney, Rosie, but you might want to first ask if she was aware of the relationships Farid had with those people," Bucky said. "See if she was suspicious of his nefarious activity."

"I agree with Bucky," Wes said. "A few days won't make any difference. Besides, you said you were going to get her to consent to obtaining private medical and mental health records. That might still be worthwhile."

"All this activity may be helpful," Thompson added. "I would appreciate if you'd keep me in the loop with anything you find."

"Of course," Rosie said. "I'll make appointments with the school principal and counselor to warn them of the lurking danger for their students. I may also touch base with Doris Simpson, and Sophie's counselor. It's possible they suspected there was more to this guy than just being an abusive man. I was going to say, 'husband,' but he never married her."

"On the way to your mother's, Rosie, let's swing by Ana's House in Gambier and try to locate the Lamberts, if they're still living."

"I'd like to do that, Bucky, but now there's no need for the Lamberts to come up for an interview since Sophie won't be tried. Although, once Sophie is exonerated, she could see them, and she will need to start over some place. On the other hand, my guess is she'll decide to get a job closer to her son and continue with counseling. Now, she has to work on starting to heal and letting go of her past."

***

Back home, as Rosie placed her purse on the kitchen table, the phone rang. She picked it up and recognized Trisha's voice before any words were spoken. Bucky took the leash from her hand and headed outside to walk Jocko.

"I hope I am not bothering you, again, Dr. Klein."

"Not at all Trisha. I wanted to talk to you anyway. But to what do I owe the pleasure of this call?"

"I spoke with Madison and Megan about the woman in the blue car who tried to talk to them on several occasions. Madison told me that one recent afternoon, the lady was standing across the street from school, leaning against her car door. There was a small camera hanging from her shoulder. They were leaving school and she called them by name, then asked if they would like to have their pictures taken for a pre-teen magazine she worked for.

"My little girl, Madison, became really excited according to Megan. But Megan was suspicious when the woman asked them to walk over to the park and pose. Megan also said her camera did not look professional. She described it as a cheap, instamatic camera. Megan grabbed Madison's arm and pulled her back behind the playground fence. The woman drove off, and Megan decided they should stay at the after-school program for a while."

"They never mentioned this to you?"

"No. I asked Megan why she didn't tell me when it happened and whether she told her principal or teacher? She said she didn't realize she needed to say anything. At the time, their teachers weren't on the playground with the kids or she might have told them. There are only after school workers who supervise."

"Well, Trisha, we've been informed by the FBI that Mr. Jordan was most likely involved in a sex trafficking ring. Would you be willing to help us apprehend these people?"

"Sounds dangerous, but yes, of course. I need my girls

to be safe. But I want to see those people put away for a long time. How exactly can we help?"

"Expect a call from Agent Ron Thompson from the FBI. He may want to set up a sting operation and you might be helpful. We don't think the ring knows we're on to them yet. And with Sophie in jail, they probably feel secure. For now, Trisha, I need you to warn Petra. Traffickers don't just abduct girls. Her boys could also be in danger. By the way, have you had any conversations with her about the people spying on the Jordan house?"

"Yes. We talked about it and we each noticed both the men and woman visiting Farid while Sophie was at work on different days. When I saw them, they came together but in separate cars. Petra and I both thought it was odd, maybe some kind of shady business deal. But we didn't want to appear like we were poking into other people's business, not until you asked us about these things.," Trisha said.

"Neither one of us thinks Sophie knew anything about it. We felt sorry for her because we could see how tired she was when she came home from work, then having to walk up to the school and back with the boys."

"Well, we now believe Sophie will be alright, but we still have to catch these people," Rosie said. "Please call me if you see any activity at the house, except for the FBI men who will also be watching."

CHAPTER 15

THE SCHOOL STAFF

Rosie parked her car in the faculty lot. She approached the side doors of DeVeaux School and entered quietly. Straight ahead was a sign on the Principal's office door. "All visitors must check in here." Rosie entered the room and introduced herself to Mrs. Gwen Kennedy, an attractive, jovial secretary. *The children probably feel comfortable with* Mrs. *Kennedy here when they are sent to the principal's office.* Rosie thought. *She certainly lights up the room with her smile.*

"Hello. My name is Dr. Klein; I have an appointment with Mr. Newman," she said as the woman looked up.

Mrs. Kennedy buzzed Mr. Newman and announced Dr. Klein was there to speak with him. She stood and ushered Rosie into his office. Mr. Newman came around his desk to shake Rosie's hand. "How can I help you, Dr. Klein?" He spoke in a clear, strong voice.

"Please call me Rosie, Sir. I'm the psychologist appointed to evaluate Sophie Jordan. I'm sure you're aware of her circumstances and the death of Ali and Omar's father, Farid Jordan."

"Yes, the boys are temporarily placed in foster care with a family living in our district, the Conrad family. They also foster other children in our school. Ali and Omar have not yet returned to school. I, for one, can understand that given the trauma they've experienced."

"I'm actually here to ask if they ever saw your school counselor, and to provide you with some other rather disturbing information."

"Oh. Well, first, would you care for some coffee? I'm about to get a refill myself. Secondly, just call me Mark."

Rosie accepted the offer of coffee, if only to establish a relationship and collect her thoughts. Mark Newman brought forward a carafe and a mug with the school logo on the side.

"Thank you, Mark." Rosie began. "The local authorities and the FBI believe there are dangers looming toward DeVeaux students. This is based on information they have developed regarding a sex trafficking ring. Two little neighbor girls of Sophie's have been approached on more than one occasion by a woman in a light blue BMW convertible. Have you noticed her near the grounds? Recently, she tried to lure Megan and Madison Small as they left school. "

"Wow. No, we weren't aware. I know those sweet little girls. But my back is to the window when I sit at my desk and the sidewalk leading to the street is not visible. Parents pull up in front to get their kids and some, like Mrs. Jordan, walk them up to the flagpole. Has anyone been abducted?"

"Not at this time. But Agent Thompson of the FBI is

of the opinion that the Jordan neighbor kids were being targeted without knowing it. We believe Mr. Jordan's boys could have been used to lure their next-door neighbor's girls and the Gonzalez boys on the other side of his house. But we have no evidence of that, nor that the boys, themselves, were aware. Mr. Jordan never allowed his boys out of the yard or out of his sight, except when he made Sophie walk them home.

Rosie continued her story. "Mark, the other day, I entered the Jordan house to retrieve some of Sophie's belongs. I was followed by two men in a black Nissan. My friend, Bucky, noticed them but didn't tell me until later. We met Sophie's attorney at a local restaurant to turn over the objects we found in the house, believing they could be evidence on her behalf. The person we were meeting there later saw the same car near his home. We believe he was followed. So, we know someone is watching."

"Rosie, earlier, you asked about whether the Jordan boys saw our school counselor. Let's call him into the office and check whether he knew Ali and Omar."

Mr. Newman buzzed Mrs. Kennedy. "Gwen, please ask Mr. Cink to come down to the office."

As they waited, Rosie explained that despite what Mr. Newman might have heard, Mrs. Jordan did not kill him, and the case remained unsolved at this point.

Mr. Cink tapped on the half open door. "Hello."

"Come in, Stan! This is Dr. Rosie Klein, a psychologist for Sophie Jordan," Mark Newman introduced him as Stan Cink and gestured for him to sit down. "Stan, do you know the Jordan boys? They're the kids who just went into foster care with the Conrad family."

"Yes, I do. I wanted the younger boy, Omar, to participate in a socialization group but his father wouldn't consent. The boy is very shy, and I thought the group would help him develop a few friendships. He seems to enjoy working on soccer skills by himself. I've watched him do it and he is quite agile, a promising athlete.

"Ali, on the other hand, makes friends by playing casual sports during recess. He demonstrates an attitude, though, when he misses shots, especially when his next-door neighbor, Miguel, is so accurate. I guess Miguel has a hoop in the driveway for practice, but he once told me Ali has never been allowed to go over to his house. I know Miguel because I coach the eighth-grade basketball team, and he's our point guard. Miguel and Ali's personalities are totally different. Ali is very humble and protective of his little brother," Stan pointed out.

"How are they doing with the death of their father and imprisonment of their stepmother?" Mark asked. "Omar seemed extremely attached to her. I noticed he would greet her with a hug when she met them after school."

"She's raised him since he was four." Rosie explained. "I've not met the boys. But I know her story from what Sophie has told me: She was lured to Toledo to become a nanny for Jordan's two little boys. She didn't realize she was being trafficked herself. When he pulled up outside her church, his deal sounded good right at a time when she was trying to start a new path in life. But once in his car, he wouldn't allow her to pick up her belongings or say good-bye to Mr. and Mrs. Lambert, her landlords and good friends. That's when she knew she was in trouble but couldn't get away. He told her he would buy her new clothes and she could mail a nice note to the Lamberts from his house.

"Based on how she was mistreated by Farid Jordan, I have come to believe she was his sex slave and beaten into submission. He threatened that If she ever left, he would harm the Lamberts who had welcomed her into their home in Gambier. When he found out the social worker at her new job had arranged for her to get counseling on her lunch hour, he ended that. He, also, alienated her from her only son, and he never married her, but let people think so for appearance sake."

"Sounds like she has had a miserable life," Stan said. "The boys may have been her only source of purpose and love. Oh, by the way, I just remembered that when I arranged for the eighth-grade boys to have their pictures taken and visit the high school. Mr. Jordan did not permit Ali to participate."

"Is there anyone else you would like to speak to, Rosie?" Mark Newman asked.

"As a matter of fact, what do you think about me talking to your school nurse?"

"I don't know about you, Mark, but I think she may have some strong thoughts about those little boys. Can we call her in?" Stan asked.

Mr. Newman buzzed Mrs. Kennedy. "Please check to see if Polly Hochwalt is in her office. If so, ask her to come and talk with us."

"I saw her come into the building. I will have her join you."

Before long, Polly Hochwalt appeared at the door. Mr. Newman invited her in and introduced her to Rosie.

"Nice to meet you Dr. Klein." Polly responded, taking a seat.

"Polly and Stan have a close working relationship," Mr. Newman explained. "They frequently see the same children by referring them to one another. The three of us often have a late lunch together and talk after supervising the student lunchroom. When Polly here suspects abuse or neglect, she asks Stan to talk to them privately. On the other hand, if a child appears to be sick or undernourished, Stan refers the child to Polly. They also engage in parent conferences together to express concerns. It's a great team we have here."

"Have you had any professional relationships with Ali or Omar Jordan?" Rosie asked.

"On one occasion, Omar's teacher sent him to see me because she noticed a lump on the back of his head and crusted blood in his hair above his left ear. I asked him how he got the lump and he said he backed into the door frame of his bedroom to avoid his brother," Polly said. "He couldn't say how the blood got in his hair. He acted like he knew nothing about it. It wasn't enough information to call the authorities and I wondered if he had been bullied on the playground. When I asked him if any of our boys were responsible, he said 'no.' But I decided to watch him inside and outside the building for a while. He was very shy, and I never observed any display of aggression toward him. Kids just left him to himself."

"I remember you asking me about Omar, Polly." Said Stan. "I spoke to his stepmother when she waited at the flagpole soon after that. She said she would keep him cleaner and blamed herself for the crusted blood. She explained he had a habit of picking his nose and depositing what he found behind his ear. I wasn't sure I believed her story. She also hadn't noticed the bump on his head and said he usually wore a knit hat, even indoors."

"How long ago was that incident?" Asked Rosie.

Polly and Stan looked at one another as if trying to put their heads together. "I think it was in January some time," Polly said. "It was cold outside, and I remember wondering why he was wearing a short-sleeved tee shirt in school when most kids were wearing sweaters. I looked for any bruises or scrape marks on his arms, but there weren't any. When I told you, I watched him during recess, I meant in the gym. The kids are not on the playground in cold weather," she explained.

"Do you think these boys may be returned to Sophie, the only mother they have known?" Stan asked. "But I don't imagine you can answer that, right Dr. Klein?"

"Sophie has been through so much. She may

want to move near her own son and start over," Rosie said. "I can see her remaining in the boys' lives on a visitation basis. On the other hand, if she stays with them, they could give her a sense of hope. If Mr. Jordan owned the home, maybe she would be permitted to live there as their guardian. Who knows at this point? I do have one more question…How was their attendance and grades?"

"I can answer that easily enough," Stan said. "Give me a minute to go to my office and pull their records."

While he was gone, Rosie asked Polly how long she had been at DeVeaux School.

"It's been six years," she answered.

"And in all my years of education," Mark interrupted, "I've not met a more committed, competent school nurse."

"Thank you, Mr. Newman," Polly said, "we have a mutual admiration society here at DeVeaux," Miss Hotchwalt smiled at Dr. Klein. "I find Mark's support immensely valuable especially when dealing with parents in uncomfortable situations. I know that Mr. Cink feels the same way."

"Okay. Here we go," Stan Cink said returning with his files. "Their attendance has been excellent with no tardiness. I guess they could never oversleep with a stepmother ready and waiting to walk them to school. Their father stopped driving them when Sophie came to live at their house, I believe."

"I suspected that would be the case," Mark Newman said.

"I do remember a few years back when Mr. Jordan did work outside the home," Mr. Cink continued. "He would drop them off in the morning, and Mrs. Jordan walked them home after school let out. She also worked at Crystal Manor during school hours at that time because we had their phone number for emergencies.

"On the other hand, let's talk about grades: Ali will attend high school next year. He has also qualified by test scores and grades for advanced placement classes. His IQ is in the top two and a half percent of children for his age group. But when we sent the kids on a field trip to the high school building recently, he was not allowed to participate. During the class visit, he could have met his teachers for Geometry, Biology, Honors English, Spanish 2, and World History. It was a shame his father wouldn't let him go. It might have helped him feel more at home his first freshman week. That's why we hold the high school visit. Sometimes, when a parent is too strict, it's not so good."

"What do you think Mr. Jordan was afraid of Dr. Klein?" Mark Newman asked. "Or was he wanting to keep a low profile for some reason? Not draw attention to himself or his kids' whereabouts?"

"Hard to say, but for whatever reason, the FBI will get to the bottom of it. For now, we have a predator contacting kids in this neighborhood, and our priority should be to protect them all." Rosie said.

"Well, we certainly hope these boys will remain in our school district either with the Conrad family or in the care of Sophie," Stan Cink said. "Knowing their history, we'll work as a team to support them any way we can."

"Now, as for Omar. It's a different story. He requires more direct supervision in a smaller group setting. The regular classroom seems too distracting for him. I see his teachers have brought this to his father's attention several times, but there has been no approval to provide extra assistance. His grades are average to below average although he has been cooperative and seems to try his best."

"Well, if they remain with us, we will approach his caretakers and make sure this little guy gets the help he needs, all around," Mark said.

"Well, everyone, I must be going," Rosie stood to leave. "Thank you all for your time and valuable input. I'll be sure to let the Judge know the situation." The staff members all stood and shook hands with her, thanking her for her interest in the Jordan family.

As she walked down the steps, the first bell rang, allowing children to enter the building and proceed to their classrooms. Rosie walked by a security guard standing beside the stairwell leading to the second floor. A bright red sign on the wall indicated the sixth, seventh, and eighth grade classrooms were upstairs.

She watched as the guard intently observed older kids mounting the stairs, barely noticing Kindergarteners passing him on the way to their own wing. He stood with his arms behind his back, feet spread wide, and did not engage in conversation with any of them. None of the children acknowledged him.

He might as well have been a statue, she thought.

Some missed opportunities there.

Outside each classroom, a teacher stood greeting the students as they entered. It seemed to be from the first through fifth grades. Occasionally, one would remind someone not to run in the hall or for boys to remove their hats in the building. Their own students said, "good morning" as they entered the room and moved toward their desks. They were obviously allowed to chat among themselves until the second bell signaled silence.

Rosie thought about going back to the office and asking Mrs. Kennedy what security company they used, and the name of the guard. Instead, she left the building and made a mental note to follow-up later in the day. She looked but didn't see any kind of official vehicle to let the public know there was security in the building. Once, she had read that positioning a security vehicle or police car in front of a school could deter potential attacks. Then, she spotted the black Nissan parked in the faculty lot. It was not near her car and had not been there when she arrived earlier in the morning.

Glancing in the rearview mirror periodically, Rosie drove home. She needed to let Jocko out and have an early lunch before going to see Sophie. As she was eating her stuffed grape leaves on the patio, the phone rang. Stepping inside, she slid both doors shut. The caller ID said "Ruth" and she grabbed the phone.

No rest for the wicked, my father used to say.

"Hi Rosie. You have three messages of importance and six others calling for appointments. According to three messages of importance, one is from Attorney Chickalette.

He desperately wants to speak to you yesterday! Ha! I figure you may want to give him a personal call back since Sophie Jordan, I mean Washington, won't likely be going to court. Looks like you can begin Chickalette's case sooner than you expected, right?"

"I guess you're right, Ruth. Maybe when I leave jail this afternoon, I'll stop by his office instead of giving him a call."

"Do you want me to let him know you'll be coming?"

"That might be a good idea, so he doesn't think we've ignored his calls. I need to inform him of the problem we might have with Judge Tucker, since his wife, Penny, is my dear friend...you know, conflict of interest."

"I know you'll be objective, Rosie. Don't you think the Judge will maintain his professionalism? After all, your testimony must convince the jury, not the Judge."

"Of course, I know he will, Ruth. Still, just the look of favoritism might seem like a conflict of interest to the public. He'll have to make that judgment call."

Jocko barked to come inside. Rosie slid open one door, and let him in, then handed him a treat, and returned to her conversation with Ruth.

"By the way, Rosie, your four-thirty client cancelled due to illness. But I filled the time slot already with Ash'lee. She grabbed the appointment when I offered it to her this morning."

"That's fine. I'll get to the Summerhill office around four o'clock."

As a beautician, Ash'lee used Mondays as her second day off, the first being Sunday. This reminded Rosie she needed a haircut herself soon. Rosie and Ash'lee bartered for services to one another. Ash'lee attended the women's divorce group at no charge, and in exchange, Rosie had her hair styled at regular appointments.

Rosie met Ash'lee at the jail many years ago when she had been arrested for possession of narcotics and was appointed a public defender. Being in an abusive marriage, she could have used Battered Women's Syndrome (BWS) as her defense, but Ash'lee insisted that Post Traumatic Stress Disorder (PTSD) be used instead, only because she understood that one. So, when a mental health evaluation was requested to prepare her defense, Rosie was appointed her psychologist, which began their friendship.

Ash'lee told her attorney back then that she had begun pushing drugs for her husband to keep him off her back. Then, she started using the marijuana herself because she found it reduced the extreme anxiety of her situation in which she felt helpless and hopeless. She hadn't been familiar with the term "BWS" back then, even though she suffered from it. So, she insisted that Post Traumatic Stress Disorder be used instead.

Actually, Rosie thought, Battered Women's Syndrome is a subcategory of PTSD. Ash'lee's husband was domineering and his physical and emotional abuse took away her freedom and self-control, the true definition of BWS. Even so, Post Traumatic Stress Disorder is a mental disorder that develops after a person is exposed to a traumatic event and continually suffers from it.

Then, again, you could argue that her

dysfunctional marriage was a tragic event. One from which she was able to escape only after being arrested for trafficking her husband's drugs.

God sure works in mysterious ways, Rosie decided.

CHAPTER 16

THE BLACK NISSAN

Ron Thompson picked up the phone on its first ring.

"Hello, Ron Thompson speaking."

"Hi Ron, Rosie Klein here; I have some news about Sophie's case. Is this a good time to talk a minute about a case?"

"Yes, let me just grab a pen...okay, what have you got, Rosie?"

"Well, the lady in the blue BMW usually stands outside the fence by DeVeaux School. She approached the Small girls, one day, and asked if they wanted their pictures taken for a pre-teen magazine. The older girl, Megan, grabbed her sister and ran back into the building and kind of hid in the after-school program to stay safe. But that seems to be at least one way she tries enticing young girls into her car.

"As for the black Nissan, I saw it parked in the school faculty lot this morning. I was there to interview the principal, counselor, and nurse, and it wasn't there when I arrived, but the Nissan was there when I left. It may belong to the security guard who stands by the stairwell to the second floor, but it's just a hunch. The sixth through eighth grade classrooms are upstairs."

"Whoa! Are you thinking the trafficking ring has a security guard in the building? That would make it easy to scout for potential youngsters. Unfortunately, it does make sense to me, Dr. Klein. Did you get the license plate number of the Nissan?"

"Yes, I did. It's a Michigan plate. Number is 776CGAL."

"Thank you. I'm pleased to tell you the car has not been seen near your friend Bucky's house or yours or Attorney Greenberg's since Sunday. I'm hoping Sophie Jordan will be able to fill in some of the blanks for us. What do you think?" Agent Thompson asked.

"I'll definitely ask her some pertinent questions this afternoon and let you know if I hear anything relevant," Rosie answered.

She decided to make one more call before heading to the jail.

"Hello, Petra. This is Rosie Klein. How are you today?"

"Just a little nervous these days, Dr. Klein. But Jose and I have been keeping close tabs on our boys and haven't said anything to them. Don't want them to be afraid."

"Have you had any contact with the woman in the blue BMW, Petra?"

"No. She hasn't been spotted since Mr. Jordan died. I should probably feel sorry for those boys; their father was weird and controlling. But I need to tell you something I just remembered: Our younger boys, Manny, and Omar were supposed to work with one other boy on a science project. It had to be a group project of at least three children. They wanted to do it with Omar, but Mr. Jordan simply would not allow Omar to come over. I think he cost his son a good grade. I don't know what excuse he gave the teacher for Omar's non-participation. "

"Well, Petra, that certainly fits the profile of a man who has something to hide. By controlling his family's contact with the outside world, he prevents being discovered."

"What will happen to the boys, Dr. Klein?"

"The Principal at DeVeaux School told me they are staying with the Conrad family. He said since they live in the school district, and have fostered other kids, they didn't mind taking in the two boys for now. At least their education won't be interrupted."

"I know the Conrad family. Mr. and Mrs. Conrad own a family business, a hardware store in the Village of Centerville. Their own kids are grown and gone, except for their oldest son who manages the store. The Conrads both have second careers now in law enforcement. Recently, they cared for two other little boys whose mother was addicted to cocaine. In that case, the mom lived at a Christian rehab home called Ana's House for a year and then received back custody of her children. As far as I know, she's doing fine even though they have since moved to a different school district to be closer to the biological father."

"Interesting. Well, thanks, Petra for contacting me. I will keep you posted to further developments in the case. Agent Thompson might call you to inquire about more details."

"You're quite welcome, Dr. Klein. I wish I had seen the faces of the men in the Nissan. I do remember how they were built. I saw them walking up to the Jordan front door. One was about six feet tall and stocky, not fat. He was white and wore a long gray, tweed overcoat, black hat, and black, leather gloves. If I am not mistaken, he walked with a limp. The other guy was shorter and slender. He wore a navy sports coat and had black, curly hair. I think he held a lit cigarette."

"Those details might be helpful to Agent Thompson's investigation. I'll be sure to tell him to call you. By any chance, did you ever see the security guard at the school? He basically stood against the wall so I wouldn't notice if he has a limp. Otherwise, he does meet the description of the six-foot guy and drives a black Nissan."

"Sorry. I have never seen a guard in the building. Be blessed and stay safe Dr. Klein."

***

While driving downtown to see Sophie, Rosie wondered about Wes now on his way to Columbus to make some inquiries about Sophie's pregnancy, childbirth, and police arrests. She also thought about Josh Greenberg and wondered if he had visited his client to break the news about the autopsy report yet?

I wonder how she reacted. The fact that she couldn't kill a man already dead, must have come as a relief... not to mention quite a shock! By shooting a dead man, Sophie would only be accused of gross abuse of a corpse and probably was only facing probation. Whereas if she had really been the cause of Jordan's death, she would have gotten years of prison time. Still, the mystery remained: Who poisoned Farid Jordan?

Arriving at LaSalle Tower, Rosie gave her car keys to the young attendant and stuffed a five-dollar bill into the palm of his hand.

"I'll be back in two hours."

Her two-block walk to the County Jail was far more pleasant with the warm Spring breeze. Sunny, blue skies had transformed the snowy, slushy sidewalks. She greeted Deputy Jeff Ambrose and placed her belongings on the conveyer belt to be scanned. She stepped through the metal detector and retrieved her briefcase and purse on the other side. Deputy Ambrose buzzed her through the secure doors to the visitation area where Deputy Jim Testerman stood. He unlocked the door and told her Officer Mitchell had been notified to bring Sophie Washington down.

"Your inmate is quite popular today. You're the third professional visitor."

"Really? Mind me asking who the other two were?" Rosie expected one to be Attorney Greenberg but was interested in knowing who else might have been there.

"Greenberg was joined later by Matthew Murphy. Can't say we often see the defense and prosecutor meeting together with an inmate."

Rosie assumed they came to see Sophie and have her sign an agreement informing her that the charges were being dismissed. That might mean she would be released soon. But released to where?

Verna Mitchell escorted Sophie to the visitation room. She smiled at Rosie and started to back out of the room when Dr. Klein stopped her.

"Officer Mitchell, it seems you have a concert coming up with Ruth, my dedicated office manager soon."

Verna laughed. "I try hard to keep my personal life to myself, yet here you know the inside scoop, Dr. Klein."

"I look forward to hearing your lovely voices. It's a patriotic concert on the fourth of July, isn't it? Well, good luck. Or should I say, 'break a leg'?"

When Officer Mitchell left, Dr. Klein turned her attention to Sophie who had placed folded sheets of paper upright on the table.

"I did my homework, Dr. Klein, and suppose you heard the news. According to my attorney and the prosecutor, my murder charges are being dropped. I can't believe it! God sure works in mysterious ways, doesn't He? And I think He had your help."

"You know, Sophie, there isn't usually an autopsy performed when there is a confession, and it needs to be ordered by someone. But somehow, one was done, and I wasn't even aware, until I heard about the results. Maybe the FBI had a hunch that paid off, Sophie."

"No one from the FBI has ever interviewed me. Do you think they will once I'm released?"

"Tell me what you've heard, Sophie, and maybe I can fill in the blanks."

"My lawyer said Farid was poisoned three hours before I shot him. The beer cans had fingerprints on them that showed Farid did not drink all three cans himself. At least, one or two other people handled the cans."

"Wow, Sophie. I didn't know that. Once it was confirmed that he was not alone, it must have allowed further investigation like ordering an autopsy."

"The prosecutor said all charges will be dropped in exchange for my cooperation in breaking up the sex trafficking ring. Dr. Klein, I had no idea Farid was that evil. I'm so happy nothing happened to the little girls and boys who lived next door. Have their mothers talked to you?"

"Yes, they have. Petra Gonzalez has been upset for a long time because Ali and Omar were not allowed at her house. Did you know Omar was supposed to do a group science project with Manny and another boy?"

"As a matter of fact, I did. His teacher stopped me at the flagpole one day and asked why Omar didn't participate. I didn't know what to say. I couldn't tell the truth, or we all would have been in deep trouble with Farid. He was mean and we would have suffered terribly."

"You were in a terrible position, Sophie. Don't blame yourself. Did the boys ever complain to you in confidence?"

"Yes. I would say their father loved them and wanted what he thought was best. I know that's what you're supposed to say. But they would tell me I was lying and stomp off. They didn't even know how much he abused me. It was always after they were in bed or when they were forced to stay outside."

"Didn't they wonder about your bed in the pantry?"

"I told them the mattress was there for a shelter in case we had a storm. They thought I slept upstairs and was married to their father. I'm glad I can now get back to being Sophie Washington."

"Where will you go?"

"I don't know. The prosecutor said Farid had three mortgages on the house. Since I was not married to him, I am not financially responsible. But I also cannot live there. You have met Officer Mitchell. She has a Bed and Breakfast not far from my old neighborhood. She offered me a small apartment if I will for fix breakfast for the guests on the mornings that she works the early shift here. She said, the apartment has its own separate entrance behind the large house. It has a second bedroom if the boys were to be returned to me. She said she would pay them to do lawn care and snow removal. Wouldn't that be great, Dr. Klein?"

"I could still work part-time at Crystal Manor just like I did before. I heard the boys are with a nice foster care family. Dr. Klein, I love those boys. I think they love me, too." If they will have me back, the boys are old enough to walk home alone and get started on their homework or chores. Will they be safe? Do you think the people trafficking kids will be arrested soon?"

"I will speak to the family services people and let them know you are willing to remain in the jurisdiction of the Lucas County family court. How will your son feel about that?"

"My son, Adam, will understand if I stay here. Hard to believe he is already thirty, and I missed all those years with him. He is busy with his teaching career and his wife. With Farid gone, I am no longer prevented from seeing him. I am interested in meeting his adoptive parents, John, and Brenda Harris. They did a great job. He seems to be a happy, responsible young man. I think we can have a nice relationship without me moving to Bowling Green. He will be such a good role model for Ali and Omar."

"Did your attorney indicate how long it will take for your release? Can I transport you somewhere?

"My attorney said it could be as soon as Wednesday. I can let you know if I need a ride.

"Okay. I will leave you my card. I think you have a terrific plan in mind. I will speak to the family services authorities to work on getting the boys back. You know they'll need counseling. You all have been through a terrible time. I'll volunteer to see them and do some family work with the three of you, if you think that would help."

"I really liked my counselor, Dr. Klein. I don't know if she realizes I quit coming because Farid found out. Doris most likely told her. I would like to continue seeing her for just myself since she knows me. Maybe you can work with us as a family. Would that be okay?"

"Of course, Sophie, may I see your homework?"

"I did my homework before I knew I would be free."

"Then, I think your answers will be different. Let me see your completion to the statement about 'I could be perfectly happy...'"

"Well, I said I could be perfectly happy 'if I never had met Farid Jordan.'"

"How would you change your answer now?"

"I could be perfectly happy 'if I could help other women avoid relationships with abusive men.'"

"That is so kind of you, Sophie. You have learned much more from your experience than you might have learned from books or classes. You have suffered such pain at the hands of Farid. I'm grateful to God that He has answered my prayers to be released from the Hell I was living," Sophie said in a soft, quiet tone with tears in her eyes.

"Let me ask you a question, Sophie: Do you have any idea what the traffickers were looking to find in your house? Did you see Farid hide anything or lock anything up?"

"He did have a safe hidden behind a framed picture of Muhammad. It was in his bedroom next to the closet door. He was supposedly praying to the East three times a day and always expected quiet and privacy."

"Interesting. Maybe there is something in that safe that would incriminate the traffickers. I will let Agent Thompson know. Did you ever see him praying?"

"One night, I passed by the room after putting clean clothes in the boys' room. His door was cracked open. He certainly was not praying. He was looking out the window toward the Small's house. Their bedrooms are on our side and he had something in his hands. I don't know what."

"Maybe he was spying on them. It could have been a camera or binoculars. On another subject, have you been in touch with the Lamberts since you left them eight years ago, Sophie?"

"As far as I know, they wouldn't have a clue where I went or how to find me."

"If we locate them, would you like to see them?"

"Oh my, yes, of course. They were genuine Christian

people. They trusted me when they had no reason to trust. I was a mess when I arrived at Ana's House. After those years, I had nowhere to go. The Lamberts welcomed me. They didn't care about my past or the color of my skin.

"Another thing, Dr. Klein, what happened to my clothes? I know you found the evidence I told you about and my get-away bag. Is there a chance when I leave here I can have my clothes and uniforms? If I don't go back to Crystal Manor, I need to return the uniforms. If I do go back, my work shoes are in the house and my employee badge."

"Don't worry, Sophie. I will get your things one way or another as soon as I leave today."

"There are a couple of other things I would like to have back, too. My one-year medal for sobriety is in a coffee can in the refrigerator. Farid didn't drink coffee, so I kept a few personal things in the Folgers can."

"If they haven't searched the house and confiscated the can, I will retrieve it. They are searching for anything that will affiliate him with the trafficking ring. Now then, Sophie, is there anything else?"

"No. I'm just so happy, even if my face don't show it. How can I thank you enough?"

"No need, Sophie, I can feel it."

Rosie stood and beckoned to Testerman to unlock the door. Sophie got up and smiled for the first time. They both exited the interview room for the last time. Verna Mitchell was positioned just around the corner and led Sophie down the hall to her cell for a couple more days.

As Rosie exited the building; the air seemed crisp and clean.

No more bleak, gray skies for Sophie Washington. The best is yet to come for that lady and thank heaven, for those Jordan boys. Rosie looked at her watch. I might just have enough time to drop by Chickalette's office before heading to Summerhill. He might be expecting me if Ruth called his office to say I would stop in.

Picking up her pace, she took a deep breath of fresh air. Each time she left the jail she felt oh, but for the grace of God go I. After her husband died so unexpectedly, Rosie had the unconditional love of family and friends, and the respect of professional colleagues to help her through that rough time. She was blessed to have that strong framework for building a meaningful future.

How sad that Sophie has never experienced such love from a family of her own, she thought. *But maybe she has a second chance now.*

CHAPTER 17

PLANNING THE STING

Rosie approached the administrative assistant seated at a glass top desk facing the door of John Chickalette's law firm.

"Good afternoon. I'm Dr. Rosie Klein. I believe Attorney Chickalette is expecting me."

"As a matter of fact, he did say to keep an eye open for you, Dr. Klein. He would like you to go right in. Can I get you water or a beverage?" the perky, young assistant asked as she showed Rosie to his office door.

"Thank you for asking. Water sounds great if it's not too much trouble."

"Not at all. I'm studying to be a court reporter and want you to know how much I admire you, Dr. Klein. I've observed your testimony and heard you testify on several high-profile cases."

"Thank you very much. I appreciate your feedback. And what is your name?"

"I'm Susan Newman. My dad told me he just met you at his school. He's the principal at DeVeaux," she said. Then, turning away, she knocked lightly on the mahogany door and opened it. "Dr Klein is here," she said to a large man behind an ornate desk.

"Ah, good, please show her in," Rosie heard a deep voice say. As she passed by Susan, she added, "Thank you. You have a genuinely nice father. Good luck in your professional goals."

"Hello, Rosie, good to see you!" John Chickalette stood and walked around the desk, all 6'3" of him. He motioned Rosie to a seat on the chocolate brown, leather chair in front of his oversized, cluttered desk.

"Good to see you again, Chick," she laughed and sat down. Chick handed her a manilla envelope and told her how happy he was she was coming on board the team for his client. He briefly explained the specific services he needed her to complete. Their discussion wasn't long into particulars of the case when he unexpectedly stood, and said he was due in Court within minutes, and would she accompany him to the lobby.

"Of course," she agreed, and left the office with him as they continued to chat while riding the elevator down to the main floor.

"Thank you," she said as they exited the elevator. "Let me know when I've been officially appointed so I can visit your client. She's being held without bail, I assume."

"Yes, Rosie. Her husband is in the Air Force, and her alleged crimes occurred in base housing and in more than one state. She needs a civilian attorney. Can we talk on Friday?"

"Absolutely, Chick. I will review the material

and let you know what else I might need."

Rosie recognized the valet who retrieved her vehicle without hesitation. As a struggling grad student, he loved her tips, and she was known to be very generous. Rosie drove to her condo to pick up Jocko and take him to her Summerhill office. Jocko was like a therapy dog since everyone loved his big, furry, docile presence. No matter what anyone was feeling, he seemed to put them at ease when they are uptight or blue.

She hurried to the office to make a few phone calls before seeing clients. Arriving, she jotted down several names. First, she wanted to touch base with Bucky.

I can hardly wait for Mom to meet him.

Secondly, she wanted to follow-up with Agent Thompson and inform him about the need to retrieve Sophie's clothes and few belongings. Then she would inquire as to whether his team found anything relevant during their search.

Bucky answered on the second ring.

"Hi Bucky. How's your day going?"

"Rosie, glad you called! Are you interested in dinner? Now that you know your way around my kitchen, I thought we could cook here tonight."

"That sounds great. Thanks again for housing me and Jocko during the threatening weekend. I discovered something interesting to share with you, but it can hold till this evening. I'm just calling to remind you to clear your calendar for our trip to my mother's the second weekend in May."

"Sure. Let's make plans tonight. What will you

do with Jocko that weekend?"

"I'm thinking about taking him with us. Would you mind? If we have his leash, water bowl, and food, he should do fine."

"Naw, that's great, I love that big dog. Does six o'clock tonight work for you, Rosie?"

"Super. I'll bring ice cream. What's your absolute favorite flavor?"

"Coffee, and I have hot fudge."

"Dinner's sounding rather good and I can't wait to see you. Later, hon."

Rosie dialed Agent Thompson's number on his business card. It went to voice mail.

"Hi Ron. This is Rosie. I was wondering if you discovered the safe behind Muhammad's picture at the Jordan house. And secondly, how might I get in to retrieve Sophie's belongings including a coffee can in the refrigerator? No rush. I am available this evening. Just give a call. Hope you get this message soon. Bye for now."

Just as Rosie was ready to lead Jocko to the car, Agent Thompson returned her call.

"Sorry, I couldn't get to the phone in time, Rosie. I listened to your message and have something extremely important to tell you. I think we should meet in person. Can I meet you at your office at five-thirty? It won't take long."

"Absolutely. I'll be done with my marriage counseling appointment by then. Just tell Ruth to send you right in, and I'll push my dinner plans back a little.

Trust me, it's not a problem."

When Rosie arrived at the office, Ruth was on the phone, so they simply acknowledged one another with a nod. Rosie filled Jocko's bowl with cool, clean water and placed it beneath the copy machine. No need for food until they settle in at Bucky's later. Her first client of the day followed her into the office and took her usual position in a comfortable, wingback, armchair.

Later, as Rosie finished writing up her session notes, Agent Thompson appeared at the door with Jocko trailing alongside. She stood to welcome him.

"Have a seat Ron. Can I get you anything? I see you have a new traveling companion. The makings of a K-9 dog, would you say?" They both glanced down at Jocko and laughed.

"No thanks. I won't take much of your time, Rosie. I came to tell you that it's vital the press does not find out Sophie has been exonerated and is about to be released. It will create turmoil with the sex traffickers who currently feel successful in framing her for Farid's death. We want to keep her innocence under wraps until we set them up to be apprehended in the act of abducting or planning to abduct a local child."

"I completely understand. What happens now? There are people who know she is innocent, you know. What about any professionals who might be involved in the ring?"

"We've vetted the deputies at the county jail and feel secure they're clean. We, especially, want it to appear that Sophie has a court date at the beginning of next week. She's been isolated from the general population and has even had her meals brought to her cell."

"What about the DeVeaux staff? I apprised them that she is just the alleged perpetrator and informed them their security guard is suspected of being part of the sex trafficking ring."

"We've met with the three of them, Mr. Newman, Mr. Cink, and Ms. Hochwalt, and their secretaries. They've all agreed to help us set-up the sting for the suspected guard. The two Small girls are going to help us by playing a little drama to entice him since we know they've been noticed by the ring. There will be agents surrounding the area every step of the way. Their mother, Trisha Small, is willing to let her girls help."

"How about the girls? Are they aware this could still be dangerous?"

"The girls see themselves as taking part in a drama. The counselor, Mr. Cink, will ask Megan and Madison to stay after school this Friday to help him organize his library of self-help books since Megan has helped him do odds and ends in the past. At lunch time, Mr. Cink will let the security guard know the girls are staying and tell him he should go ahead and lock the doors when he leaves at the end of the day. Cink will explain that he'll let the girls out the front doors at four-thirty, when some parents are coming to see him for a conference. The guard will know Mr. Cink will remain in the building and will think the girls are walking home alone. It would be the perfect opportunity if he's our guy. His black Nissan will have a tracker on it in case he actually gets them into his car."

"Sounds like a plan. Knowing by lunch time this is going to happen allows the guard time to contact the woman and his other partner, so they can nab the girls. Right?"

"Yep. Correct. If they use the BMW, then our agents will follow them."

"Meanwhile, Attorney Greenberg will let Sophie in on the plan. He'll explain that she needs to stay in jail until the end of next week after this plan goes down. So far, everyone believes she has a hearing on Monday anyhow."

"Did you get my message about the safe behind the Muhammad picture, Ron?"

"Yes. As soon as I heard the message, I called my guys. They went back an hour ago and found the safe. They said the combination was simple to crack and there was a movie camera, movie projector, and some reels of film in it. Apparently, he was filming the Small girls through their second-floor bedroom windows. The traffickers like to see potential victims and these movies definitely would depict two precious, beautiful little girls during their evening routines."

"Why are their routines important?"

"If the girls are practicing an instrument, listening to music, reading, or watching television, the traffickers use those interests to find ways to get their attention. They'll hang out at any nearby library, or bookstore, for instance, to find out if the girls take vocal lessons at a music store."

"Oh my. I had no idea the trafficking business goes about investigating kids that way."

"It will raise your awareness now, Rosie. It truly is a business, and the traffickers are profoundly serious about it. From now on, you'll probably find yourself looking around for people who look like predators when you visit public places where kids may gather."

"You're right. I'll be far less casual when I sit in a bookstore browsing through magazines that I don't intend to buy. Incidentally, Sophie's asked me to retrieve some of her belongings. She's thinking about returning to her job at Crystal Manor and needs her uniforms and shoes. I hope they haven't emptied the refrigerator yet because she keeps valuables in a coffee can."

"I'm sorry. We don't want you anywhere near the house. I'll advise my female agent to gather all women's apparel and grab the can from the refrigerator. She can bring it to you over the weekend. Can you think of anything else Sophie would like to have?"

"No, not at this time. Once I have her belongings, I'll let Sophie know her things are safe with me. I won't alert the social worker, Doris, at Crystal Manor about her circumstances until the traffickers are captured."

"Well, thanks for your time, Rosie,"

They both exited Rosie's office building with Jocko wedged between them. Agent Thompson couldn't help glancing up and down the street for sight of a black

Nissan or the fancy blue BMW.

"I'll let you know when we have these rats in custody. You know, we couldn't have broken this ring without your help. Can't thank you enough; and your community will always be in debt to you. Your practice will, probably, overflow with private clients once word gets out, and the legal community will flood you with appointments to family and criminal court cases. At least I hope so, and I'll be your best referral source."

"Only too glad to help," she said modestly.

CHAPTER 18

TIME OUT

Rosie arrived at Bucky's and released Jocko from his leash. He ambled up to the front door with Rosie tagging along behind. Bucky met them with a smile and gave Rosie a sweet, warm kiss.

"How long before dinner, Bucky? I have an exceptionally long tale to tell you. Do we have time to sit over a drink?"

"Absolutely, Rosie. I don't mean to insult you, but you look like you've been through a wringer. Please sit down and I will pour you a tall, cold beverage. Wine can wait for dinner."

"Thanks. I don't feel insulted. Our communication is definitely open and honest. It shows how genuine you are, Bucky, a gentleman and a scholar."

Rosie proceeded to share the details provided by Agent Thompson. Repeating them helped her to digest what was about to come down. Bucky listened attentively without interruption."

"Do you feel safe staying at your own place, or do you think you should stay here with me?"

"I think I should stay at home. I don't want them to be alerted that anything is coming down. Now that I won't be in Sophie's neighborhood, they will likely think my role as any kind of investigator is complete. I want them to believe I am simply evaluating her for sentencing."

"Well, I could stay with you. They will think our relationship is progressing. Ha."

"You do sound logical at times. Usually, I tend to be more on the emotional, intuitive side. Emotionally speaking, my appetite just peaked. It happens when I am distracted from the tasks at hand by the flavorful smell of good food. Otherwise, I go all day without eating and don't think much about it. What are you cooking?"

"I am fixing my special chili recipe, to be served with spinach salad, steaming hot, crusty, Italian bread and your favorite dark red wine for medicinal purposes. How does that sound? Or should I say, how does that smell? My intuitive side thinks you will love it."

The meal was great. The evening wore on. Rosie became relaxed and decided to call it a night. She anticipated a big day coming up on Tuesday. Teaching at the University two days a week demands a bit of preparation. No matter how many times her courses are offered, she continues to insert new material into her lectures. She doesn't want to put the college kids asleep in her afternoon classes. For some it is after lunch, for those who slept in, it is after strong coffee.

"Thank you, Bucky. You always come through when I need tender loving care. Will I see you on campus tomorrow?"

"Absolutely. Would you like to see a movie tomorrow night? It was fun last time, right?"

"Yes, it was. What film you have in mind?"

"Angels in the Outfield. It is a baseball movie, of course. It's about the worst team in the major leagues and how an angel, in the form of an eleven-year-old boy, shows up to assist the Coach."

"Gee, Bucky. It sounds great. How many hankies do I need?"

"It has a happy ending, Rosie. You will have my hand to hold. That will be sufficient. Or do you cry with happy endings, too?

"Maybe."

"How about we leave your car on campus and go to an early show with a real dinner after?

"Well, since we have to consider Jocko's needs, leaving my car makes that difficult. Don't you agree?"

"Okay. Go home and take care of Jocko's simple needs. I will pick you up and we will take off from your condo. Not having a pet, I tend to forget about that sort of thing. As for your needs, let me walk you to your car. I know you don't need me to be your bodyguard with that large companion of yours."

"I would be honored. Come outside and look at the full moon." They stepped outside arm in arm. "I noticed it as I pulled up earlier. There is something about the moon that has always fascinated me. How about you?"

"Actually, I have always been intrigued by the stars. The first star of the night depicts the end of a lovely day with you. I must say the majesty of the moon shining on your face makes you look stunning. Back to earth. Don't forget your leftovers."

"You are so sweet. What leftovers? You are sending me home with your specialty chili?"

"You didn't think I would eat that entire pot, did you?"

Bucky opened her door, turned her toward him, held her shoulders straight, and kissed her on both cheeks, European style. Jocko jumped into the backseat with no regard for his humans' silly antics. He cleared his throat and said softly, "You know, Rosie, I am not a wealthy man. But I can promise you, your life with me will never be boring."

Rosie found herself speechless. Tears welled up in her eyes. "No doubt about that, Bucky." She slid into the driver's seat, placed the insulated bag filled with the chili and extra bread on the passenger seat and whispered, "Thanks for a lovely evening." She blew him a kiss and headed home with a feeling of contentment not experienced since her husband died.

***

Rosie's week progressed without any glitches. Her classes on Tuesday and Thursday left her invigorated. Students remained alert and responsive. Participation was lively. She loved being on campus in the Spring. There were yellow daffodils and red tulips in bloom along both sides of the paved walkways. Students lounged in small groups on the grass or sat together on stone ledges, absorbing the warm rays of the sun. This was in total contrast to the harsh winter months when they preferred the student union with hot chocolate or their favorite lattes.

Rosie hustled quickly to the baseball diamond where the University of Toledo was playing Bowling Green. She spotted Bucky in the dugout, holding his clipboard, and addressing his team. It was going to be his last season as head coach. His promotion to athletic director would begin in August. Bucky had mixed emotions about moving on while his own recruits were still on the team. He remembered the sense of abandonment he felt as a ballplayer at the University of Dayton when his coach left for a larger university down South.

The good thing is, these players know their new coach, Luke Matthews, well. He is currently the assistant coach, respected and well-liked by everyone. Rosie recalled meeting Luke and his wife, Julie, at the team Meet-n-Greet. Bucky told her Luke was a physical education major at Ohio University where Bucky was a graduate assistant. When Bucky became the baseball coach at The University of Toledo, he brought Luke on board as assistant coach.

Rosie caught Bucky's eye and waved. She joined Julie, Judge Lincoln, and Darlene, in the bleachers. Rosie found it to be such a coincidence that her boyfriend and Julie's husband work together. Julie manages an indoor tennis facility where Rosie has taken lessons and played in a few leagues through the years. More recently, Rosie's focus has been totally consumed by her career and occasional opportunities to visit her family.

Rosie and her new co-leader, Linda Willis, decided

to meet with Rosie's Post Abortion support group the weekend prior to Mother's Day. Linda, a long-time close friend, and school nurse with a mental health background, agreed to co-lead. A few of Rosie's clients still suffered from PTSD after after the loss of a baby, even if it was long ago. It still hits them hard near Mother's Day. They wonder where their child would be, developmentally and what their own lives would have been like, as well. Rosie's thoughts shifted to her mother and taking Bucky to meet her.

Rosie noticed Julie was seated beside Sean Simmons' parents. She met them before the season at the Meet-n-Greet and was impressed to hear they both worked for the Sylvania Fire Department. Sean's dad is a Captain, and his mother is an EMT. Bucky told her that Sean's decision to pitch for Toledo was partially based on staying local so his parents could watch him play. He said Sean is very humble and appreciative of the sacrifices his parents made for him to develop his pitching skills. After that pre-season team party, they recapped the evening on the deck of her condo. Bucky also told her Sean is a Senior and going on to graduate school in music and sound mixing. He will be attending school in California with the blessing of his parents.

The game ended with Sean striking out the "bottom of the Bowling Green line-up". Bucky had explained to Rosie that teams win when the last three batters get on base. That is what he calls the "bottom of the line-up." He also said Sean was one of the few pitchers who could hit well. He is last in the Toledo line-up which makes him their secret weapon. The opposing teams don't expect the last batter, let alone the starting pitcher, to be a great hitter.

"It helps having a left-handed pitcher when he is faced with left-handed batters. When Sean throws a curve ball, it curves away from the lefty. If the batter is right-handed, it doesn't make much difference. But for a left-handed batter, it means a swing and a miss. Ha!" Bucky chatted outside Rosie's car door after the 4-3 win for Toledo.

"So, are we joining the others for a victory drink and pizza at Marion's?"

"Absolutely, Rosie. I hope you don't mind. It is a tradition, win or lose. Do you want a lift, or would you rather meet me there?"

"Let's meet there. You probably need to go back to the locker room with your players."

"That's very polite of you, Rosie."

"Actually, it helps me. I need to make a couple of phone calls." Rosie mentally made note of who she wanted to touch base with before the close of business: Greenberg, Agent Thompson, and Big John.

As she crossed the square located between the ball fields and the faculty lot, she prayed silently about the safety of the Small girls and Sophie's future with the Jordan boys. She felt blessed to be in a relationship with a sweet, sensitive man who seemed to offer her a future filled with love and adventure.

Rosie heard her name called from behind her. She turned around and saw Charles Lincoln and his girlfriend, Darlene, moving quickly toward her. "Hi, Rosie. We didn't have a chance to talk at the game. What did you think of Bucky's team?" Asked Darlene.

"I was so impressed, and not simply because they won. You could see the bonds between the players. The older guys seemed to encourage the younger members of the team and the young players saw the upperclassmen as role models."

They parted as Rosie reached the faculty lot. The Judge and Darlene were parked on the street across from campus. They refused Rosie's offer to give them a lift to their car. As Rosie pulled out of the lot, she was filled with gratitude that Judge Lincoln had introduced her to Bucky.

CHAPTER 19

SOPHIE: FINAL INTERVIEW

Sophie was already seated in the visitation room when Rosie arrived. Officer Mitchell stood outside the door, casually chatting with officers Testerman and Ambrose.

"Good morning Officers. T.G.I.F. or do you have to work shifts this weekend?"

"Testerman is lucky. He gets to play his first round of spring golf. I have a 7-7 shift in the morning," Ambrose said. Testerman took an imaginary golf swing and laughed.

Verna Mitchell responded. "I'm performing at the Toledo Museum of Art with your office manager. It's a 'Merry Month of May' concert. Would you like to come?"

"I must say, Verna, you know more about Ruth's personal life than I do. What time is the concert?"

"It is at 2:30 p.m. on Sunday with lemonade and cookies served afterward. The museum doesn't allow dark liquid of any kind to protect the artwork. That's why they chose lemonade."

"Thank you. Do I need tickets?"

"I happen to have two in my uniform pocket. I would like you and a friend to be my guests. Ruth has tickets to sell. I'm surprised she hasn't hit you up to buy them already. The concert will benefit the children's orphanage, Saint Anthony's Villa."

"I appreciate your kind offer. If you won't let me buy them, I'll gladly donate to the orphanage. I was just telling my boyfriend about it. His church festival raised money for them. Do you know George Emmanuel? He's the man who provided Christmas gifts and circus tickets every year when Sam and April lived there. Remember, Angel Morgan? She was a friend of Sam and April who were raised in that orphanage, then, tragically murdered some years later. Such an incredibly sad case."

"I remember Angel, and Song, too," Verna said. "They were housed here before sentencing. It's very thoughtful of you to donate to the orphanage. The reason there are so many fund raisers is to prevent the orphanage from closing. It's not a government sponsored facility, so they're totally dependent upon community support. At the art museum, they'll have an auction of Mother's Day gift packages. Why don't you just bid on those and give your mother a present?"

Rosie's thoughts brightened. "Great idea, Verna. I'll spend a little time with Sophie now." Rosie opened the door and sat across from Sophie who had observed the conversation through the glass windows. Her posture had improved. Now, she sat straight instead of slumped and her hands were folded on the table. Her eye contact and smile told it all. She knew she would soon be a free woman. What a difference having hope made.

"Good morning, Dr. Klein. I'm so happy to see you. My lawyer said you would come back one more time."

"It looks like it won't be long until you move out of here. Any information about what happens with the boys?"

"I had a visit by this nice lady from Children's Social Services, Louise Meyer. She asked me if I wanted to remain in the house I lived in with the boys. She said Lisa Turner could have Farid's mortgages paid off from some victim witness fund. I hate to disappoint Officer Mitchell. It was so nice of her to offer me a job and little place to live. I just want to do what's best for Ali and Omar. What do you think?"

"I'm sure Officer Mitchell will understand. There's nothing better than to live in a place where the mortgage has been paid off."

"I told the Children Services lady that I would like to live in Farid's house, if the neighbors are okay with me returning. They all know I shot him, Dr. Klein, even though I wasn't the one to actually kill him."

"If you want me to, I'll speak with Trisha Small and Petra Gonzalez. From what they have told me, I think they'll be happy to have you back. They like the boys and don't see you as a danger to society."

"Yes. Please, ask them. I have the Children's Services lady's card to give you. Her name is Louise Meyer. She said she knows you and would like you to call her. She wants to introduce you to Ali and Omar. I believe she wants you to counsel them about all of this nasty stuff."

"I would be glad to give Mrs. Meyer a call." Sophie slid the card across the table. Rosie was pleased to remember that the woman was a golfing buddy she sometimes played with on weekends.

"You'll need transportation, Sophie. Can I pick you up when you're released?"

"That would be great, Dr. Klein. I would be more comfortable with you than walking out with my lawyer. Don't get me wrong. He has been incredibly good to me."

"I'll bring you all clean clothes. Agent Thompson is delivering your belongings, including your Crystal Manor uniform and your work shoes, to my house later today. He's waiting until the traffickers are apprehended, just to be on the safe side. We don't think they're watching me anymore, but he's being cautious, none the less."

"Thanks. I'll call Crystal Manor as soon as I'm released. Hopefully, I will get my job back."

"It's a good idea to wait. The fewer people who know your background story, the less likely it is the traffickers will try to harm you. We're still uncertain about their motive for poisoning Farid."

"I might be able to help them with that. Farid seemed protective of those girls next door. Maybe, it was because he was attracted to their mother, Trisha."

"That's new and useful information, Sophie. I'll pass it on to the authorities." Rosie slipped a hand into her handbag and pulled out several breakfast nutrition bars and a bottle of Gatorade. "I brought you these. You might get hungry in here. The drink restores electrolytes."

"About three o'clock in the afternoon I tend to be a bit hungry. Lunch is flimsy and supper is often served cold. The Gatorade is a real treat. Thank you, Dr. Klein."

"It won't be long, and you can cook whatever you

desire. Did you cook for Farid and the boys?"

"Not much. He had certain foods he wanted to eat all the time. Mostly rice and overcooked lamb. He sent me to the market for vegetables and milk and always waited in the car."

"Unless you want to go to Mt. Vernon or Gambier to look up the Lamberts, you should be back in your own home for Mother's Day weekend. I wouldn't be surprised if you hear from Adam this year."

Rosie thought her own trip to visit her mother just became simplified by not having to take Sophie to visit the Lamberts. That reunion could wait until Sophie got settled with the boys.

"I would like to see them at some point when I can travel independently. I plan to get a driver's license. For now, I'm excited to have my own bedroom and be able to decorate the whole house. I'm sick of dark shades on all the windows. I want pretty curtains with sheers you can see through."

"What are your thoughts about Adam?"

"I forgot to tell you. He visited me, but it was during a dark period in my mind before I knew I was going to be free. Until then, I never thought I would see him again. He forgave me for giving him up and said he would remain close for good."

"Now that you are free, he won't have to travel so far. You can be a real grandma. He has kids, right?"

"Oh, my, yes. God has been so good. I hope to be baptized in Adam's church. I believe Jesus has a good plan for my life. The chaplain here, Lisa Turner, has met with me almost every evening. There is a peaceful little chapel here and Officer Mitchell has walked me there a couple of times to be with Chaplain Turner."

"Lisa Turner? She's the victim advocate employed by the Lucas County Public Defender's Office. Are you telling me she moonlights as the County Jail Chaplain?"

"I didn't know anything about her day job or her personal life until the Children's Services lady, Mrs. Meyer, told me she's the one getting the house paid off. I just appreciate her so much. She gave me a Women's Devotional Bible and taught me to pray and trust God's love."

"I have a feeling you'll give back to others the kindness you've received here. Not only that, but you can also teach by example, what happens when one makes poor decisions. I have to leave now, Sophie, but I'll see you soon."

"I'll look forward to it, Dr. Klein. Meanwhile, I'll pray for your safety and tell Chaplain Turner and Mrs. Meyer to expect a call from you. Right? After supper, I'm helping Chaplain Turner pray with the "ladies of the night" who were arrested on the streets last evening."

Rosie stood and hugged Sophie. She exited the visitation room and wished Officers Ambrose and Testerman a good afternoon and nice weekend. Verna Mitchell smiled as she escorted Sophie back for lunch with the other female inmates. There was a good feeling in the room, and everyone could sense it.

CHAPTER 20

THE STING

As Megan and Madison approached Mr. Cink's office door, he stepped into the hallway. He'd been waiting for them, only not for just the reason they thought he'd invited them to come.

"Oh, hi girls. I'm glad you agreed to help me rearrange my personal library," he said while holding the door for them to enter the office.

"Well, here we are. Where do you want us to start?" Megan asked.

"Let's start by taking all the books off the shelves and dusting," Mr. Cink answered smiling. The girls were too young to notice anything but a friendly smile.

"I love to dust," Madison chimed in happily. The girls were both eager to help and have something other than schoolwork to do. Mr. Cink handed each one a microfiber towel and the can of wood polish.

"I bet you're a big help to your mother, Megan."

"I wouldn't go that far," Megan laughed, and ruffled her little sister's hair. She loved her sister and would do anything to keep her safe.

They were naïve and unaware of the operation that was beginning. Being young and trusting of an adult, they began removing books from the shelves. Madison dusted. Megan alphabetized and they replaced the books in neat order. Mr. Cink catalogued each book by title and author while keeping up light, funny chatter.

"I brought some soda in a cooler and some of my wife's homemade chocolate chip cookies. Let's sit around the table and eat before you leave.

"Wow! Thanks Mr. Cink. Chocolate chips are my favorite," Madison said while reaching for a cookie. "This is great, Mr. Cink. It's kinda nice hanging out with you."

"I think that, too, Madison. What are you girls doing for the rest of the day?"

"We're heading to Mom's beauty shop. She's works until supper. Hey, does your wife go to our mom's shop for her haircuts? I bet she does, doesn't she?" Megan asked.

"You know, I'm not sure, Megan. She's never mentioned her hairdresser's name. But I know she looks great when she comes home from an appointment, though. Then she insists I take her to dinner. I always figure the cost of dinner is added to the price I pay for her haircut," he laughed. The girls chuckled, too, feeling comfortable sitting and talking to a trusted grown up. By the time they finished and collected their backpacks and rain jackets, the sky was filled with dark clouds. Mr. Cink walked them to the door, gave them each another cookie, helped them on with their rain jackets and slipped their arms through the straps of their backpacks.

"Thanks again, girls. Try not to get wet and have a great weekend."

"You're welcome, Mr. Cink. Thanks for the soda and cookies. Tell your wife,' thanks!'"

As the girls neared the curb in front of the school, the rain began to fall. They put up their jacket hoods and began the five-block walk to their mom's beauty shop. As they neared the corner, the friendly lady in the blue BMW was standing by her car, holding a large, orange umbrella. She gave them a big smile and called them by name.

"Hi Megan. How are you today, Madison?" The woman said with a sweet tone. "It's going to rain hard soon; this is just a cold drizzle. I was just at your mom's beauty shop and she asked if I would give you a lift there after you finished helping your counselor."

Megan took Madison's hand and answered reluctantly. "I guess so, if Mom told you it was okay. Madison just got over bronchitis. I don't want her to get sick again." Still a little hesitant, Megan began to reason: It must be okay if Mom told her to give us a ride. And it's raining. It should be okay. Her growing willingness to trust the woman came from the fact that she knew so many details about their family.

The woman opened the passenger door. Both girls slung their backpacks into the backseat and jumped inside. Once in the driver's seat, she pushed the child lock button to secure the girls inside. They were unaware of her action, her intent, or the sleeping bags on the floor.

***

Agent Thompson and his rookie partner, Agent Liza Cunningham, looked for the black Nissan. It was nowhere in sight. The tracker indicated it was parked approximately two miles away in a commercial park just South of the Michigan line. From their vantage point in an unmarked, beige SUV, they watched the girls get into the blue BMW, then began following it when it pulled away from the curb. As expected, instead of turning left on Secor Road where the beauty shop was located, the woman took a right turn at the traffic light. The sisters were talking softly to each other and didn't notice the fact that the car had taken a wrong turn and was now heading directly North. They listened as the woman "called" their mom to say they were on their way. But they didn't know the phone call went to alert the men in the warehouse to be ready and open the doors. Meanwhile, Trisha waited impatiently to hear her girls were safe.

Agreeing to go along with this plan is upsetting me. My girls and I are taking a big gamble to put these people behind bars. Dear God, keep them safe, and let this turn out right, Trisha prayed silently.

The BMW turned left, passing a blacktopped parking lot and a large warehouse with metal, overhead doors, high enough to allow an eighteen-wheeler to pull in. The BMW drove on by but circled back toward the warehouse. An unmarked police car with two local officers sat unnoticed around the side of the building. The tracker had indicated the black Nissan was parked inside the warehouse.

When both girls looked up and realized they weren't at their mother's shop, Megan asked, "What are we here for? Why are you stopping in here?"

"I have to pick up a chair I ordered from Sears. This is where it has been delivered," she said still with a kind voice.

"How can you fit it in your little car?" Megan asked innocently.

Before she could answer, the woman quickly drove into the dark, musty smelling building. The police knew they could not allow the doors to close or they would lose access to the girls. The officer behind the wheel abruptly hit the gas pedal and followed the BMW through the doors. Two other police vehicles appeared from nowhere and also followed them inside, blocking any vehicles from going anywhere. The two traffickers in the Nissan now sat with arms raised in full view. One was Clyde Tipton.

From the beige SUV, Agent Cunningham exited her side of the car with weapon drawn, using the open door to protect her from any forthcoming gunfire. Then she carefully approached the BMW as she was joined by her partner.

"Get out with your hands in the air!" The two backup officers apprehended the two men in the Nissan with no weapons exposed.

Agent Thompson exited his vehicle in time

to grab the scrubby, little accomplice standing by the doors. As Agent Cunningham neared the driver's side of the BMW she ordered the woman to get out. She obliged without resistance. Agent Cunningham then commanded her to release the childproof button so the girls could exit the vehicle.

She put her arms around the girls' shoulders and walked them over to her SUV. They clung to her as she assured them, they were safe and would be reunited with their mother very soon.

"You girls did really good," Cunningham said. "You've helped put some really bad people behind bars where they can't hurt other little girls like you."

"Do you think they know Mr. Cink?" Megan asked trying to make sense of it all.

"Yes, I do. Why?"

"Because he never asked us to help after school like that before. I just thought it was funny that all this happened on the same day."

"The cookies were real," said Madison.

"Yeah, but not much else, little sister."

CHAPTER 21

THE ABDUCTION

The hayride had been fun, and Alex was having a good time. She carefully jumped down from the side of the wagon and swept the hay off her thighs and butt. But she failed to notice the strange man who was watching her. Her thoughts were on smoking a cigarette and sharing a beer with her friend, Mr. Tipton, the stable attendant after he unhitched the horses from the wagon and returned them to their stalls. She always went to see him after taking a trail ride on her favorite horse, Nuts 'n Bolts.

This evening before the hayride, he had indicated he would be waiting for her, as usual, but tonight, he had said she could bring a friend. She and Violet had been driven out by Vi's father and Alex's mom was going to pick them up at ten. That left plenty of time for them to enjoy cigarettes and a beer with him behind the barn.

Meanwhile, the parents thought the girls would be having hot cider and donuts by a campfire after the hayride. That's what the brochure said was included in the cost.

Alex grabbed Vi by the arm. "Follow me. Mr.

Tipton will be waiting for us."

"Okay, okay," Vi said. "Don't pull on me. I'm trying to keep up. My balance is a little off after jumping down from that rickety wagon. I don't want to trip. It's really dark back here."

As they rounded the corner of the barn, they could see Mr. Tipton leaning against the open passenger door of his truck. The headlights were on and shining in the girls' eyes. He appeared to be holding two cans of beer in one hand and a pack of cigarettes in the other. Alex figured they were cigarettes because that's what he always offered her. But she had never shared a beer with him before. She didn't really like its bitter taste, but she was determined to be "grown up" tonight.

In the past, she had sneaked a swig from her mother's bottle while helping clean up after one of her mother's parties. Her mother didn't entertain men, just her lady friends who played mahjong. Otherwise, her friends were from church or golfing. Since Alex's father had died tragically from a botched gallbladder surgery, her mother had never looked at another man.

The girls were a little out of breath from running to reach Mr. Tipton, but just as they did, the lights suddenly went out on the truck and they were grabbed from behind! Something terrible smelling was pressed against their nose and mouths. Within seconds, they were woozy, and barely felt the rough, horse blankets thrown over each of them. Had they been conscious, they would have felt the ropes being tied around their legs, but both girls were out cold.

As Alex would recall later, Mr. Tipton had not said a word. He had stood there in front of them before they lost all sense of time and place. Nor could they identify the strong men who bound the blankets around their ankles and tossed them into a bed of hay in the open back of the truck. Sometime later, however, as they slowly regained consciousness, they both remembered finding themselves traveling at high-speed going who knew where, as the night grew colder.

***

A search of the warehouse found a small room with two narrow cots, a table and two chairs in it. There was also an empty vending machine, a microwave, and small refrigerator with a half-empty twelve pack of Bud Light. Adjacent to the room was a portable toilet like those used by construction site workers, but no evidence of anyone else in the building.

"They had no electronic devices like computers or phones here," Thompson said. "They didn't want anything traced back to here."

Two Sheriffs' vehicles arrived to transport the prisoners to Lucas County Jail. The woman was separated from the men to avoid any collusion during questioning later. The Agents didn't want any of their stories to be coordinated untruthfully. The Nissan and BMW were towed to the impound lot to be searched by a team of officers.

Thompson and Cunningham introduced themselves to the police officers who had formed their team. "Hi. I am Ron Thompson, and this is my partner Liz Cunningham. We can't thank you enough for your role in terminating this heinous criminal activity." They shook hands all around.

"I'm Jack Conrad, and this is my partner, Jessica Conrad." Thompson's eyebrows went up.

"We know it's unusual for a married couple to be police officers, let alone partners. But the Chief trusts us to work together at times. Ordinarily we have opposite shifts, so one of us is home helping the kids with homework and meals.

"We're grateful to have been assigned to help you." Jessica Conrad said. "How about if we transport the guy who guarded the doors?"

"Sounds good, if It doesn't interfere with your other shift work," Thompson said.

"No problem. We'll see to it that he gets booked."

"Say, by any chance would you two be foster parents?" Liz asked.

"Funny you should ask. As a matter of fact, we are. Why?" Jack questioned.

"Actually, I think I heard your names mentioned regarding the two boys associated with this case. Ali and Omar Jordan," Thompson said.

"That's true. We've been caring for the boys since their dad died," Jessica said.

"We have reason to believe their dad was poisoned by these culprits. It looks like he was part of their trafficking ring. We just don't know their motive for killing him yet," Thompson said.

"You're kidding . . . What about the step-mother shooting him?"

"It isn't public knowledge yet, but when she shot him, after years of abuse, he was already dead in his chair from the poison. She just didn't see that before she pulled the trigger," Cunningham said. "So the most she can be charged with is 'abuse of a corpse.'"

"Geez, that's one for the books. So, what happens next? Will she face time, or probation?" Jessica asked. "And will she get the boys back?"

"It's likely. I imagine you two will be the first to know. Right now, we need to be sure the entire trafficking ring has been apprehended. Sophie will be released when it's safe for her to be back in public view again. We're also working with a psychologist by the name of Dr. Rosie Klein. She'll be providing family counseling for the boys and Sophie. She's also been on this case from the beginning. Can she call you for information on the boys?"

"Absolutely. We want to help in any way we can. Right now, they're about ready to return to school," Jack said.

"It looks as though Sophie and the boys will be living in their old house and remain at DeVeaux. The counselor, principal, and nurse were helping us with this Sting operation."

"We know them well. They're great people. Our own children and other foster kids have attended

DeVeaux over the years. Good to know they were part of something so important. Well, we better get going. Nice meeting you. Hope there's an occasion to work together again," Jack said as Jessica checked on their prisoner, preparing to leave.

The girls were waiting together in the beige SUV. Agents Thompson and Cunningham drove the girls to their mother's beauty shop by a direct route this time. Trisha Small was waiting with open arms and agreed to have more questioning done with the girls in the comfort of their own home.

"I want Dr. Rosie Klein there with us," she said. "That's my only condition. My girls have been through enough with strangers."

***

Rosie Klein's phone rang.

"Dr. Klein. If you can spare a little time, could you please meet us at Trisha Small's house? We arrested the traffickers, and the girls are heading home with their mother. We'd like you to debrief them and begin whatever counseling they'll need. Fortunately, they don't appear too traumatized. They had one another for support throughout the ordeal," Agent Thompson reported.

"What good news. I would be glad to come right away. Would you like me to call anyone? I think Mr. Cink and the Principal and Nurse will be relieved to hear this news."

"That would be great, Dr. Klein. We'll also notify Attorney Greenberg. He can tell Sophie her release will likely occur on Monday. By then we should know if there are any other traffickers associated with this ring of monsters.

"From the information we've received, the DeVeaux security guard was the BMW woman's older brother, Clyde Tipton. Her name is Bonnie Tipton. He was dishonorably discharged from the Air Force National Guard, for sexual harassment. His unit was housed at the Toledo International Airport, and he's listed in Michigan as a sexual predator, but that info somehow did not get transferred to Ohio. When Lobers' private security company hired him, he ended up assigned to DeVeaux School. But Lober is a reputable guy and obviously did not know about Tipton's history in Michigan."

"I agree that his company is reputable. Our department has cracked cases where Lober was involved," Dr. Klein said.

"Good thing you noticed the Nissan in the school parking lot. Tipton was tracked after his shift at the school today. His phone was taped and we know he did make a call to his sister when he heard the girls were staying after school to help Mr. Cink. There's plenty of evidence to convict him as an accessory to this horrific crime."

Rosie called Bucky to share this turn of events. Her call went directly to voicemail. "Hi Bucky. I know you're at ball practice. I'm heading to Trisha Small's house to talk to the girls. Everything went down as planned. The traffickers have been arrested. Stop by there if you get this message in the next hour. Love you."

She hoped they could celebrate later that evening. There were a number of things for which she had a grateful heart.

CHAPTER 22

SECRET OF THE STABLES

Rosie pulled up to Trisha Small's curb, turned off her engine, and pulled her briefcase across the passenger seat. She no longer felt the need to check her rearview mirror before exiting the car. Two vehicles were parked in the driveway. One she recognized as the unmarked car that Agent Thompson drove and the other belonged to Trisha.

The front door was open, and the girls were visible inside. She tapped on the screen door and heard Trisha shout for her to come inside. Megan and Madison were cuddled side by side in an overstuffed chair with a floral design. Megan had her arm around Madison. Trisha, Agent Thompson, and his rookie partner, Liza Cunningham, were sitting in three separate chairs that complemented the chair where the girls sat. The adults stood to welcome Rosie. Agent Thompson introduced her to his partner.

"Rosie, I'd like you to meet Agent Cunningham."

"Just call me Liza. It's a pleasure to meet you," Agent Cunningham said. She was a petite but muscular brunette with a ready smile.

"Okay. And call me Rosie. I'm wondering if we have met before. You look familiar."

"I agree. Where did you go to school, Rosie?"

"I graduated from Toledo, actually, three times. I'm much older than you, Liza. I think you may have been an undergrad when I was a graduate assistant in the counseling department." Then it hit her. Now I remember. I observed Liza behind a one-way mirror when she was being counseled by a student working on a master's degree in Counseling. Uh-oh. This is confidential information. How do I get out of this one?

"On one hand, you hit the nail on the head, Rosie. I got my Bachelor of Arts degree in criminal justice from the University of Toledo. On the other hand, I can't remember seeing you around the department. Sorry."

They laughed and Rosie turned her attention to the two little girls who narrowly missed being trafficked. They had hopped out of their chair and stood hand in hand in front of their mother whose hands were on their shoulders.

"Well girls, Dr Rosie would like to talk to you for a few minutes. We should offer her something to drink." Trisha Small put her arms around both girls pulling them close.

"Dr. Rosie, would you like some lemonade?" Megan asked politely.

"Sure. Then I would love to see your rooms. I've heard you decorated them yourselves. Would that be okay, girls?"

"Oh yes! I have drawings to show you," Madison said as she took Rosie by the hand to lead her upstairs. "My favorite class is art, but Megan likes gym because she likes boys."

Megan handed Rosie a glass of lemonade and they both followed Madison up the stairs. Rosie glanced back at the grown-ups, smiled, and waved. Trisha breathed a sigh of relief.

Upstairs, Madison ushered Rosie into her room where a small, round table sat in the corner. It was in front of a window that faced the Jordan house. She had colored pencils and scented markers in a shoebox on the window ledge. The scene she had drawn on manilla paper was of a girl on a horse in a field of multi-colored wildflowers.

"This is simply beautiful. Do you ride horses, Madison?" Rosie asked.

"Yes, I do! The Stoney Lake Stable truck picks us up at school on Thursdays. We ride in the back part with straw until we get to the barn for a lesson. Want to see my boots and helmet?"

"Sure."

"I want to put them on for you. The horse I ride is called 'Laddie.' This summer, Mom said she will let us lease horses for a month! She says it's expensive but not as much as owning your own horse. Megan rides better than me. Her favorite horse is called 'Pepper.' Pepper is white with black spots, and they've won blue ribbons . . . I didn't win any yet."

Madison pulled the tall, black boots on and

strapped the snug-fitting helmet under her chin while Megan rolled her eyes. "She's horse-crazy, Dr. Rosie. She saves her allowance for riding on Saturdays. I haven't been riding much because I help Mom clean up at the beauty shop. She's buying out the owner and going to rename it for us."

"Really? How nice. What will she call it?"

"She says, 'Megginson's' will be in honor of both of us. Do you like it?

"I do," Rosie said as a red flag came to her thoughts. She quickly excused herself saying she had to use the bathroom, but she really wanted to catch the agents before they took off. Hurrying down the steps, she caught them on the front walkway.

"Hey. Wait Ron," she called out to Agent Thompson. "It's not over. The case is not closed."

"What do you mean, Rosie?" Ron asked, his eyes locked on her strident manner.

"I remember seeing the Stoney Lake Stable logo as the license plate holder on the Nissan. Could be the security guard also works at the stable where Madison rides. It's on Secor Road just before the Michigan state line. Again, no record of his shady background in Michigan, but that would give him access to children who take lessons, or board horses, or pay to ride by the hour."

"We'll head out there right away before the stable is notified of his arrest. The stable and the warehouse are located near each other."

"Great Ron. Sounds like they could gain all

kinds of information out there. Even if the parents transport their kids, the registration cards have their addresses and places of employment, enough to sound trustworthy to a young one when offering them a ride home or to the parents' work. It would be easy for the security guard to know enough to tell a child that he's supposed to give them a ride, just like his sister did in the BMW. Then it would be easy to transport them from the stable to the nearby warehouse, and from there, who knows where? How many other children have gone missing in this area?"

"Enough for us to know there's something organized going on. Stoney Lake could have hired him just like Lober's security company, without enough background history. The stable owners might not even be guilty or aware of the trafficking operation," Liza added.

"Let's get going, Liza. We'll interview the owners without sharing details."

"Bye guys. I'm hitting the bathroom and heading back upstairs. I also need to let Trisha know the news and advise her not to take Madison out there riding tomorrow. Please keep me posted."

Trisha came into the house through the patio door. She had been relaxing in a hammock connected to two oak trees and appeared startled to see Rosie standing there.

Rosie spoke first. "Trisha, I have to tell you something. The school security guard may have worked at the riding stable where Madison takes her lessons.

Agents Thompson and Cunningham are on their way out there now. It doesn't mean the owners are involved. But if he does work at Stoney Brook, he just might have been gathering leads on potential victims by operating independently out there just like he was at the school."

"Oh my gosh, Dr. Rosie. All those times we let Madison and her friend, Lilly, wait for us to pick them up. They literally sat on a bale of straw by the road. Lilly's mom will never believe this. We never thought anything about their safety. Do you suppose the owners are involved?"

"Why would you think that Trisha?"

"Well, they have hayrides at night and bonfires. We haven't allowed our girls to stay because it seems as if it's more geared toward junior high kids. Megan hasn't even expressed an interest. I remember hearing about one girl who ran away from home after telling her mom she was staying for the hayride. Her Mom went out to pick her up and she was nowhere to be found. That case has never been solved."

"Can I have that child's information, Trisha? She may not be a true runaway. It's more likely a question of who grabbed her."

A short time later, Rosie took a moment to call Mr. Cink and let him know everything went according to their plan.

"Hi Stan. The girls are fine. You played your part perfectly and the police picked up the perpetrators, including your school security guard, Tipton."

"That's great news, Rosie. Do the girls know I

was playing the 'good guy' part?"

"We didn't tell them all the details, yet, and I'm still at their house. I don't have time to tell you everything, but will you be available later?"

"Absolutely. I'll wait for your call. Do you want me to notify Mark and Polly?"

"Yes, I'd appreciate that. Let's talk later. The girls are looking for me. Oh, one quick thing. When I call back, I would like to hear what you know about Stoney Lake Stables."

"Okay, Rosie." She made one more quick call to Attorney Greenberg. It was his private, after office hours number.is; She decided to leave a voice mail message.

"Hi Josh. This is Rosie. The bad guys were arrested. But it's not certain we have everyone in the ring yet. Thompson is on his way to talk to the owners of Stoney Lake Stables. Have you heard of it? There's a missing girl who was last seen at a hayride out there. I'll call you back when I know more. I'm with Trisha's girls and their looking for me. More later."

Rosie went back upstairs while Trisha called Lilly's mom and tried to find out more about the missing girl. All Trisha knew was that she was an only child, from a single parent family, and her mom worked late as a manager in an upscale restaurant. They lived in Sylvania Ohio.

"Megan, do you remember ever talking to Mr. Tipton at school?"

"Not really. At school he stood stiff as a board in the halls. I thought he was rude and sort of creepy the

son said. "I see him at school
e. He's always super friendly
e horse, Laddie. Megan just
o. He told me it's his job to
il still by the stairs at school
don't notice him."

a saying you knew him

ometimes, and he said if I
could sit up front and help
nd the farm. I thought it'd
would say, "no way" until I

that the girls had been
e so quickly, they apparently
had not seen Clyde Tipton being arrested in the Nissan.

"Megan, did you know a girl supposedly ran away after going to one of the hayrides?"

"Yes, Dr. Rosie, and I knew who she was. She used to smoke behind the barn with her friends."

"Why would she have run away? And how? The stables are in the middle of nowhere."

"I don't know," Megan said. "No one else was missing that night. As far as why? I didn't know her well enough to figure that out. It was near Halloween. She was in the eighth grade and her name was 'Alex.'"

"You girls are in the fifth and seventh grades, is that right?"

"Megan will be thirteen on June 14th and I will

be eleven on July 11th," Madison said. "Next year Megan will be a big wheel in the eighth grade, and I'll finally be in middle school on the second floor with her. Sixth grade will be neat with changing classes and having lockers."

"Well, girls, it's good to talk about all this with you. But I need to get to work now, so, I'm taking off. Would you like to come and see my office one day? I have banner paper, colored chalk, and scented markers that smell like fruit."

"I definitely want to come visit. I'm thinking about studying psychology, Dr. Rosie, like you. Or maybe be a school counselor like Mr. Cink. That would be so cool," Megan answered.

"Me too! Ask Mom," Madison said. "Oh. Do you like girl scout cookies? Chocolate Mint, maybe? We have twelve more boxes to sell by Mother's Day."

"Okay, I'll buy two from each of you. I'm meeting with a women's group in my office in the morning and they'll enjoy them with coffee. I'll take a couple of boxes to my own mother on Mother's Day." Rosie reached into her billfold and took out a twenty-dollar bill. "Will this cover them?"

"They aren't that expensive, Dr. Rosie. We can give you six boxes for that much. Thank you," Megan said. She left the room and returned with six boxes of assorted girl scout cookies. "We're raising money to go to camp for a week."

"Thanks, girls. Please tell your mom to call my office and tell me when you can visit. You can make cards for her for Mother's Day. Okay?"

"Okay, it's been nice getting to know you," Madison said standing and hugging Rosie.

At the bottom of the stairs, Trisha stood with a forlorn look on her face.

"I spoke to Lilly's mom, and she said the missing girl's mother has no clue what happened to her daughter, but she refuses to believe she ran away. The Lucas County Sheriff's department has jurisdiction because the stables are outside the Toledo city limits. They've coordinated efforts with the Michigan State Police since the Michigan line is less than a mile from where she was last seen.

"The girl's name is Alexandra Pappas, known as 'Alex,' and her mother's name is Katrina Pappas. Alex is enrolled in the eighth grade at Liberty Country Day School. Mrs. Pappas used to volunteer at Alex's school library, but she's now on leave of absence because she can't bear entering the building since Alex's disappearance."

"Well, that says a lot, Trisha. Since Alex didn't attend DeVeaux, the link between her case and the attempted abduction of your girls, must be Clyde Tipton. I hope Agent Thompson and his colleagues can find Alex and round up any others in the trafficking ring," Rosie said hopefully. Her phone rang, and she motioned to Trisha that she was taking the call.

It was Bucky. Trisha gave a wave good-bye and headed up the stairs to check on her girls as Rosie strutted quickly out to her car.

"Hi Rosie. Are you okay? Are the girls safe?"

"Everything's fine, I'm happy to tell you, Bucky. Well, sort of. It seems there's another young girl who went missing from the stables last fall. The police and other authorities assumed she was a runaway. But now, it seems possible she was abducted."

"That's horrible. Anything I can do for you?"

"As a matter of fact, yes. Can you meet me at home and walk Jocko with me later?"

"Absolutely. See you about six. We can order Chinese if that works for you. I know you like pepper steak and I prefer sweet and sour chicken. How about fried rice and egg rolls?"

"Yup. Great idea. Oh, and don't forget to request the fortune cookies. I'll fill you in on all the details. I hope you don't mind if part of the evening is interrupted by phone calls. There's a chance I'll hear from two attorneys, Greenberg and Chickalette."

"Not a problem, Rosie. I want to be there for you."

Rosie drove home hoping this new aspect of the Jordan case would not hamper Sophie's release. The authorities don't want to let the cat out of the bag regarding her innocence until they successfully close the case. She felt overwhelmed by all the new information about the school guard's involvement and his connection to the stables, as well as to Alex's disappearance. Rosie was hopeful that a search would be re-convened by local, state, and federal branches of law enforcement.

As she pulled into her attached garage, the phone rang and her dog barked, simultaneously. She accepted the call and walked into the laundry room to the friendly greeting of Jocko.

"Big John!" she said, recognizing his deep voice, bold but jovial.

"Hey, Rosie. My courier delivered the discovery packet of my client, Hannah Fields, to your office. Ruth said you were holding a counseling group in the morning and I am hopeful you will have time to begin reviewing the materials."

"Your timing is perfect. I'll read the arrest reports and interviews and get back to you by Tuesday. Does that give you enough time to have me appointed by Judge Tucker?"

"You already have been appointed, I'm happy to say. The order is in the packet, so you'll have easy entry into the court building to see Ms. Fields."

"That's great. If that's it, I'll talk with you next week. Have a nice weekend and bye now." There was a knock on the door behind her, and Bucky stepped into the laundry room with his hands full of dinner. The aroma was downright delicious.

"Oh, Bucky, I'm so glad to see you . . . for all the right reasons," she smiled.

CHAPTER 23

SOPHIE'S FATE

Sunday morning brought an opportunity to take Jocko to the dog park by the river. He loved to romp with other dogs, big and small, along the shoreline. Rosie slung the ball into the water and Jocko scrambled down the bank, dove in, and swam out to retrieve it. He happily delivered it to his owner in hopes of repeating this exercise over again, as many times as she would.

Rosie paid the attendant to give Jocko a bath while she enjoyed a frothy, vanilla latte and waited for her dog to be returned.

This was a first for Bucky who loved watching his beloved Rosie play with the dog. He hated the stress she had been under with the trafficking case. Then, last night, when she suggested going to the bar scene to look for potentially trafficked girls, he knew she needed a break.

"Don't let your coffee get cold, Bucky. It only takes fifteen minutes for them to wash and dry Jocko. I didn't expect you to dash out here from church. Sorry I overslept. I would have gladly gone with you."

"Charlie and Darlene would like to meet us later at the Greek restaurant in Perrysburg. I know you're reviewing your new case material, but I'd like to go. Can you fit it in your schedule?"

"I'll make it work. I need two hours and a little time to clean up. What does your afternoon look like?"

"I have paperwork to do for the team. Their scholarships are partially based on a B average. Their professors turned in their winter quarter grades, and it's my responsibility to compile them."

"Good. I hate to think I'm messing up your lovely day off."

The animal bath attendant brought Jocko to them on his leash. Rosie commanded him to Sit. When he obeyed, she patted him on the head, handed him a dog biscuit, then tipped the attendant.

"You smell really good, Jocko," she said to the fragrant-smelling dog as she scratched him behind both ears. Now when you shake off river water, I won't mind so much," Rosie said. He looked at her and cocked his head as if he wasn't sure what she wanted him to do. Bucky reached down and petted the animal on his head fondly.

"Where's your car? I'll walk you there."

"Thank you. It's in the lot to our left. Yours?"

"Not far from you."

"What time should I be ready and what are you wearing?"

"Darlene said it will be casual, but to bring a sweater in case it's cool in the restaurant. What is your favorite Greek dish, Rosie?"

"I love it all. Spanakopita. Gyros. Moussaka, and Dolmades. You?"

"What are Dolmades?"

"Stuffed grape leaves. My grandmother and I used to ride the local bus to a park near the river, pick the leaves, ride the bus back home, boil them, stuff them with ground beef and rice, and bake them all within a few hours."

"Wow, good for you. What is Moussaka?"

"Stuffed eggplant. Same sort of filling but some people use ground lamb and add cheese on top."

"I'm sure as long as I'm in such good company, I'll be eating great food."

"Good company? Oh, you mean Charlie, your best friend, right?"

"I wasn't referring to Charlie, sweetheart." They laughed together and enjoyed the moment.

Rosie shoved Jocko into the back seat and sat herself behind the wheel. Bucky leaned down, brushed her hair back from her face, and kissed her.

"See you around five, okay? Oh, and save some room for Baklava. Don't be surprised that I know all about Greek desserts."

"You're such a character, Bucky, but I love that about you. Have a nice afternoon. And thanks again for showing up here. Jocko and I loved being with you."

"Back at cha,' he said with a wave and strolled off.

***

On Monday, Rosie arrived at the office and instantly absorbed the aroma of freshly brewed coffee. Rosie released Jocko from his leash and he promptly walked over and snuggled close to Ruth's side. She smiled as she patted Jocko's shaggy gray forehead and turned back to her duties. Rosie was eager to get Jocko settled and begin reviewing the case history of Hannah Fields. But it wasn't to be.

"Call on line one," Ruth called over the intercom.

"Rosie, this is Josh Greenberg. You'll be happy to hear that Sophie was released this morning. They let her out the Sheriff's exit and a woman by the name of 'Doris Simpson' picked her up."

"That's great news, Josh. Why the back door? Do they think she's in danger?"

"Not really," he explained, "It avoids the Press and it's just to be on the cautious side. We don't want her back in her house alone just yet. Doris arranged for her to temporarily live at Verna Mitchell's bed and breakfast for a short time."

"Good to hear. I'll touch base with our Sophie. I assume this means she'll have her job back at Crystal Manor, and receive guardianship of the boys," Rosie summarized hopefully.

"Definitely. She has her uniforms and shoes already. Doris made her an appointment to see her counselor, Maria. Her son, Adam, is coming to see her on Mother's Day. By then, we may permit her to be in her own home with the Jordan boys."

"I couldn't be happier for her. I believe she wants to return to the only home Ali and Omar have known. It doesn't hold fond memories but with a little redecorating, she can make it cozy and warm.

"By the way, Rosie, we're making some headway on your leads. It may result in the return of the Pappas girl, Alex, or at least some closure for her mother."

"I hope by closure, you aren't implying that she's not going to be found alive."

"No. Actually, Agent Thompson put out a poster with her picture and a reward for information resulting in her return. No telling where traffickers may have transported her. Between you and me, someone thought they spotted her at a nearby mall last Christmas. It doesn't seem anyone's followed up on it."

"Any chance a pimp has changed her appearance and is using her in the Toledo area?"

"Anything is possible, Rosie. She is a little young but with makeup they could create the appearance of her being at least eighteen-years old. Some perverts don't mess with minors. They pick up young women and make themselves think it's a mutual arrangement."

"Terrible. Maybe Bucky and I will go bar-hopping tonight and keep our eyes open for illegal activity on the street outside the clubs. Now that we have an idea, you never know what we'll notice around there."

"Everything helps, Rosie. That would be great, but don't put yourselves in danger. If you identify someone or something, please call 911."

"Will do, Josh. It has been a pleasure working with you. I'll recommend you to my friends and professional colleagues."

"I'll do the same, Rosie. There are times when a weeping woman comes to see me for a divorce but needs to just talk to someone like you. I know if anyone in my family needed therapy, it would be your card I'd slip to them."

CHAPTER 24

ALEX

On Wednesday, the call finally came: The missing girls, Alex Pappas and Vi, had been rescued on a lucky tip from a blackjack dealer at the casino. Agent Thompson told her to expect another call from Agent Cunningham to set up an appointment to evaluate Alex. She was a lucky one, but her girlfriend, Vi, hadn't been. Everyone was hopeful they would learn more about what happened during the girls' captivity and possibly the source of the heroin.

"Vi won't be able to talk for a while. She certainly got the worst of it and isn't communicating with anyone right now. Hasn't said a word since we got her back."

"How did you actually rescue them?" Rosie asked with relief.

"We had a tip from an American blackjack dealer living in Michigan who dealt cards at the Windsor Casino every night. Her position was in the high rollers' lounge. On several occasions, when walking to her car after her shifts, she noticed a group of well-dressed, young ladies leaving in a van about four o'clock each morning. She kept an eye out for them and saw them hovering over the wealthy men as they gambled. She found it interesting that they all wore long sleeved dresses. In her experience, it usually was a sign of drug use or cutting. Since they traveled together in a van, she realized they were not individually accompanied by any of the gamblers.

"One night on her break, she recognized one of her regular customers entering the elevator with one of the young ladies. The high rollers had their room suites comped with their meals delivered to their rooms. Thank God, this caring woman decided to let the authorities know about her suspicions of forced prostitution, possibly of minors."

"Yes, that was one huge blessing, for sure. What kind of symptoms is Alex displaying? I know what they do to those girls and since she was abducted around Halloween, it's been about six months now. "

"Well, the docs at the hospital think her detox can be handled at home because her addiction appears to be relatively mild. They hate to get her on a Methadone program that can lead to further addiction. With therapy and a supportive, calming environment, they say the prognosis for her is outstanding, Dr. Klein."

***

"I was so afraid and ashamed to have gotten poor Vi into this mess. What was I thinking?" Alex said to Agent Cunningham. Following her dramatic rescue from the seedy motel, she had been taken to the hospital for a physical exam. Now, she sat on the edge of the hospital bed and Agent Cunningham sat in a chair facing her.

"Don't blame yourself, Alex. Try the best you can to tell the rest of the story."

"Finally, the truck stopped, and they carried us into a motel room that smelled moldy and smokey. They threw us onto some beds and untied the ropes from our ankles. I took my horse blanket off and looked over at Vi. She was just as scared as me. I clutched the blanket to keep from shaking in the damp, cold air, chilled to the bone. Vi stayed curled up in a little ball and cried quietly. I could see her body shaking under the blanket."

"You both had to be terrified. What happened next? What did they look like and what did they say?"

"There were three of them once Mr. Tipton entered the room. He must have parked the truck. One was tall and his face looked like he grew up with acne. He wore a brown knit hat and a camouflage-colored jacket, like for hunting. The other guy was smaller but real stocky. He wore a Detroit Tigers baseball cap and the same type jacket. He never took his gloves off. They said not to think of escaping or calling for help because the room phone was not working and one of them would be outside guarding the door and windows all night. If we screamed, the tall guy threatened to tie us down and wrap our mouths so we couldn't talk. Other than that, we could sleep until they came for us in the morning." Alex's voice quaked and her eyes began to tear up. She wiped at them with her fingers.

Agent Cunningham felt empathy for this poor,

traumatized girl. She reached forward and gently took both of her trembling shoulders and squeezed them saying, "You're doing a great job, Alex. If you need a break, I can get you a soda and snack."

"Thank you. I would like a drink, but no food. My stomach is queasy, and I need to take a nap if it's okay with you. When do I get to go home and see my mother? "

"Let me buzz the nurses' station to bring the soda. You try to rest. I'm sorry to say, the doctor plans to keep you overnight for observation, but your mother is being brought here by my partner, Agent Thompson. She can spend the night with you and the doctor will let you go home tomorrow. We want to keep you safe and well."

"What about Vi? Is she here too?"

"Yes. She's staying in another part of the hospital." *It's not my place to explain that Vi is in the psych unit. Apparently, she is not verbally responding to anyone and making no eye contact.*

"I am sorry to say you can't see her today. Don't worry. She's safe now and being well taken care of. Although her parents are divorced, they are on their way here together. Both of you were considered runaways, you know. But now, it's a blessing to your parents and everyone that you returned alive. Not everyone is so lucky," Agent Cunningham said in a gentle voice.

The nurse arrived shortly with the soda and a smile. "Here you are. Just call if you need anything else. The doctor will be in later to see you."

Alex nodded as she sipped the cool, refreshing

drink through the straw. She repositioned herself under the covers, closed her eyes and sighed. She wondered if they knew she would crave the drugs they had forced upon her by daily heroin injections.

Agent Cunningham quietly left the room, heading for the lobby to wait for Alex's mother to arrive. The last communication she had from her partner, was that he would be getting to the hospital in forty-five minutes. She no sooner sat down when the elevator doors opened, and a woman rushed out along with Agent Thompson.

"Mrs. Pappas, this is my partner Agent Cunningham," Thompson explained. "We'll be driving you and Alex home tomorrow. We don't think you're in danger, but to be cautious we'll be taking you."

"Nice to meet you Mrs. Pappas," Cunningham said in a steady voice. "Your daughter is resting but is anxious to see you. Let me take you to her."

"Is she injured? Is she sick? How in the world did you find her?" Mrs. Pappas spoke with happy concern.

"Physically she's fine. But her mind seems to be in another place. Once you get home, we would like Dr. Rosie Klein to evaluate her for emotional distress and give us a diagnosis. Dr. Klein is a wonderful psychologist and instrumental in finding your daughter. The human trafficking ring has been broken and twelve girls were rescued, including Violet Grant."

"Violet Grant? How wonderful! We thought they ran away because they were mad at us. Violet's mother and I had slapped a ten o'clock curfew on the girls. I was picking them up after the hayride, but I guess you know the story. No one knew of their whereabouts and no one from the stable took responsibility. The police labeled them runaways once a couple of kids told them the girls were complaining about their mothers. Then the investigation just seemed to stop."

"Violet's parents are on the way. You might see them once they've checked on their daughter and consulted with her doctors. She's being kept in another hospital unit," Cunningham said without going into further detail.

Mrs. Pappas quietly entered her daughter's room, then extended her arms as she quickly approached the side of the bed.

"Mama!" Alex screamed when she opened her eyes. "Oh, Mama, I'm so glad you're here." As they embraced, Agent Cunningham quietly left the room and closed the door.

***

Dr. Klein knocked on the large, Oak front door of Alex's house. Surprisingly, Alex came to welcome her. She looked like a normal, enthusiastic fourteen-year-old girl. Her long black hair was pulled back in a ponytail and she was wearing a dark blue sweatsuit with her gold school logo across the chest.

"Hi, Alex. I am Dr. Rosie Klein."

"Come in, Dr. Klein, we've been expecting you. My mother had to take a business call, so I offered to welcome you and take you to our den to talk. Would you like anything to drink?"

"No thank you, Alex," Dr. Klein said as she sat down on a white leather loveseat and placed her briefcase on the Berber carpet beside her.

"I'm so relieved you came here this morning. I still feel anxious when I first wake up. Then I open my eyes and realize I'm safe at home with my mother. But there is lots of stuff I need to talk about. I saw a counselor for a while after my Dad died and that helped me a lot."

"I can assure you, Alex, that what we talk about will be confidential unless you indicate you are thinking about hurting yourself or others or know of someone who is thinking that way."

"That's good. I don't want my mother to worry and if she knows about some of my flash-backs she will definitely feel horrible."

"Why don't you begin where you feel comfortable? Can you explain your routine, Alex?"

"Yes. I was made up to look like eighteen but as you can see, I haven't started to develop. No boobs. No hips. So, the rich, older men were suspicious of my age. Well, it turned out, they used me like a go-between and had me introduce them to my friends who looked more developed and experienced, if you know what I mean."

"I understand. You must have felt terrible setting the other girls up for forced prostitution. Were they mad at you?"

"We were all under the influence of heroin and demands of the guys who told us they owned us. They threatened to kill my mother, so I was willing to cooperate; but they didn't treat me as bad as they could have. They wanted me to look healthy and not strung out when I worked the high rollers' room."

"Next time, I would like to discuss your flash-backs. For today, I've brought you a journal and a special pen with a flashlight on one end. Have you ever kept a journal?"

"Yes, when I was in counseling before. I can't thank you enough, Dr. Klein. Is it okay if I draw in it, too? My counselor told me that writing thoughts is second to talking to someone *about* your thoughts. If I draw some pictures, then I can remember what I want to talk about when I see you."

"Of course, it's perfectly okay. I plan to have you do some drawing as well," Dr. Klein said as she stood to end the session for the day. "I'll come back the day after tomorrow if it fits your schedule and you mom's, too. You're a courageous and smart girl, Alex." "Oh, Dr. Klein, I'm so sorry I had to learn the hard way."

***

It was late when Rosie returned home, greeted by Jocko. After a light meal, she settled into her favorite chair and, at last, pulled out the file on Hannah Fields, her next case. As usual, it was a most unusual case, one that would be talked about for a long time.

PART TWO

HANNAH FIELDS

CHAPTER 25

HANNAH'S STORY

The following morning, Rosie was still engrossed in the file on Hannah Fields when her ringing phone jarred her back to the present. Bucky's name displayed in green.

"Hi Bucky."

"Hi Rosie. What's your morning look like?"

"For starters, I'm reviewing a stack of materials related to Hannah Fields, my new lady defendant . . . including her handwritten confession. It seems she suffocated her two daughters. What's even worse is the two crimes were a couple of years apart, so she repeated her action."

"That's terrible, Rosie. What's your take on her motives?"

"Well, she's lived a troubled life, that's for sure. Sadly, no one intervened in this young woman's life before the senseless murders of her poor, infant daughters. She even attempted to suffocate her infant son because someone in the grocery store mistook his darling little face for a little girl. She has some real underlying issues."

"Sounds like she has something against baby girls. Was she mentally ill and her husband didn't notice, or did he ignore the signs?"

"Well, not that he's mentioned anything in the records. The first death took place in Alaska and was deemed a crib death. Any time an infant suffocates, Sudden Infant Death Syndrome (SIDS) is an assumed diagnosis without an autopsy, and just appears to be a tragedy. The second death took place when they were stationed here in Ohio, just a few years later."

"So, they were a military family?"

"Yes. Mr. Fields enlisted in the Air Force as a young high school graduate. It appears he's was making it a career."

"Where did you say they are from?"

"A small town outside of Springfield, Ohio. Her mother sent Hannah to live with her maternal grandparents during her junior year in high school because of her father's violent, unpredictable nature. She met Jerry Fields, and was charmed into a high school romance. She blossomed and even became homecoming queen. At that point, she seemed like a normal young woman. Meanwhile, her boyfriend, Jerry, had graduated and was in Texas for basic training while she was still a senior in high school. After he completed his training, they were married, partly because she was pregnant."

"Do you think it's normal for a mother to send a young woman to live with her grandparents?

Was there something dysfunctional about her own family, Rosie?"

"You could be right," Rosie said. "But currently, I'm thinking we'll never be able to separate fact from fiction because of her delusional belief system. From the little her attorney shared with me, her memories are skewed because she needs to see herself as a victim.

"Doesn't sound like a victim to me," Bucky said.

"I know, but I'll need to see her and listen to her story before I can understand why she did it. She apparently was trying to 'save' her daughters from something. That's grounds for a potential insanity plea, I think. How could anyone who takes the lives of innocent children to 'protect them' be deemed sane? If she was in her right mind, how could she live with herself realizing she'd murdered her own two daughters, for any reason?

"Good questions, Rosie," Bucky said. "How is someone viewed as legally insane?"

"Well, legal sanity means the person understands the wrongfulness of their acts at the time of commission. In this case, being temporarily insane cannot be a factor of consideration because sanity can't be turned on and off like a light switch. It seems to me that long term mental illness looks more appropriate, at least now at the onset of my evaluation. The question is how could so many professionals have missed it?"

"Such a tragedy, and heavy stuff to be reading. You know you can call me anytime, don't you, if you need a break?

"I do, and I will, if I need to; thanks, you're really kind to think of it."

"Not to change the subject, too quickly, but I'd like to know how to pack for the visit to your mother next week-end."

"Well, Bucky, why don't you just pop over for lunch later, and we can talk about it. You're on campus today, right?"

"I am and can happily do that. Want me to bring food?"

"No, I have all the makings for an overstuffed ham and cheese sandwich on rye. Sound good? I even have apple sauce for dessert."

"Sounds great, Rosie. Hope your reading gets better this morning. See ya about 12:30."

"Perfect. Oh, my other phone's ringing, Bucky; got to take this call. Bye for now." It was Agent Thompson calling.

"Thought you'd want to know we found Alex Pappas, the missing girl from the stable. She's beat up from her ordeal, but safe, just in need of treatment to restore her sound mind. Some detox, rehab, and therapy, but we found her, thanks to your lead on this."

"How did you find her so quickly? Did you arrest her traffickers? She wasn't a run-away, right?"

"No, she was not. Got 'em all. The Stoney Lake Stable owners knew nothing about it. Clyde Tipton was the go-between. Tipton turned State's witness to save his hide. We suspected they were crossing state lines, but it didn't occur to us this could be an international ring. The bridge to Windsor, Canada was a short drive up Interstate 75."

"I never thought of that either." Said Rosie.

"They had twelve girls working at a casino in Windsor, Ontario. Alex Pappas was one of them. Housing them in Detroit, they passed 'em as eighteen-year-olds with makeup and outfits. And the abductors kept them dependent by inducing heroin habits. The girls picked up high rollers who had complimentary rooms at the casino. "

"Do they know where the other girls were abducted? Ohio? Michigan? Ontario?"

"Not yet. They're being examined by a female gynecologist, then they'll be carefully interviewed prior to transport to a detox center in Michigan. Have you heard of 'Ana's House'?"

"Yes. I believe I have heard of it. Christian, long-term residential facility, right?"

"With permission from their parents or legal guardians, the girls who require long-term care will be able to continue their education and receive in-depth therapy there for a year."

"Have you actually seen our girl, Alex, or given her mother the good news?"

"No, to my having seen her. Yes, to going with my partner to Katrina Pappas. She was overwhelmed with relief and collapsed in my partner's arms."

"I think I'll call Wes Hall, my investigative reporter, and let him know about all this. He's been researching Columbus-based trafficking operations and may not be aware of the international ring."

"Being from Toledo, myself, I would hazard a guess he's heard about this ring. He may have even been suspicious when our girl was classified as a runaway last fall."

"Well, thanks again, Ron; let's talk again soon. I'm reviewing materials on another sad, murder case today. The defendant confessed to suffocating her two little daughters. I'm suspecting some mental illness in this case.

"I figured you'd get appointed to that one, Rosie. It may even be a federal case. I played a small role in her arrest and spoke briefly to her Air Force husband. I must tell you, I was far from impressed. These men must surely have heard of post-partum depression and the potential for it following births of babies. You'd think they'd be concerned about watching for any unusual depression in their wives. Yet because of their egos, they don't seek help; they just continue on as before, making more babies. Makes me darn mad."

"Well, Ron, statistics show that most women who kill, suffer from delusions that lead them to commit murder. So often, they justify their acts as 'providing a greater home in heaven for their poor, innocent babies, and children.' But since you've spoken with her, I may have questions to ask you when I've read the arrest reports. Would you mind if I give you a call before I go see her?"

"Not at all. Don't mind a bit; I'll be glad to

assist. Have a nice day."

Rosie closed off, picked up her coffee cup and gathered the materials. She decided to get more comfortable, then give Wes a call before beginning to read.

***

"Hi Wes. It's me, Rosie. How are you?"

"Just returned from Columbus, Rosie. And how about yourself?"

"Great. I wanted to bring you up to date on the sex trafficking ring here in Toledo. Have you been made aware of any of it?"

"Only that Sophie is being released, and didn't actually kill her husband. He was in a local sex trafficking ring. But guess what else I found?"

"What?"

"He was also involved in the Columbus ring. It encompassed the entire state, not just Toledo. That's why he happened to be in Mount Vernon when he picked up Sophie."

"How interesting. She was, indeed, trafficked even though she was much older than most victims."

"He didn't want to go home 'empty-handed,' so to speak. He, also, had a need for someone to care for his little boys."

"Did you know the Toledo operation was actually international, Wes? The Feds found twelve girls in Windsor Ontario at a Casino. One of the girls, Alex Pappas, disappeared last fall after attending a hayride at a place called Stoney Lake Stables."

"I remember that, Rosie. The mom, Katrina, goes by the name 'Kat' with her friends. I understand she put out all kinds of posters, ads, and rewards for information leading to the return of her thirteen-year-old daughter. It looked like the two of them were bonded with no apparent friction. She was a single mom, and Alex was her only daughter. It must have been really hard on her."

"Get this Wes: The school security guard, Clyde Tipton, worked at the stables on weekends. The owners knew nothing of the ring, but turns out, he was the go-between for the traffickers and victims. His sister, Bonnie, was the woman in the blue BMW who engaged the girls in conversation. Ultimately, she was the one who transported them to the traffickers."

"As far as Sophie's story, this is breaking news and will make a fantastic front-page column in the Sunday edition of The Blade. It'll be a real Mother's Day tearjerker."

"Yes, it will. Sophie will be reconciled with the Jordan boys and become their legal guardian. They think of her as their mother and want to get back to life at home and school and they want the chance to make new friends. Farid never allowed them to have friends. But now they realize how bad his actions were, yet, as their father, they'll probably still mourn his death."

"Well, that's all the shop talk I can handle on one call. How about lunch on me, soon?"

"Sounds like a plan. See you soon, Wes."

***

Rosie took note of the potential interviews she wanted Ruth to schedule and put in a call to her.

"Morning Boss," Ruth said in a jovial tone.

"And a pleasant morning to you, too. I have some interviews related to the Hannah Fields case that I need you to schedule. Give them an option to come to Summerhill or the LaSalle office, okay?"

"Sure enough. I have a pad and pencil ready."

"You won't need it; the list is quite long. Watch for a fax with their telephone numbers. Let's begin with the grandparents who helped raise Hannah. From what I've read, they live on a small farm outside of Yellow Springs, Ohio. They're her mother's parents, the Michaels. There is also Hannah's uncle who also lived there at times. Maybe Mr. and Mrs. Michaels can provide his contact information. His name is Ty Michaels."

"How soon do you want to see these people and can Ty come with his parents?"

"I'm thinking about next week. Bucky and I'll get back from Mother's Day weekend late Sunday. If they come to Summerhill, Monday or Wednesday are the best days since I teach on Tuesday and Thursday. Obviously, if they prefer to come downtown, Friday works best."

"No problem. You have two-hour blocks of time open on all three of those days, Rosie."

"Great. Following those interviews, I want to see Hannah's husband, Jerry Fields. And on a separate occasion, I want to speak to his parents privately. Jerry and Hannah lived with them when they returned to Ohio from Alaska."

"Should I wait to contact him?"

"Yes, I want to see Hannah a couple of times first. Her input will be useful in my line of questioning to him. Bye for now, Ruth. Watch for the fax and their contact information. I need to get going so I can serve Bucky lunch later. "

"Check back with me this afternoon, Rosie. By then I should have some appointments scheduled. It's terrific to hear about the trafficking ring being apprehended, and Sophie set free. I bet you're relieved."

"What a turn of events, Ruth. Who would have predicted such an outcome? God works in mysterious ways. The best I expected was a verdict of not-guilty due to self-defense for Sophie and we received so much more."

"I was worried she would die in prison, Rosie. Being middle-aged, I wouldn't think she was exactly in the best of health, not that prison at any age is good for anyone."

CHAPTER 26

PLANNING NEXT STEPS

Bucky came through the foyer with Jocko trailing along beside him. "Thanks for inviting me to lunch. What are you up to?"

"I just faxed Ruth some contact information for the upcoming interviews," Rosie said, then set the table for their informal lunch. She brought plates in holding their ham and cheese sandwiches.

"Wow, this looks delicious. Didn't think I was hungry 'til now," Bucky said. "Can we say a quick 'Grace'?"

"Of course," she said bowing her head and closing her eyes.

"Thank you, God, for this food we eat; thank you for this day. Thank you for keeping us safe and helping us on our way."

"That's lovely, Bucky. I'm really grateful you're such a strong believer," she said, smiling at him. Rosie passed the bowl of chunky, homemade applesauce and picked up her water glass to toast their upcoming weekend at her mother's. But before she could speak,

Bucky interrupted her.

"Let me raise a toast to you, Rosie. You wear so many hats between counseling, teaching, your court work, and caring about your mom and friends, I'm really impressed."

"Thank you, Bucky, but you've also brought spice to my rather mundane, routine life."

"Are you kidding, Rosie? You're the sassy, spunky one in this duo. I love you 'to the moon and back' as kids say now-a-days."

Rosie felt her face blush, so she quickly began sharing the itinerary for the weekend.

"For starters, let's drive down to Oakdale on Friday afternoon. My parents moved there when my dad retired. He had a good friend, Gus Andros, who managed The Oakdale Club, known by many as the best restaurant in Montgomery County, Ohio. Anyway, Gus invited my dad, his old pal, to help him order the spirits and maintain his liquor inventory. He claimed he didn't have anyone else trustworthy enough. Dana, his assistant manager, was on maternity leave and it was to be temporary. Dad agreed to step in for five months. But, after a few weeks, my mom noticed for the first time that he came home short of breath."

"Then, what happened?"

"She made him go see a cardiologist and it turned out he needed a minor heart procedure. It wasn't long after that when he suffered a fatal cardiac arrest in the hospital after undergoing the scheduled surgery."

"You and your Mom must have been devastated."

"It was the call you never want to receive in the middle of the night. The interns tried to revive him, but his kidneys shut down and he ended up in a coma for nineteen days. They put him on dialysis, but he never regained consciousness. The ICU nurses kept his favorite Stan Kenton music playing on the CD player the entire time. They even turned on the Dallas Cowboys football game that final Sunday. But he never woke up. He finally died peacefully the following evening. It was the Monday after Thanksgiving."

"It doesn't seem like much time for your Mom to have lived in Oakdale and develop much support in the way of friends, right?"

"Fortunately, they had joined a lovely church, Washington Heights, and the pastor spent time with Dad while he was in the hospital. He prayed with my father the night before he arrested. It was customary for our pastor to visit parishioners for prayer and encouragement. From what Mom said, they had a nice little relationship."

"Obviously, your Mom decided to stay in Oakdale. Did you encourage her to move back to Toledo to be near you and your husband?"

"She said, 'you can't follow your children, Rosie.' So, when their circumstances changed, she stayed there and volunteered at the hospital in the surgical waiting room. She still maintains old friendships in Toledo and visits them . . . and me . . . about every three months. Her Toledo friends invite her to play in golf outings and she invites them down to Oakdale. They are all widows."

"How long ago did your dad pass?" Bucky asked as he help clear the table.

"It was five years ago. They were about to celebrate their fiftieth wedding anniversary. My little brothers and I were going to throw a small party here in my clubhouse. It was at Thanksgiving and they would not have been suspicious about getting together at the clubhouse. When you add the rest of my brothers' families and close friends, this condo would not have held everyone comfortably. The clubhouse would have been perfect."

"You come from sturdy stock, Rosie. Your mom is a really a strong, determined woman, isn't she?"

"I'll let you decide. You can make up your own mind when we get down there on Friday. I would like to take her to the Oakdale Club for Mother's Day brunch after church, if that's okay with you. Dad's friend, Gus, is still the manager. He took our reservation and can't wait to meet you."

"Absolutely." Bucky gave Rosie a sweet little kiss. "Will I see you on campus tomorrow? We have a home baseball game at 3:00."

"You can bet on it. Watch for me in the stands. Am I invited to the after-game shindig at Marion's?"

"You can bet on it," Bucky said as he patted Jocko's head on his way to the door. Then, he waved and closed the door softly behind him.

Rosie smiled and settled herself into her comfortable chair to resume reading and highlighting the Fields arrest reports and witness statements. Before long, the phone rang.

"How was lunch, Boss?" Ruth asked with a chuckle knowing it was great if she was with Bucky.

"Let's say the marble rye bread was toasted a bit too crisp, but he didn't seem to notice."

"Love, sweet love. By the way, I have the info you requested, Rosie."

"I have my appointment book. Let me hear it."

"Uncle Ty will drive the grandparents to the Summerhill office next Wednesday at 1:30. Can you see Hannah before that?"

"I plan to go day after tomorrow. I may see her twice before next Wednesday. Good job, Ruth."

"Oh, that's not all. The reluctant husband will come downtown to the LaSalle office next Friday at 10:00 a.m. I'm referring to the Friday after Mother's Day weekend. He didn't sound like a happy camper."

"Have I told you lately what great work you do, Ruthie, dear?"

"Have I asked you for a raise, lately, Rosie dear?"

"Well, with the income from these two new court appointments back-to-back, I'm willing to discuss that. How about breakfast tomorrow, on me, for starters? Meet me at First Watch. Does 8:30 work?"

"I can make that happen. No reason to clue my sweet, understanding husband in on it. He will assume I'm leaving early for the office. Good assumption, right?"

"See you then, Ruthie," Rosie smiled to herself. She shook her head, took a deep breath and let it out slowly. She does deserve a raise. Honestly, what would I do without her?

As Rosie returned to her reading, her phone rang again. "Hello . . .This is Dr. Klein."

"Good afternoon, Dr. Klein. This is Big John."

"Oh, hi, Big John, I didn't recognize the phone number. I'm reviewing the Hannah Fields material as we speak."

"I won't keep you long, Rosie. Just wanted to report that I visited our gal in the County jail this morning. She was very weepy. I took my associate, Dee Wakefield, with me since Hannah appears uncomfortable being alone with men. I went over the charges with her. She is now charged with one count of murder and one count of attempted murder. The Feds have dropped the charges of the first murder in Alaska in exchange for the new charges.

"I, also, got a hold of Dr. Dyer, the jail medic to get some meds prescribed for depression. The chaplain, Lisa Turner, was just coming to work as I was leaving and I asked her to stop in to see Hannah. Told her about the charges and Hannah's moods."

"That's good. Let me ask you before I go interview her: Is she a danger to herself? Do they have her on suicide watch?"

"No, they don't. If you think it's needed, call me after your first visit."

"I absolutely will do that."

CHAPTER 27

HANNAH: FIRST INTERVIEW

Rosie handed her car keys to the valet in the LaSalle Building underground parking lot. "I will be back by noon, Geoff."

"It'll be sitting right here when you return, Dr. Klein," Geoff said smiling.

He's so attentive. I need to remember to tip him generously, Rosie thought. *College students never seem to make ends meet by the end of the month.*

Rosie hustled down Spielbush St. to the Court Building. She nodded to acknowledge other pedestrians who appeared familiar. Entering the building, she laid her briefcase on the conveyer belt along with her blazer and walked through the metal detector. As she was claiming her property, someone tapped her on the shoulder and she turned quickly.

"Good to see you, Dr. Rosie." Attorney Greenberg was standing next to her with a pleasant look on his face. "What brings you to my stomping grounds this morning?"

"Oh, hi! Good morning, I'm here to interview

Hannah Fields. How about you? Don't you ever take a vacation?"

"Just asking myself the same question. Can't stay away," he laughed. "I'm here to see a new client. It's a domestic violence case. In contrast to the Sophie Washington Jordon case, I'm representing the alleged perpetrator this time. I think he's been set up by a vengeful ex-wife."

"Well, then, he can consider himself lucky to be represented by someone as conscientious as you, Josh," Rosie said.

"I might need an expert witness, Rosie, to educate the jury about Battered Women's Syndrome. Also, to explain that not every wife or ex-wife suffers from this condition. Would you be available, if I do?"

"Sure! You know how to reach me. For now, I'd better get going. Hope to talk with you soon." Rosie headed for the elevator going to the fourth floor where women defendants charged with federal crimes were housed.

The young, female deputy on duty saw Dr. Klein approaching her desk and used the intercom to call for Hannah Fields to be brought to the visitation room. She knew the reason Dr. Klein was there: to evaluate the Fields woman. Despicable, she thought. Can't believe a woman would take the life of an innocent baby, let alone two of them.

"Good morning Dr. Klein. You can put your things in there. It's unlocked." Deputy Kremer pointed to a spacious room directly across from the elevator.

"No need to worry about any women housed on the fourth floor escaping. The elevator doors don't open, nor will the elevator buttons work without a deputy's key inserted."

"Thanks, Kremer." Rosie winked as she entered the visitation room. Deputy Kremer's first name was Diane, but she preferred everyone to call her "Kremer." Working in a predominantly male profession, she felt that being addressed by her last name lent more authority to her position.

Rosie turned to see Hannah standing in the doorway without an escort. A small, slender twenty-nine-year-old Caucasian woman, she was wearing green, dollar store slippers, a gray prison uniform pants and a V-neck tee shirt with the jail logo on the left front breast pocket. Her dark brown hair had natural curl, and her expression was curious.

"Hello, Hannah, my name is Dr. Rosie Klein, and your attorney has appointed me to work with you on your court case. I must tell you what we talk about is not confidential, but it is meant to help your lawyer defend you better."

"Sure. Why not? I think I can trust a woman. Men have only caused me hurt and pain." Hannah quickly took a seat at the heavy steel table in the room commonly reserved only for visits from professionals. Dr. Rosie followed her in and sat opposite the young woman.

"It's totally boring in here. The television is pre-set to Fox News, and the other women look at me like I'm the Devil incarnate. Last week, I was transported to the emergency room because I was having really, awful bad periods, practically hemorrhaging with clots." She was silent a moment. Rosie looked at her expression. *She's very talkative. That's interesting.*

"I could hear the nurses on the other side of the curtain, call me the Baby Killer. "

"That's horrible, Hannah. Did they mistreat you at the hospital?"

"No, they didn't know I heard them. I kept my eyes shut as if I was sleeping. I was exhausted from the painful cramps. They gave me something they said was for pain. Then they connected me to an IV because I heard them say I was dehydrated. It was okay there, but then they returned me here . . . to my final resting place."

"Final resting place?"

"Well, I mean it won't be here in the County jail, but it will be in prison . . . somewhere . . . without my little boy or my husband."

"In your opinion, do you know why you were arrested, Hannah?"

"There was this Air Force investigator, Mr. Jackson, he interviewed me and told me to tell the truth and not to worry. He said my son was fine and he'd love to raise a sweet little boy like that. I told him my story. I love my children, Dr. Klein. I wanted to protect them. I knew a boy could make it, with the help of a good father, but I doubted the baby girls could survive, at least not mentally. I was suspecting they were being molested by my husband, Jerry. When I was molested by my dad, my mom didn't believe me, or didn't care. Every time Jerry changed a diaper, I know he had bad thoughts. I suspected they were being molested by him."

"Did your dad molest you when you were in still in diapers?"

"I can't remember that, but I remember him getting into my panties when I was about five. One night, I went to bed early with a tummy ache and he came up to check on me. He touched me between my legs. I didn't like it at first, but he said it would help my tummy ache."

"What happened after that?".

"It felt a little good, but somehow, it made me feel . . . not good. But he was my daddy and I guessed he knew what was right. He told me it was our little secret. Still, I started to pee my pants after that. I told my mom that he was touching me, but she didn't understand. She said he was probably 'cleaning me' and all I got was spanked."

Rosie began asking more questions and went through Hannah's history up to the eighth grade. It seems her health was good, her school attendance and grades were fine. She only attended one school and the family appeared stable.

"Hannah, I would like you to fill out this form on your health history. Then complete the endings of these forty sentences. Just fill in the first thoughts that come to your mind. Don't think a lot about each answer. It's more about what you feel. We've done good work today, but I think these sentences will help a lot. I'll be back to see you next Monday. Is there anything I can bring you?"

"Would you bring my Bible if you can? If you see Jerry, ask him to bring it to you. Only doctors are permitted to give anything to an inmate. Other visitors are frisked and can't even bring candy. If he won't do it, bring me any Bible. I don't want to go to Hell. Do you think I am doomed to Hell for what I have done?"

"I will be happy to bring a Bible, Hannah. And it's not for me to say where you'll spend your after-life. That conversation is between you and God. But promise me you won't try hurting yourself. Many people care about you. And you've been given life. That means you are worthy to be on this earth. I am seeing your grandparents and uncle next week. If you want to write a letter, I brought you some paper and a pen." Rosie slid a couple pieces of college-lined paper and a pen to Hannah. "I can pick it up when I see you next."

"Thank you. I would love to write a letter to them, and to my little boy. My husband has been here only once. I don't understand. He knows how much I love him and our family."

"I'll see what I can find out. Meanwhile, I brought you a journal so you can write your thoughts and feelings down. Sometimes, it helps to get your mind off things. Would you like to have it?"

"Thank you. The turquoise cover is beautiful. I will treasure this and share what I write with you soon, Dr. Klein."

Hannah opened the cover and began to write

in her new journal. First, she wrote her name and date inside. Then, she turned to the first page and Rosie could see she was writing a simple prayer, asking God for forgiveness. Rosie rose quietly and beckoned to the officer on duty to release the lock on the visitation door. She heard the click and stepped out. Kremer unlocked the elevator. Hannah remained in the visitation room, head bowed, writing her heartfelt thoughts. Rosie stepped into the elevator and the doors silently closed behind her.

Outside, the fresh air and sunshine was inspiring. Rosie slipped a twenty to Geoff, and drove off, heading to the woods behind the home where she grew up. She felt blessed that the family who bought it from her parents only lived in Summerhill in summertime. The remainder of the year they lived in a senior retirement community known as The Villages in Florida, leaving her to drive past her childhood home at will.

A narrow path behind the two-story, charcoal-colored frame house with white shutters, led down to a narrow creek whose sides crested each spring from the onslaught of daily showers. She remembered often sledding down the snow-covered hill, always praying to stop before slipping into the icy creek. Right now, she needed to think, and preferred thinking on her feet, so she parked along the roadside and walked into the wooded area.

Walking among the squirrels, the birds, and other small, wild critters, expanded her mind and offered her insight. It also made her feel peaceful and calm after talking with someone, like Hannah, with such a hardship story. There was some research on sexual abuse from within a family she needed to do. She knew the effects were always life-changing and a serious matter. Did Hannah's terrible actions stem from her own childhood experiences? Probably.

Her father was another story completely. If he could have known that his actions would result in the future deaths of his granddaughters, would he have stopped himself before molesting his daughter? Probably not. Sex offenders rarely think of anyone but themselves.

CHAPTER 28

SOMETHING'S WRONG

Bucky rang the bell and heard Jocko's response before Rosie could unlock the door. Her week-end bag sat in the foyer beside a black cloth sack with gold Dorothy Lane Market logo on both sides. Not surprisingly, it contained cans of moist dog food, a stainless-steel bowl, and a bright red plastic bowl for Jocko's water.

"Hi there, old buddy," Bucky said, leaning down and scratching the top of Jocko's head between deep set, brown eyes. He saw a calmness come into the dog's eyes. Bucky had seen this done to calm a horse once and began repeating it whenever he thought Jocko needed to be quieted down. The dog needed to be relaxed during their three-hour drive to Oakdale. He knew Rosie felt compelled to pamper him now.

"I guess I'm as ready as I will ever be. It's not like we'll be gone all week." Rosie kissed Bucky full on the lips. "Hello, sweetie. I thought you'd appreciate that more than a scratch on your head like Jocko got, right? That's your reward for calming him down."

"You are so insightful, my dear. I'll stash your

stuff in the trunk and we can be off for our big adventure. Maybe down around Lima we can stop for a burger and fries."

"Sounds good. We need a place that's pet-friendly so he can stretch his legs, too. At least they need to allow dogs on the patio."

"I know just the spot. Rather rustic, but I think you'll like it. Like milkshakes? I like peanut butter and chocolate, myself. What do you think of that combination?"

"Not bad. I would say my favorite is coffee and chocolate. Speaking of peanut butter, did you know they don't have peanut butter in Austria? I found that out when I was there on a short-term mission trip. They asked all volunteers from the United States to bring peanut butter. That way, they could make peanut butter cookies for mid-afternoon treats for the European students and staff. By the way, is it okay with you if we have brunch tomorrow with my Adrian college roommate, Marlene? She lives near my mother. After college she married a rabbi and they'll be moving to Jerusalem next month."

"Sure, I'd love to meet her. She can fill in some blanks for me. What kind of a girl was my Rosie in college? Did you stay in touch after you left Adrian?"

"Yes. We ended up in grad school together. When they get to Jerusalem, Marlene plans to open a language institute and teach English."

Lunch with milkshakes hit the spot. The server brought a whipped cream cookie and placed it on the pavement for Jocko. It was gone in two seconds.

It was about four o'clock when they pulled into Esther's driveway. She swung open the door and stepped onto the stoop.

"Come on in and let the celebration begin! It's five o'clock somewhere and not too early for a glass of wine . . . I'm so glad to see you and so excited to meet my future son-in-law. Hi, Bucky. Just call me Es."

"Hi Mom. No need for formal introductions, I see." Rosie threw her arms around her mother's shoulders and squeezed tightly.

"It's an honor to be here, Es," Bucky said with a broad smile and an extended hand.

"Oh, we don't shake hands with family," Es said, giving Bucky a warm hug and a pat on the back. "Just take your stuff upstairs and meet me on the porch." Es pointed to the French doors opening to the screened porch off the side of the living room.

Bucky noticed the baby grand in the corner by the doors. "Do you both play the piano?"

"Rosie plays a little. Her father played honky tonk, jazz. Rosie and I were the dancers in the family. Weren't we?"

Rosie laughed and headed up to the second-floor loft with Bucky trailing behind.

"Will Jocko stay down here with me?" Es asked. "No need for him to climb those steps. I'd love to have him sit at my feet."

"Jocko. Stay with Es," Rosie commanded. The big dog looked at her, then at Es and promptly sat down. "He loves enclosed porches with a slight breeze like you have right now. He'll love it downstairs tonight."

Rosie sat her bag on the Cherrywood hope chest at the foot of the bed. It was given to her on her sixteenth birthday to collect things of personal value. Sadly, she had never managed to move it to her own condo in Toledo, but it held great sentimental value. Bucky followed suit, then took her hand.

"What a neat guest room she has set up here. But I imagine all your memories can't fit inside your girlhood trunk."

"It's called a 'hope chest,' Bucky. Girls loved putting things inside related to their hopes and dreams. Most of my memories, some painful, are in that hope chest. Maybe I will bring my yearbooks home with us. How very perceptive of you. Ready to join my mother?"

"Sure. Point me to the bathroom first if you don't mind."

"There isn't one up here, sorry. It's at the bottom of the stairs, straight ahead."

"I'm going to text Marlene and let her know we here. Then, I'll be by Mom to hear how she views her future son-in-law. Ha."

Rosie texted Marlene and asked her to call about nine thirty on Saturday morning to confirm breakfast and make plans to join her. Then she started downstairs and heard voices.

"Hope you like shrimp cocktail, cheese, grapes, crackers, and peanuts. Help yourself while I get you a drink. Name it."

"A cold beer might hit the spot, if it isn't too much

trouble, and you have it on hand."

"Of course. Ahh, Rosie, how about you? A glass of red wine for medicinal purposes as you say?" "Yes, let me help you, Mom."

Bucky reclined in the plaid-cushioned wicker chair, patted Jocko, and glanced around. Little by little he was becoming better acquainted with the life and loves of Rosie Klein.

Dinner was served with a delicious meatloaf, mashed potatoes, peas, and spinach salad. Strawberry shortcake rounded out the hearty meal. Most of the conversation involved Esther asking questions and Bucky answering to the best of his ability. Rosie sat quite amused by their interchange.

Later that evening, Rosie was invited to sleep with her mother. Something they hadn't previously discussed, but she should have realized would happen. She thought the invitation had more to do with old-fashioned values than to participate in a late-night slumber party. But that's actually what it evolved into. Rosie and Esther shared a few laughs, a nightcap, and a few tears long after Bucky had called it a night. It was a chilly night and, earlier, as Bucky headed up to the loft, Esther had adjusted the heat and told him to open his heat vent upstairs.

It was just dawn when Rosie got up quietly and ambled out to the living room to snuggle with Jocko on the couch. She felt a little wobbly on her feet and wondered why her head was throbbing. She knew it wasn't a hangover, and didn't feel feverish or cold, still she wrapped a warm shawl around herself, then, waited to hear from Marlene about breakfast arrangements. Sure enough, Marlene called as scheduled.

"I can't believe my mother and Bucky are still asleep. I'll wake Bucky in a while and we'll see you at eleven at Bob Evans." Oh my gosh. Now, I'm feeling nauseous. "Call you when we leave, Marlene."

Rosie started upstairs to the loft. She held on to the rail and fought off lightheadedness. "Rise and shine, Bucky. It's going on nine. You must have been worn out by my mother's interrogation."

"I never sleep this late. Where's the shower? I'll hustle and be ready when you say."

"It's in the basement. I don't feel so great. Let me sit in the recliner till you come up."

As they headed down the steps, Bucky said, "I feel dizzy myself, Rosie, and a little nauseous. Maybe I'll feel better after I get cleaned up. Grubbiness is another symptom."

Rosie rested until she heard the shower water turn off in the basement. Ten minutes passed and Bucky still hadn't appeared. She headed down the basement stairs and knocked on the door of the knotty pine room that held the shower stall. She turned the knob, but the door wouldn't budge. She called out for Bucky, but only heard him moan. Then, she realized his body was wedged against the door.

"Don't move, Bucky. I'm calling 911! There's something wrong in this house. I should wake my mom, too."

Rosie made her way upstairs and called 911 on the house phone.

"My fiancé has fainted in the shower and we're both nauseated. Please send help right away," she said, giving their exact location. The dispatcher asked if they had smoke or carbon monoxide detectors.

"I don't know; this is my mother's house."

"Open all the windows and get everyone outside if you can," the dispatcher said. "Help is on the way."

"Mom. You need to get up. We need to get out of the house," Rosie said, trying to rouse her mother from the bed. Lethargic, her mom staggered out from under the covers.

"What? Do I have time for a cigarette?"

"No! We need to get Bucky out, too. The medics are coming. It's carbon monoxide!" Rosie slipped her mom's feet into her loafers, snatched her purse from the dresser, and carefully led her by the arm. Bucky slowly mounted the basement steps to the kitchen. He had a gash on his forehead above his left eye and was holding a washcloth against the wound. Outside, they heard the approaching sirens. Multiple sirens.

"Oh my, Rosie, there are three ambulances," Esther shouted, looking out the window.

Within minutes, firemen and EMTs were at the door, now opened wide. They rolled in three gurneys and teams of two attended each of the three adults. One by one, they were asked to lie onto the rolling stretchers and buckled in. Bucky's head wound was quickly dressed after everyone's blood pressure was checked

233

and oxygen masks were placed over each of their faces. Rosie saw a TV stations van pull up outside as she was wheeled out the doorway.

Within minutes, her gurney was shoved into the back of an ambulance, the paramedics closed the door, and the ambulance pulled away from the curb. She heard someone tell the driver that Toledo Hospital was the closest. She heard sirens and knew Bucky and her mother were in the parade. Then, she began to pray. Gratitude was the first thing on her mind. If they had not visited, her mother would have died in that house.

***

The hyperbaric chambers sat side by side. They were each receiving high-pressure oxygen therapy and feeling better within a short time of their arrival and treatment. The three of them could wave at one another. Rosie thought they looked like glass coffins. Bucky was watching a baseball game on a wall-mounted television across from his chamber. Esther remained silent with her eyes closed. Rosie lay still with her arms crossed over her chest, hands clasped together, resting and in prayer. Their treatment took most of the day and the physician on duty said they would stay overnight for observation.

Without my phone, I can't get a message to Marlene. How will she know? After that, Rosie was able to give Marlene's number to her nurse who called and left a message.

Later that afternoon, a fireman visited to inform them that Esther's gas furnace had a slow leak. Before the oxygen therapy, her level of carbon monoxide had been measured as being the highest, followed by Bucky's. The furnace was in the basement and had probably been emitting the odorless gas for the past few days. The loft where Bucky had spent the night, had also received the toxic substance.

"After discharge tomorrow morning, Mrs. Klein, you'll need to find someplace to stay," Dr. Bailey said. "You can't return to your house until the furnace is replaced. Meanwhile, if you all make a list of what you need, we'll send firemen with masks to bring your things to you. Include your car keys. Your car will be in the emergency room parking area, Mr. Walker. You're lucky, the dog nosed open the door and slept on the porch last night." He was encouraging and said none of them had any notable permanent damage.

"Mom why not come home with me while your furnace is replaced. You can ride in the front seat and I'll sit in back with Jocko." Rosie slipped her arm around her mother's waist.

"Tomorrow night, the three of us can stay at the Hampton Inn in Dayton," Bucky said. "I can get a free suite with my points from all my baseball traveling. It won't be a problem and actually, I insist." He had been lucky, his head wound only required six stitches. Hearing there was no concussion was even better news.

"Maybe we can still do brunch with Marlene tomorrow if we are released early enough, Rosie said. I'll call her now and see if she received the nurse's message." Marlene picked up the phone after two rings.

"I'm so happy you're all right. What a scare! When you didn't show up at Bob Evans, I went by your mom's house and found the firemen going through it. When I told them, I was a friend of the family, they asked if I could take care of Jocko. I have him with me now."

"Oh, Marlene, thank you so much! I had a nurse try to call you, but she only could leave a message."

"I must have been at your mom's house. I found the message when I came home. Care if I stop by the hospital now? How about if I bring pizzas from Marion's? You heard me right, Marion's is a franchise now."

"That would be fantastic as long as you let me pay for them. Make mine veggie, please, and Bucky's a meat lover. Mom will eat either one. What about you? Bring Stan with you, too."

"I'll split your veggie. Stan has a committee meeting tonight at the Temple."

"You know, Marlene, your morning call may have saved our lives. We could have slept our way into oblivion. I'm kind of surprised that Jocko didn't wake me up, although he slept on the porch."

"Get some rest, Rosie, is the nausea gone? How about your headache?"

"I am fine. Can't wait to catch up on the directions our lives have taken since grad school."

With her mom feeling a little woozy, they decided to eat in her room. Their rooms were adjacent and the nurses' station was directly across from Esther's room.. After two pieces of veggie pizza, Esther asked if she could get some rest. Rosie, Marlene and Bucky moved to the waiting area by the elevator for a little more visiting. Marlene inquired about Bucky's life since she wanted to know more about who her dearest friend was going to marry. After all, she was moving to the other side of the world and had Rosie's best interest in mind.

"At some point, I would like to bring Rosie to visit you in the Holy Land," Bucky asked. "Would that be okay?"

"More than okay. You just went from an eight to a ten, Bucky," Marlene rose to say goodbye and hugged him, winking at Rosie over his shoulder. "You picked a good one, Rosie." She smiled back, looking at two people she cared about deeply. Imagine that, after such a harrowing day, this evening has ended on a real high note.

CHAPTER 29

ROSIE'S MOM

Once Esther was settled into her bedroom in Rosie's condo, and Bucky and Rosie had walked Jocko, Bucky excused himself to check on his own house and take a couple of Tylenol tablets. His head was still sore from the gash he had received when he blacked out at her mom's house. He also hadn't told Rosie the nurse practitioner revealed to him privately that he had sustained a mild concussion from his fall. But there was no way he was going to allow Rosie to drive them back from Oakdale. *Somethings are better kept to oneself,* he reasoned.

But the idea that he had put them in some danger by doing the driving back to Rosie's with a concussion, never occurred to Bucky. Fortunately for everyone, they arrived safely.

***

Rosie began to plan her interviews with Hannah Fields' family member for early the in the week ahead. She had already let Ruth know by phone what had happened at her mom's house and that Es had come back to stay with Rosie for a while.

"How did your Mother's Day concert go?" she had asked on the phone to Ruth.

"A lot better than the weekend you had at your mom's place," Ruth had quipped.

Now, with her legs tucked up under her, and hands cupped around a steaming mug of pure peppermint herbal tea, Rosie felt grateful. She silently thanked the Lord for their survival and safe return home. Using a yellow sharpie, she began highlighting written statements provided by Hannah's grandparents, Mr. and Mrs. Michaels and their son, Ty. They had also given personal recollections of their granddaughter's life to help Rosie fill in details and assist in her assessment of Hannah Fields' mental capacity.

The phone rang. "Hi Rosie. Just checking on you. Are you and your Mom feeling okay?"

"Yes, fine, Bucky. It's good to hear your voice. How are you after driving all the way back from Oakdale?"

"Fine. I dozed off while reading the paper. Other than that, I'm ready for work with my team tomorrow. By the way, have you seen the paper? Wes' story on the sex trafficking ring made front page headlines. And you, my dear, are quoted throughout.

"Really? I'll have to go outside and get my copy from the driveway."

"I'll bring over my copy tomorrow. Your mother may want to save it. Not every mother can say her daughter is famous."

"Ugh, if that's what it takes to make somebody 'famous,' I'll pass. Besides, I might take Mom shopping over at Lion Store in Westgate where I worked during my high school and college days. If I know my mom, she can always use another pair of shoes."

"Well, buy yourself something too, Rosie. I would like to take you gals out to Alfie's for dinner. We never got to celebrate Mother's Day. What do you think?"

"Mom would love it. Let's meet at six. That'll give me time to come home and walk Jocko, and change clothes."

"By the way, when are you seeing the defendant's grandparents?"

"Not until Thursday. I'll see the grandmother then, and her husband, downtown on Friday. First, I'll hustle over to the jail tomorrow. It's looking like Hannah suffered what we call "The Sleeper Effect." It's a delayed post-traumatic stress reaction, usually quite severe.

"How so?"

"Well, after traumatic sexual abuse by her father, she moved out of danger from her own home to her grandparents' house where her teen-age life appeared normal. She was a cheerleader, homecoming queen, and fell in love. But her symptoms seriously manifested after she gave birth to her first child. The birth brought up repressed memories of her own victimization. She might not even have been aware of why, but she dealt with them by smothering her own infant daughter so the little girl wouldn't one day suffer the fate of being sexually abused. In her mental illness, Hannah thought she was protecting the child."

"That's unbelievable. She can't be considered 'in

her right mind' doing that, could she?"

"No, but that's not the worst of it. Her baby was determined to have suffered Sudden Infant Death Syndrome (SIDS) and Hannah was not seen as someone who killed her child. So, she didn't get the help she desperately needed at that time."

"Didn't another child of hers die the same way? Kind of unusual?"

"Yes, a couple years later, she did the same thing to their second daughter. By then, they were stationed back home in Ohio. That's when her husband began to suspect something wasn't right with Hannah's thinking. It was the first time he sought help for her."

"Geez, how sad. To lose two baby daughters. I, honestly, can't imagine the pain."

"Me, neither. So, I'm working on all this today, so I'm ready for my interview tomorrow."

"Well, I'll let you get back to your reading. Love you. See you tomorrow."

***

Rosie awoke with a start. It was a sunny, new day and Jocko's nose was prodding her arm. She found herself covered by the lap blanket her mother had knit for her after Rosie's husband died. She had fallen asleep on the couch after sipping peppermint tea, so her mother must have covered her to be sure she was warm enough.

"Good morning, Mom," Rosie said, glimpsing her mother on a stool at the kitchen counter.

"Top of the morning to you, too. Did you sleep okay with your blankie tucked around you?"

"Yes, thanks. How about you? I see you figured out where the coffee and filters are."

"Yep, and there's something I need to tell you. My friend has arranged for a new furnace to be installed tomorrow, so I'll be leaving on Wednesday."

"Already? My day is chock full on Wednesday with interviews and my women's group."

"No need to worry, Rosie. I know how busy you are. He's picking me up."

"He? Mother, your friend is a 'he?'"

"Well, yes. I meant to break the news when you took me to brunch, but the accident happened and there was no proper time to tell you."

"Where did you meet him, and what's his name?"

"His name is Caleb Davidson. We met at church, and our spouses died within months of each other. His wife had Alzheimer's and lived in a memory care home. Your Bucky will like him. He's been involved in sports all his life. Football, basketball, and baseball, the 'big three' as he calls them."

"Ask him to come tomorrow so we have a little time together. I can stay at Bucky's and the two of you can spread out in the condo."

"Well, that would be nice. I would like you two to meet. Let me call and ask if his schedule permits. That way, he won't have to drive both ways in one day."

"Absolutely, Mom. I need to go downtown for a couple of hours later today to see a woman in jail. Then I was hoping we could go shopping at Westgate. What do you think?"

"Sounds great. Would it be okay if I walk Jocko around the grounds while you are gone?"

"Absolutely. First, how about an onion, sesame bagel with cream cheese? Then I'll shower and get out of here."

"Fabulous. You know, sweetheart, it hasn't escaped me how very blessed we are, you know?"

"Yes, Mom, we certainly are."

CHAPTER 30

HANNAH: SECOND INTERVIEW

Rosie approached the jail's professional visitation room with an interview plan in mind. She had to ask Hannah questions without seeming too aggressive or judgmental. She, certainly, didn't want to shut her down emotionally. Officer Kremer was standing by the door.

"Good Morning, Kremer," Rosie smiled. "Have a nice weekend?"

"Actually, I did Dr. Klein. It was the first weekend I've had off since before Easter."

"What do you do in your spare time?"

"Well, I'm actually in college and working on my master's in psychology."

"Really! Do you plan to leave law enforcement?"

"No. I want to go into the FBI Intelligence Division, and their requirements are stringent."

"Well, good luck. Let me know if I can help you in any way."

"Thanks. I'll call for Hannah Fields to be brought to the visitation area. In our Monday morning conference meeting, I heard she had a bad weekend. On Sunday, she couldn't breathe and was taken to the Infirmary. It turned out to be a panic attack. I was hoping you would be here to see her today. The medic would like to speak with you when your interview is over."

"That's fine. When I stand up to leave, perhaps you could call him?"

"Oh, the medic is a woman. Her name is Argie Dyer. People think her name is 'Archie' and that she's a guy. It's funny to see their expressions when they meet her face to face." They shared a laugh, and Rosie's eyes strayed down the hallway in time to see Hannah round a corner and walk toward her. She was walking slowly with her head down, arms hung in front of her, fingers intertwined tightly.

Hannah spied Rosie entering the visitation room and silently followed her. They seated themselves opposite each other as they had for the first interview.

"Good morning, Hannah. Thank you for meeting with me again. How are you feeling?"

Hannah lifted her head and looked at Rosie through tear-filled eyes. "I think I'm having flashbacks, Dr. Klein. Not dreams. Actual memories, and they are awful and so scary."

"Would you like to tell me about them?"

"I remember lying on a sort of table and being injected with something in my arm. Then, these metal instruments were inserted inside me. It was a long time ago before I knew Jerry or lived with my grandparents. I remember being worked on down there, and then it felt like something was stuffed inside of me. Somebody told me it was to 'stop the bleeding.' I think I missed school for a while. I, also, remember my mother bringing me meals on trays, chicken soup, mac and cheese, oatmeal. Soft stuff like that. Then, I was taken back to the doctor and these like-bandages were taken out. It was a scary memory. But I remember my dad never touched me after that. It made me feel dirty. I didn't feel like he cared about me anymore. Strange, he's the one who suggested that procedure."

Hannah's eyes had been filled with suffering at the memory, now she put her head down on the table and sobbed. Dr. Klein reached across and gently smoothed Hannah's hair. She noticed Hannah had not brought her homework or her journal.

"Hannah, you are the beloved daughter of God, and there are many people who love you. I'm meeting with your grandparents this week and understand they would like to come and visit you."

"Really? You don't think they don't hate me for what I have done?"

"No. Their love is unconditional. Do you know what that means?"

Hannah lifted her head from the table. "No, not really. What does it mean?"

"It means you are loved regardless of what you do, or don't do in your life. Can you tell me more details about your memories? Who took you for the procedure?"

"My mother took me to the doctor and kept saying she was sorry. I couldn't figure out what she was sorry about. She mumbled something like 'the only way to prevent a divorce.'"

"Do you think she meant your father forced her to arrange this?"

"Maybe. She was probably thinking of my little sister and brother. She couldn't afford to raise them alone."

"How soon after that did you go to live with your grandparents?"

"As soon as the school year ended. They picked me up, and we packed all my stuff into their Chevy pick-up truck. Dad was at work so he couldn't help, not that he would have anyway. I remember hugging the other kids and Mom, and off we went. It turned out to be the best summer of my life."

"Is that when you met Jerry, and fell in love?"

"Yes, it was his senior year and my junior year. He was the starting quarterback of the football team. He could have gone on to play college ball, but he worked in his dad's hardware store. They had some big difference of opinion, so he enlisted in the Air Force. It was just after the Christmas of my senior year."

"I understand you were homecoming queen that year. So, your grades were good?"

"I was thinking about becoming a dental hygienist . . . but then it happened."

"What happened, Hannah?"

"I got pregnant. So, Jerry and I got married when I graduated. We moved to Alaska and lived in base housing at Elmendorf. That was the name of the base. The base hospital and doctors were great."

"That was probably a relief. Your daughter was born healthy, and you were fine?"

"I thought our family was off to a good start. My grandmother came out to help me for about three weeks. I was nursing and it was tough to make it through some of the nights. She would get up and change the baby's diaper. Then give her to me so I could feed her. Jerry needed his rest to go to work early the next morning."

"I see. What happened next?"

"When my grandmother left, I began to feel isolated and lonely. There were times when Jerry's unit was called away for training missions. TDY, they called it. I guess, despite being a new mom, I really felt depressed. Some nights, I was afraid to sleep because of bad dreams and horrible thoughts in my mind."

"I can understand. Can you describe the thoughts and dreams, Hannah?"

"At first, I dreamed someone was hiding in the closet in Amy's room. So, I usually sat in the rocker, held her tightly, and breast fed her around two in the morning while keeping the closet door open. Then, I would feed her again about five. One night in my dream, she was missing when I came for the five o'clock feeding. It scared me that I hadn't heard her cry. But I woke up and realized it was a dream. Still, I was edgy a lot and didn't know what to do. Jerry was out of town."

Hannah squeezed her hands together. She squeezed so tightly that her arms began to shake. Rosie reached out and covered her cold, shaking hands to warm them.

"Can you tell me what happened next?"

"The dreams changed. When they began, I would look in the empty crib and search for her everywhere in the room: under the crib, behind the rocker, and in the closet. Then, I would wake up feeling sweaty and panicky, dash to her room and see her sleeping with her little thumb in her mouth."

"What changed?"

"After a while, I would see myself, instead of Amy, in the crib and my father leaning over me. His eyebrows were always knit together with his squinty eyes glaring into my face. I wouldn't recognize him, so I would scream for my mother, but she couldn't hear me. Then, he would clap one rough hand over my mouth and one behind my head and tell me to 'Shush.' He would lift me up and shove me onto his lap facing him. That's when I would wake up."

"That had to be terrifying. What must you have been thinking?"

"I don't know what I was thinking in the dream. But each time I woke up, I remember thinking how to protect my Amy from a future childhood like mine. I thought about it a lot. Finally, I knew what I would do."

"What was that?"

"I waited for a night when Jerry worked the night shift. Then, I fed her and rocked her at two a.m. She fell asleep in my arms. I gently placed her back in her crib on her tummy. I covered her mouth and nose with her pink blankie with satin trim. First, she squirmed and made a few sounds, but at least, I didn't have to look at her sweet little face since she was on her tummy. Pretty soon, she stopped moving. I sat back down in the rocker and thought: 'Now, she's safe.' Then I went back to bed. Jerry found her at seven the next morning."

"What did he do?"

"He screamed and told me to call 911. He asked me if I had fed her at five. I said no, I guessed she slept through the night after the two o'clock feeding. Dr. Klein, he believed me. And the nightmares I had about her being missing . . . they stopped. Then, my thoughts of protecting her stopped. I knew she was in heaven. But..."

"But what?"

"The nightmares about my father got worse. I kept getting older and what he did became so terribly mean and hurtful."

"Did you tell anybody, or get counseling after Amy's death?"

"No. Jerry's answer was to have another baby. I got pregnant almost immediately, but I miscarried before the end of the first trimester. The next year, we had another little girl and named her, Hope. The doctor ordered a breathing monitor for her due to the SIDS death of Amy. That's what they said happened to her. Then Jerry got assigned to Ohio."

"How did you feel about the transfer?"

"I couldn't wait to see my grandparents. I didn't get to see them right away. We lived with Jerry's parents until we could get into base housing in Toledo near the airport. He was gone long hours again. He also commuted to a base in Dayton. It was two hours from Toledo by car, but mostly Jerry was shuttled by helicopter to and from that Air Force base."

"Was his mother helpful with Hope?"

"Yes, I have no complaints. She just wasn't my mother or grandmother. Once we moved to base housing, we joined a little church in Swanton and got involved. Our life changed some. Jerry became a deacon. Then Hope was christened. My grandparents came to that. By then, my mother had divorced my dad and moved out of state."

"Your parents got divorced?"

"I think he was messing around with a lady from work. They're married now. She has two little girls. If I could warn her, I would. Those girls could be his next victims, Dr. Klein."

"Do you resent your mother for not protecting you back then?"

"I sort of resent her. She couldn't or wouldn't believe he got me pregnant. He wanted her to think I was messing around with every boy on the block just like she did. But she didn't really do that, Dr. Klein. I think my father had the problem. Even though I was born ten months after they got married, he never treated me like I was his own little girl. He was much nicer to my little sister and brother. When he got me pregnant, he told my mother they were not raising another bastard baby. That's why she took me to the clinic to have the abortion. I think she was on Ativan or something for anxiety and there were times she mixed it with alcohol."

"Do you think she took you to your grandparents to live so she didn't have to face the truth every day? She may have felt guilty about what happened and not protecting you."

"Probably. All my grandparents knew was that my dad was very mean and cruel to me and my mother. They didn't know about the abortion. I faked being a normal, happy teen-ager and pushed everything that happened to me to the back of my mind. I just focused on cheering and school."

"What your father did was criminal. You don't have any proof, do you?"

"I have my diaries. I hid them under my mattress and took them to my grandparents' house. They're probably still there under the mattress in my grandparents' extra bedroom. After I left, my grandmother transformed my room into a sewing room or guest room. It was more useful than staying idle as a teenager's room."

Rosie made a mental note to inquire about the diaries. If mitigating factors included proof of incest and child abuse, they could factor into Hannah's conviction and sentencing. She also reminded herself to check with Argie Dyer and Lisa Turner. Their observations of Hannah, while in jail, could be powerful validation of her post traumatic stress disorder and mental illness.

"Were your grandparents back in your life after the christening?"

"Not really. They lived far away from Toledo. And you will never guess I was pregnant again, and my grandmother noticed right away. Privately, in the lady's restroom of the church, I cried and said I didn't know how I could handle a toddler and a new baby."

"Was she aware that you had miscarried after Amy's death?"

"No. I didn't want to cause her more heartache."

"What did she say?"

"What could she say? She said she was just a phone call away and to call her day or night. I told her Jerry wanted me to put them in the church nursery and work there full-time. All I could think of was how in the world could I work fulltime and still meet his standards in terms of housework, cooking, and . . . other needs, if you know what I mean."

"Did you go to work?"

"Yes, I did and that's another story. I will say that Jerry said if we had a healthy little boy, he would get a vasectomy. When we had Ty, Jerry kept his promise and got a vasectomy."

"Do you want to talk about working at the church?"

"Not today, if you don't mind. You will come back, won't you? I'll bring my homework with me next time, promise. I've been writing in the journal pretty regular and I filled out the sentences the best I could."

"That's really great, Hannah, I will be back after I see your grandparents and uncle this week. Is it okay if I ask her to look for your diaries?"

"Yes, that would be really good. Tell my grandpa and uncle I really, really appreciate them. They are the kindest men I have ever known. Without them, I would always have been bitter toward guys. I'm learning about myself every day, Dr. Klein. My biggest regret is what I did to my two beautiful babies. I was not in my right mind. I didn't see any other options. I should be punished for what I did. But I thought I was protecting them from being taken advantage of, like I was. I will be sorry for what I did for the rest of my life."

CHAPTER 31

FAMILY INTERVIEW

Hannah's grandparents found Dr. Klein's office easily, and were on time for their Thursday appointment at 9:30 a.m.

"Dr. Klein, Mr. and Mrs. Michaels are here. Shall I bring them back?"

"Thank you, Ruth. I'll come up and receive them. Have you offered coffee?"

"I'll do that right now. For the record, they seem to be genuinely nice people."

"Sounds good. I'll be there in a couple of minutes after finishing some session notes from my interview with their granddaughter."

Rosie greeted the Michaels in the waiting room and introduced herself. Ruth asked if they wanted coffee or tea. They agreed to coffee with cream, no sugar. Rosie escorted them to her office.

"Please, make yourselves comfortable. I appreciate your willingness to travel all this way to meet with me."

"We are happy to be able to help our sweet Hannah in any way we can. Please, just call us James and Betty. You were highly recommended by Mr. Chickalette." They sat side by side on the loveseat across from Rosie's overstuffed chair.

"I'd like to begin our interview with how you came to be her guardians. She came to you as a junior in high school, correct?"

"Yes. Her mother, our daughter, wanted to prevent her husband's abuse from escalating. He was physically and mentally abusive from the time she was just a small girl."

"Did anyone know that at the time?"

"Unfortunately, no, or something would have been done about it."

"She has two younger siblings, right?"

"Yes, she does . . .a younger sister, Faith, and a little brother, Jonathon."

"Were they mistreated too?"

"No. Actually, we think Hank doubted that Hannah was his child, but we are certain she was, Dr. Klein, there is no way our daughter, Suzanne, slept with anyone before Hank and Hannah was born ten months after they were married," Betty Michaels said, her eyes beginning to moisten.

"Faith was the apple of his eye," James Michaels said. "She loved sports, and he helped coach her Little League team. Jonathan was a clone of his father in appearance and behavior, a real tough little guy. We thought he kind of ignored Hannah."

"So, Hank was tough, then? Were either of you aware of Hannah's molestation accusations?"

"Not at all. We did see bruises on her arms and cheeks, but she would say she fell off her bike. She never mentioned any abuse at all, certainly, not to us. After all this time we've had to think about it, we think she was afraid her father would molest her little sister if she told anyone or didn't do exactly what he wanted her to do."

"How did she do in school before and after she lived with you?"

"Her grades improved dramatically after she came to live with us, and she took college prep classes. We were so pleased with how she applied herself to studies. She even became interested in careers in medical fields."

"How did she do socially?"

"She was a pretty little thing and well-liked. She was a cheerleader and in her senior year, she was voted homecoming queen. Then, she fell in love with Jerry Fields who was a year ahead of her. We thought she would move on after he joined the Air Force and was in Texas for basic training. That was in the second half of her senior year."

"But it lasted, and they got married as soon as she graduated. Unfortunately, by then she was pregnant, so the thought of further schooling was over. Dr. Klein we should have noticed she was looking paunchy, but we didn't and neither the school, I guess. Once Jerry became assigned to Elmendorf Air Force Base in Anchorage Alaska, we couldn't even see her anymore. They lived in base housing, and when their daughter, Amy, was born, I went out to help Hannah for about three weeks."

"How did she seem?"

"She seemed fine. She was nursing the baby and you could see how bonded she was becoming. There was no doubt she loved her little Amy."

"How did she take it when you left?

"She cried some and clung to me when we hugged good-bye. Jerry wasn't home much during our visit, and when he was home, his expectations were a little too high, in my estimation, for a new, young mother who was up through the night nursing a baby."

"Did you hear much from her after you returned to Ohio?"

"Once I left, she seldom called. I just figured she was busy trying to keep up with everything. Besides, it was a short summer. Then winter came along. Hannah did write one letter describing how miserable Alaska was in January. The sun comes up at 10 in the morning and sets by 3 in the afternoon. What kind of day is that? She said you almost had to wear long underwear in the house. It only had aluminum siding with a little insulation. They used a space heater in their tiny living room. She also said it snowed a lot and was very unpredictable. I can imagine with all that and not even six hours of daylight, those conditions certainly didn't help her mood. The next thing I heard, the baby died of SIDS, and it devastated us all. You can see the letter if that would help."

"Yes, I would, thank you. So, there were no signs of abuse out there?"

"Not toward the baby, but, yes, mental abuse

toward our granddaughter. One night, I overheard them in the bedroom. He called her names like "worthless" as a wife and mother. She was weepy the next day. If my husband had been there, he would have had words with Jerry. Right, Hon?"

"You can bet on it." Mr. Michaels had remained composed, and silent until then. Now, his fists were clenched as he looked down in thought.

"How about when the second daughter was born . . . did you help then, too?"

"No. We knew they wanted a second child to help overcome the grief of losing little Amy. But to us, it seemed too soon. Hannah said Jerry had insisted, but I felt he did not understand the grieving process or even the healing needed after having a baby. The pediatrician ordered a monitor for little Hope, due to the previous SIDS death. They named her Hope because it made them hopeful of having a family. Then Jerry got transferred back to Ohio."

"They lived with his parents until they were eventually admitted into base housing by the Toledo airport. He was assigned to a base in Swanton, Ohio, near Toledo, two hours away. Can you imagine? Sometimes, he flew home during the week but usually only got to his parents' house on some weekends."

"The next time we saw Hannah, again, was at Hope's christening at their church in Swanton. I noticed Hannah looked, well, kind of paunchy. She confided she was five months pregnant again. I couldn't believe it. I didn't surprise me that she cried and said she didn't know how she could handle a baby and a toddler. Jerry said if they had a boy, he would have a vasectomy. That was good news because I thought he was pushing her too fast to have a family. It just didn't seem right."

"Jerry seemed downright gleeful at the christening. By then, he was a deacon in the church. His answer to her concerns about the kids was to put them in the church nursery and work there herself. She wondered how she would ever meet his standards in terms of housework and meeting his needs, you know what I mean."

"A few months later, their son, Ty, was born and Jerry did have a vasectomy. I was not asked to come to Swanton to help her. Although we talked on the phone. Honestly, she sounded pretty desperate."

"When did her lying begin, and did you believe what she told you?"

"Aside from small childhood lies, I noticed she started telling 'stories' while they were still in Alaska. She said the neighbor had raped her in her backyard. When I became alarmed and asked if she had reported it and gotten help, she backed down and said, it wasn't true. Why would someone fib about that? Then, I noticed even worse things after they lost little Hope to SIDS, again. How does that even happen . . . twice? Then, when she said that an intruder tried to rape her in the basement of the church in Swanton, I began to suspect she wasn't mentally well. She even cut her cheek with a razor which was found in the trash of the church's ladies' room. When authorities questioned her, she said it happened while she was trying to protect the little children because she had seen an intruder in the building earlier in the week."

"I am so deeply sorry for your tragic losses. What you have shared is not just informative but extremely useful to me and most certainly to the Judge. Did you bring Hannah's journals by any chance and can you bring her Bible to me?"

"Yes, I'll also bring her Bible and the letter I mentioned, next time. After you called, I did find these journals. When she was just a tiny girl, she drew pictures of things that would happen to her. Would these be helpful to you and her case?"

Mrs. Michaels handed the journals to Rosie.

"No doubt about it, Betty. Thank you so much. I'll return them after Attorney Chickalette, and I have reviewed them. He may want to photocopy some or all her writing and drawings. Thank you. Now, I would like to speak to your son, Ty, if you don't mind."

"Absolutely. He drove us here and is eager to help his niece in any way he can." Obviously, a man of few words, James Michaels seemed glad to offer this information as his wife wiped her eyes with a tissue, nodding in agreement.

Rosie escorted them back to the waiting area and called young Mr. Michaels in. "Ty, please join me, and by the way, is there anything any of you want to drink?"

"Not for us," James answered.

"I could use a refill of black coffee, if it isn't too inconvenient," Ty said.

"Coming right up. I'll bring it back to Dr. Klein's office for you," Ruth said while in earshot of the conversation.

Ty followed Rosie to her office, seated himself in a plaid wing chair facing her desk, and sighed deeply. "I'm relieved to talk to you, and thankful you called us to participate in your evaluation of my niece. She's been a troubled young woman for a long time."

"First, I want to thank you for bringing your parents here today. Secondly, I'd like to hear why you believe she is a troubled young woman. Can you explain?"

"When she came to live with my parents, I was away for five-months basic training in the Ohio Army National Guard. When I returned, she seemed to have blossomed. Previously, she had always been quiet and subdued, but when I came home at Christmas, she was helping Mom bake cookies, and we decorated the tree together. She brought this young guy to church on Christmas Eve, Jerry Fields. He seemed okay. He was a senior and Hannah was a junior. But I felt she was too young to be serious about any guy."

"You thought they were serious? Did she seem happy to you?"

"Yes, but, by her senior year, she seemed a little too dependent on him, in my opinion. I was glad when during her second semester he went off to basic training and I hoped Hannah would see others, especially after being voted homecoming queen. I thought that would build her confidence. But she confided in me that she believed the only reason she won was because her boyfriend had been the starting quarterback during her junior year when they were dating."

"Really? Is that what she told you?" Ty nodded his head in agreement and swallowed hard.

"I was hoping she would go away to college and have a great college experience. I never did because my grades weren't super good. I was a jock. Going away for National Guard training was not the pleasant experience like being a freshman living in a college dorm. Not by a long shot. Ha."

"What happened about her education?"

"The Christmas before he left for training, Jerry gave her an engagement ring on New Year's Eve. She was so proud to wear that sparkly, little diamond. I knew then, she would not be going to college."

"Did she share any of her plans with you and with her grandparents?"

"Only that she was going to take typing second semester to be better qualified for an office job. She planned to marry Jerry and join him wherever he was assigned."

"From speaking with her, I guess she did just that. She was soon pregnant, but the plan was already in place before she knew it, correct?"

"Yup. She graduated on a Friday evening. They were married on Saturday. I was his best man, most likely because he had no close friends. They left for Alaska on Sunday. She had no worldly belongings, so it didn't take much to move. They just drove off in a Chevy station wagon."

"When did you see her again? I know your mother went out there to help her when Amy was born."

"I didn't see Hannah until they were transferred back to Ohio. By then, their first baby, Amy, had died of SIDS and my niece, was toting another baby girl, Hope. We were at Hope's christening. My mom noticed she was pregnant again. We were upset, to say the least."

"Did you have a relationship with Jerry? After all, they named their son after you, right?"

"From what I heard Hannah had to beg him to name the little guy after me. Jerry finally agreed, probably because he thought it would look good to name his son after his best man. To answer your question, we did not have a relationship. We never even spoke separately other than in the presence of my parents or my niece. He was tight-lipped and never shared anything personal. Like I said, I was the best man because, in my opinion, he had no one else to ask. My niece did have a best friend who acted as her bridesmaid."

"Do you remember her name?"

"Sure. It was Carly. I think her real name was 'Caroline,' but they called her Carly. She lived down the street from my parents and she was a cheerleader with Hannah. She was a bigger, stronger girl so she held Hannah on her shoulders in some of the routines."

"Interesting. I'll look her up."

"She married a mechanic by the name of Brett. I heard he works for Brondes Ford in the service department."

"Great. You have been extremely helpful. Would you like to visit your niece?"

"That would be amazing. Can you help us arrange that?"

"I can and I will. It will likely be a week from Saturday. Does that work for you and your folks?"

"We will make it work."

CHAPTER 32

OUTDOOR CONCERT

Dr. Rosie said good-bye to the Michaels family and sat back down to call her mother. Her mom's new boyfriend, Caleb, was very impressive. Dinner last evening had been lovely, and both men found they had a lot in common, namely their love of sports.

Just as her mother predicted, baseball, football, and basketball conversation seemed to create instant bonding. Something about "speaking the same language" her mom had suggested. But, as it turned out, Bucky and Caleb also shared the same favorite college and professional teams. The evening had ended with Bucky explaining his new position as athletic director and offering Caleb tickets to any University of Toledo game he might want to attend. Of course, mom was invited as well, he had added. Caleb was touched. Now he and her mom were driving home to her house.

"Hi Mom, how ya' doing? Almost home?"

"Hi Rosie, . . . it's such a beautiful day we've taken a little side trip to Indian Lake. There's a nice walking path along the lake, and a McDonald's where we plan to sit outside and watch the boats pull up to order food. Almost there now."

"Sounds nice, Mom. Hope you enjoyed the run of the condo last night. Does Caleb like dark red wine?"

"Of course. By the way, we turned on the gas fireplace and enjoyed the darting, blue flames. I must say it's a much different experience than the wood-burning fireplace you grew up with. No sweet smells or crackling sounds. Nice ambiance, just the same."

"So glad you did that, Mom. When I come home each evening, I usually get wrapped up in my responsibilities, like walking Jocko or writing reports. What I ought to do when I walk in my door, is to flip the switch and relax in front of the fire for a half an hour."

"You definitely should do that, dear. Please thank Bucky for a lovely dinner at Alfie's. I'll get back in touch soon."

"Good. We dodged the bullet this visit, didn't we? You'll have to get a carbon monoxide detector now, don't forget!"

"Yes. My life was spared because you came to visit. God is good."

Ruth tapped on the door and peeked in just as Rosie was hanging up.

"Hey, Boss, remember you have your women's group later? You said you wanted to see how Mother's Day went for the gals. I duplicated the handouts you plan to distribute. Need food or anything?"

"Thanks Ruth. I'm stepping out for a while and plan to stop to get snacks. How are we set for cold beverages? Some of the ladies don't drink coffee late in the day."

"We have a two-liter bottle of diet coke and a two-liter of regular. There might be some caffeine-free drinks in the fridge, too."

"Okay. I'll be back before you leave for the day."

Rosie saw another call coming through. It was Mr. Charming, himself.

"Everything go okay with your Mom and Caleb? Did they get underway back home?"

"Yup. Guess what? They used my fireplace, and this afternoon they're taking a side trip to Indian Lake. We used to rent a cottage there when I was a kid. You seemed to enjoy chatting with Caleb at Alfie's."

"I did. Mostly I enjoyed the fact that you stayed at my place."

"I loved being with you, too. Pretty soon, we'll be an old married couple."

"Can't wait to grow old with you, Rosie; it'll be our adventure together."

"Your game is away tomorrow, right?"

"Yeah, and quite a road trip for the team. We play Marshall and that means going by bus to West Virginia and back. We'll feed the team a nice meal, win, or lose. Sorry our best cheerleader can't be there."

"If I didn't have class, I'd love to ride along. But the movie I'm showing this week takes two class periods . . . On Golden Pond . . . part of a take home exam. Once they've seen the movie, I'll give them essay questions to complete at home. I want them to show how the four main characters express humor, anger, communication, and love. They'll get their blue books after the film to write their thoughts and answers."

"Are you teaching summer school, by the way?"

"Not this year. I need to participate in Hannah's trial, then will be appointed as an expert witness on a new case. I won't be meeting with the defendant in that one which will make it interesting."

"Sounds like it. We have a league tournament coming up after our semester ends. Some other schools are on quarters, so their year goes into the first of June."

"Will the dorms remain open for team members?"

"They'll be open anyway since the summer session will have begun. A few guys are actually taking classes so they can graduate on time next spring."

"What about Friday night, Bucky? Anything special you would like to do?"

"Yes. I would like to be with you. That's extremely special."

"You say the sweetest things, Mr. Walker. How about going to the first outdoor concert of the season at the Ottawa Park dome?"

"Of course! I'd love to go. Who's playing?"

"Would you believe Willie Nelson?"

"You're kidding. Right?"

"No. I am dead serious. A client I see pro bono gifted me two reserved seat tickets. I'm working for no financial payment because she ran out of insurance and I really wanted to see her get justice."

"Awesome. What time should I pick you up?"

"How about six o'clock? We can catch dinner at the food trucks. I'm buying."

CHAPTER 33

MEETING JERRY FIELDS

Rosie was looking forward to interviewing Hannah's husband, Jerry Fields today. He was due for his appointment at one-thirty. She put her briefcase down and glanced in her personal mailbox cubicle for correspondence. There was none.

No need to make coffee at this time of day, she thought, and knew she was taking a chance by not having backup staff at the LaSalle office during the interview with him. But, somehow, she didn't see him as a threat to her safety.

After retrieving a few insignificant messages on the phone, she put the receiver down just as someone tapped on the door. She opened it to find Jerry Fields standing there holding a box full of materials and his briefcase.

"Hello! You must be Mr. Fields. Come on in and make yourself comfortable." She pointed to the inner office door which was propped open. Tinted windows from the floor to ceiling allowed afternoon sun to provide warmth without a glare.

"It's nice to meet you, Dr. Klein. I brought some medical records I thought might be pertinent to Hannah's case. I have my own set of copies, so these are for you." He placed the box on the coffee table and sat down across from her large, oak desk. Rosie seated herself behind the desk and took out her pen and legal pad.

"Thank you, that was very thoughtful and I appreciate your efforts. Attorney Chickalette has provided me with quite a few medical and legal documents already. However, yours may be more complete. Can I offer you a bottle of water or can of soda before we get started?"

"I am fine, thanks, I just had lunch."

"Okay, well, please tell m your version of events leading to your wife's arrest. I have no particular line of questioning."

"I have to say it has been a nightmare since our baby girl, Amy, died in Alaska."

"Can you start at the beginning? What exactly happened there?"

"Hannah was nursing Amy so I couldn't lend much of a hand when I was home. She was always exhausted after two feedings during the night. One night . . . the night it happened. . . I came home from my night shift and opened the door to our bedroom. Hannah was sleeping peacefully. Then, I opened the baby's room to check on her and saw Amy lying on her stomach. We were always told it was best for babies to sleep on their backs so their airways couldn't be blocked. It surprised me to find her on her stomach, so I moved closer."

"How was she?"

"Amy seemed very still. I could see her tiny facial skin appeared blue. I panicked and I picked her up. Her little body was cold, stiff. I shouted loudly to awaken Hannah and began CPR. When the ambulance guys came, I cried that I wasn't doing it right. But one of them told me quietly that I had done okay, it just wouldn't have helped because she had already been gone for a while. Hannah and I followed them to the hospital where Amy was formally pronounced dead on arrival. We were completely devastated." His voice wavered and tears filled his eyes. Then, he bent his head and shoulders forward.

"I am so sorry for your loss, Mr. Fields. How very tragic."

"The doctor said no one was to blame. They said she died from Sudden Infant Death Syndrome . . . 'SIDS,' he called it. They still don't know why it happens."

"Did any family members come visit to help you and Hannah with your grief?"

"No. We thought we could tough it out. But winter came and those long, bleak Alaskan months are horrible, even under the best of circumstances. We struggled, but we had each other."

"What happened next?"

"I wanted us to have another daughter as soon as possible. You know . . . I thought it would help us get over losing Amy. Hannah wasn't on board with that, but I convinced her it was for the best. Within a year, we had another daughter. We named her, Hope, for obvious reasons. Then, I was transferred to a base near Toledo, Ohio, which is only about two hours from my parents. That helped us avoid living through another harsh winter in Alaska. We lived briefly with my parents, until we could be admitted to base housing in Swanton just west of Toledo."

"That was probably very comforting to have your family nearby."

"Yes, it was quite nice although we seldom needed their assistance Hannah and I joined a church in Swanton. It's a small town, and we soon became actively involved. They admired my leadership skills, and I was voted to serve as a deacon. They seemed to appreciate Hannah's office skill sets, too."

"You mean with a little one at home and adjusting to a new location, Hannah chose to work, too?"

"I thought it would be good for her to get out of the house, so I sort of suggested she do it. She seemed to handle it alright. It was just part-time and the baby-napped."

"I understand you knew Hannah suffered from depression. Did she receive treatment at that time?"

"No. Our family doctor on base in Ohio seemed to think she could manage it with diet and exercise. Hope's pediatrician put her on a monitor since we had the history of SIDS. That eased our fears."

"When did the two of you decide to have a third child after that?"

"We wanted a son, . . . well, truthfully, I wanted a

son, and promised Hannah that I would get a vasectomy if we had a healthy baby boy. The doctors agreed and said that was best because Hannah was too young to have her tubes tied."

"How far apart were Hope and your son?"

"Thirteen months. Some people thought they were twins. We had a double stroller and Ty was a big boy while Hope was petite. We named him Ty after Hannah's uncle. She always felt close to him and convinced me it would be a blessing. Her dad was horrible and neither of us wanted our boy named after him. I blame him for this whole mess."

"How is that?"

"I think she suffers flashbacks and severe depression because of being repeatedly abused by him from the time she was a small child."

"I see. Hannah didn't get counseling after Amy's death. Has she ever been in therapy?"

"No. We didn't realize that the root of her problem stems from early childhood until only recently. When we met, she seemed very well-adjusted. She was popular in high school and was even voted homecoming queen."

"Right. But you didn't really know her until she came to live with her grandparents, did you?"

"No. She had lived in a different school district. She didn't know anyone in our school, but she had the courage to go out for cheerleading as an entering junior. That sounded like a normal, outgoing girl to me. Doesn't it to you?"

"Absolutely, Mr. Fields."

"Please, just call me 'Jerry,' Dr. Klein."

"All right, Jerry. So, where is your son, Ty today?"

"Hannah's good friend, Sandy from our church, is watching him. She has a little boy, too. He would be the same age as Hope would be now. He's just a year older than Ty."

"Will she be your permanent childcare plan?"

"To tell you the truth, I see a future with this lady. It looks like Hannah will go away for a long, long time. Ty will need a loving mother and a family unit."

"What are you saying? Are you romantically involved with Hannah's friend?"

"We're taking it slowly, but yes, we are involved. Her husband died in a helicopter accident on an Air Force training mission. She's raising her son alone and he's already attached to Ty, and to me as a male role model."

"Does Hannah know about your relationship?"

"No, actually, I haven't said anything. Why upset her before her trial. There will be plenty of time later. But, no, Dr Klein . . . Rosie . . . I don't see a future anymore with Hannah."

"How do you define 'later,' Jerry? Do you mean by mail instead of in-person?"

"I haven't really thought about it. Hopefully, she'll be sentenced to a federal prison or better still a hospital, within a day or two driving distance so when Ty becomes older, he can visit his mother."

"I see. So, let's move on to other matters. Help me

get this timeline straight, Jerry: Hannah graduated from high school in June,1990, and you were immediately married. Amy was born in Alaska in August,1990. Just before Christmas that year, at the age of four months, Amy presumably died of SIDS. "

"That's correct, Dr. Klein."

"The last day of December, 1991, Hope was born. Hannah got pregnant rather quickly after the loss of your daughter. How was that decided?"

"We needed to put the past behind us. I thought Hope would keep Hannah company through the dark, winter months in Alaska."

"But you actually got transferred to Toledo in January 1992."

"Yes. Right after Hannah's six-week check-up, and Hope's as well. We avoided another miserable winter. We lived with my parents in Clifton, Ohio and I commuted to the base in Toledo."

"When did you finally move your family into base housing?"

"We moved to Toledo in May, just before Mother's Day that year."

"And in August, 1992, Hope was christened in your church there. Right?"

"Yes."

"Was Hannah pregnant with Ty at that point?"

"Yes. As I've mentioned, we wanted a son and didn't know if she was having a boy, yet."

"In January of 1993, Ty was born. How did you feel now that you had a son?"

"We were happy. It seemed our little family was complete. I went ahead with a vasectomy as we had planned."

"Did Hannah go to work at your church?"

"Yes. She worked three days a week from the time we joined the church. After Ty was born, both kids were in the nursery of the church daycare and pre-school."

"So you think Hannah showed no signs of depression at that point?"

Jerry Fields shook his head "no."

"Bear with me. Tragedy struck again in December of 1993. It was almost exactly three years after your first daughter, Amy, had died. Hope was two. Was she off the monitor at that point?"

"Yes. She had been off the monitor for months. She showed no respiratory issues since she was a little older than the average SIDS patient. It was Ty who was on the monitor at that point."

"Did you see any signs of depression in Hannah that December?"

"Some. But she hid it well. She and Sandy worked out at the base gym on the days she didn't work at church. I think she even put lipstick on and combed her hair before I got home from work, so I didn't think she was depressed at all."

"Who is Sandy, again?"

"That's the friend of ours who is watching Ty today. We helped her through her own grief after her husband's death. She and Hannah shared some tears from each losing someone close."

"You mean the friend with whom you are having a romantic relationship?" He looked at Rosie before sheepishly nodding his head, "yes."

"And then unbelievably, our little Hope was found dead in her crib. It was ruled a SIDS death, again. I have to say that I found it very difficult this time."

"Was there an investigation into Hope's death? Did they know about Amy?"

"They did know about Amy. That's the reason Dr. Daniels, the base pediatrician in Ohio, put Hope, then Ty, on monitors. Looking back, I can see there was some suspicion of monkey business, but nothing anyone could put their finger on. Hope appeared to have died peacefully in her sleep. Again, it was thought to have been about five a.m. There were no signs of a struggle."

"What was the straw that finally broke the camel's back?"

"Well, it was actually when someone at the grocery store stopped Hannah and complimented Ty as being a real 'pretty little girl.' He was wearing a blue parka, but the customer must not have given that much thought. He has small features but is visibly a little boy. Even so, this must have triggered Hannah's irrational thinking again."

"What did she do to Ty?"

"From what I was told by, Captain Jackson, the base investigator, she quickly took Ty home from the store. Apparently, her confused thoughts ran rampant. Ty had fallen asleep in his car seat. She placed him in his crib and sat in the rocking chair and wept. Then she walked over, covered his face and head with a small pillow, and held it there. But, he was big enough that he struggled and lifted his head fighting to breath. He looked her in the eyes and said 'Mama!' She freaked out and immediately stopped what she was doing. She told me she then took him to the ER. She tried to explain it to me when I arrived at the emergency room. But I didn't quite get it until after she was arrested. I still can't wrap my mind around what she was thinking."

"Were the doctors in the Emergency Room familiar with your family at all?"

"No. We were on a different base than when we had Amy. It's not like she took our kids to emergency rooms or doctors' offices every time. To my knowledge she calmly cared for them when they were sick and appeared to be a doting mother. Never would I have guessed she was so sick, herself, that she would do these horrific things. Now that I know what her father did to Hannah, I blame him for being the cause of everything she did. I hope he rots in hell!"

"I can't imagine the pain and suffering your family has been through. Hannah was a victim, too. Do you have any message you want me to take to your wife? I will be seeing her the first of the week."

"Honestly, I'm speechless and numb, at this point. I really can't think of anything to say to her other than not to worry about Ty. We'll be okay. Maybe you can tell her to stay safe and take care of herself. Sometime jails are not all that safe. Oh, there is one more thing.

I'm leaving the Air Force but joining the Ohio Air Force Reserves. That way there won't be any more transfers. I'll report for duty one week-end a month and two weeks in the summer."

"Are you saying you will pursue another career in Toledo?"

"Yes. I have an offer from an elder at our church who owns and operates a small factory. They produce buffing pads used to polish airplane windshields, cultured marble sinks and tubs and automobiles. I'll be the sales director and he'll continue managing production at the factory. There will be some travel, but I have it covered."

"And he will release you for reserve training?"

"Sure. I'll have more than two weeks of vacation and Sandy will watch Ty when he's not in daycare with her son at the church."

"I see. It all sounds well planned out."

"I also have my parents, and Hannah's parents, near enough to help when I travel on business or with the Guard."

Rosie hoped her own opinion of this man didn't show on her face. While she tried to be professional about every interview, she realized the part that Jerry Fields had played in the destruction of his own family never even entered his mind.

That he pushed his young wife too fast and too far to have children, even before the grieving for Amy had a chance, then insisting she go to work with a toddler and while pregnant after moving halfway across the country, would take anyone down. He has no clue what he has done. Nor how he never helped his wife at all to cope with any of it. What a shame. Rosie tried to clear her emotions and managed a smile.

"Here's my business card. If there's anything else you would like to share with me, just give me a call. Sometimes when people are no longer upset, they recall something they forgot to mention."

Jerry Fields stood and extended his hand. "Thank you, Dr. Klein. I'll do that." He retrieved his briefcase and let himself out.

CHAPTER 34

THE PRISON MEDIC

Rosie headed home with her mind cluttered and the bus load of materials that Mr. Fields had given her to review. It was a tremendous amount of information to digest and process. She was not in the mood after interviewing him about the tragic life of his wife, Hannah. She walked in her condo and grabbed Jocko's leash off the hook by the door. He wagged his tail vigorously while standing perfectly still beside her. He knew what was next..

"I see you want to go for a walk. Let me change my shoes and we'll go." Her phone rang and she hoped it was a personal call rather than business. But . . . no cigar. It was Ruth.

"Hi, Boss Lady. I have Jerry Field's parents scheduled in your Summerhill office on Monday. Does that sound good to you?"

Oh, brother, she thought."Thanks, Ruth, that should be the last face-to-face interview with Hannah's family. I do want to connect with the medic, Argie Dyer, and check on Hannah's moods. I also want to check with Lisa Turner who is wearing multiple hats. Did you

283

know she's a chaplain at the jail, Ruth?"

"Can't say that I did, Rosie."

"Perhaps, Lisa will want to have lunch Friday."

"Maybe so, Boss Lady. You're in the downtown office Friday and she works at the jail down the street. Want me to set it up?"

"Let me ask her when I call. I think John Chickalette and I should also talk at the end of next week. I should have all my interviews all wrapped up by then."

"One last thing. I hate to burden you on a Friday, Ruth, but a new name came up in my interview with Hannah's uncle, Ty. He mentioned a high school friend by the name of 'Carly' or 'Caroline.' She was Hannah's bridesmaid."

"You just want a telephone conference call with her? I'll call Mrs. Michaels and see if she knows where Carly lives. If I reach her, I can work the call in on Monday before or after the Fields couple arrive."

"That would be great. No big deal though. If you can't find her, I can track her down by asking Hannah about her on Wednesday.

"I hear carbon monoxide can leave you like that. Anyhow, if you're overloaded and want to beg off leading the morning group, I can have Linda cover it alone. No problem making that happen, Rosie."

"No, Ruth. I'm fine. Bucky and I are going to a Willie Nelson outdoor concert this evening. But I almost forgot. When you call Mrs. Michaels, please tell her I need to bring Hannah her Bible on Wednesday. If I must, I'll pick it up from Mrs. Michaels before Wednesday."

284

"I'll ask her, Rosie. One way or another, I am sure it will work out. Have fun tonight. You have had an extremely trying week coming up. Enjoy the fresh air and music."

"We will. No need for you to come in this Saturday. See you Monday."

Jocko was patiently waiting at the door. Rosie picked up the dangling leash and took him outside. The fresh air was invigorating, and they walked around their usual path while he sniffed and explored and did his business. Then, they returned to the condo.

She decided to check messages before reviewing the mound of materials. There was a call from Argie Dyer wanting to touch base with her. Rosie kicked off her shoes and picked up a pen and a legal pad. Then, stretching out her legs, she dialed the number Dr. Dyer had left on the message.

"Good afternoon. Dr. Dyer's office. How can I help you?"

"Hello. This is Rosie Klein returning Dr. Dyer's call. Is she available to speak to me?"

"Of course, Dr. Klein. She was hoping to catch you before the weekend. Do you mind holding for a couple of minutes?"

"No. That's fine." At this point, Jocko was positioned on the floor glancing up at his mistress. Rosie scratched behind his ears.

"Dr. Klein, I'm hoping we can chat about Hannah Fields. She signed a release for me to talk to you. Do you have time?"

"Yes, of course. Please call me, Rosie. I was hoping you might have some sense of Hannah's mental capacity and whether she could take the witness stand in her own defense."

"Well, she's articulate, but sincerely believes she's committed no crimes. Her story is consistent, but she shows no remorse."

"I had the same impression. In terms of her moods, is she stable or fragile or what?"

"I don't believe she is suicidal, but I put her on an antidepressant. Right now, she holds out hope the jury will set her free to raise her son and be reunited with her husband. She doesn't seem to grasp the reality of the situation. I think it's extremely irrational thinking."

"I'd say so. After my interview with Mr. Fields this morning, I can confirm that he is moving on and not looking back. While he does not see her as a danger to their son, he also does not see a future with Hannah after what she has done. He did say he plans to have the boy visit her in prison, or a psych hospital, as he gets older."

"I doubt that the son visiting would last long, Rosie. The husband will get transferred in the Air Force and have the perfect excuse not to bring their little boy to see her any longer."

"He is resigning from the Air Force but I'm sad to report that he already has a new stepmother picked out for Ty. She's a young, widow friend of theirs who is babysitting Ty now. He's already involved with this lady, himself."

"That could really put Hannah over the edge."

"I was thinking the same thing. It's probably good that he is not taking Ty to visit his mom now with all this stuff going on. The little guy could accidentally let the cat out of the bag by telling Hannah how much fun he is having with Sandy and her son."

"How long before your evaluation is completed?"

"I will see her mid-week, after I receive her Bible from her grandparents. The Michaels will also bring me her journals. In them, Hannah said she wrote about her abuse over the years. The jury should be allowed to see what she wrote as a child. It will cast a different light on their opinion of her. Mitigating factors like that should definitely influence the sentence imposed by the Judge."

"That certainly has been my experience, Rosie."

"If we can have lunch before I submit a report, I would really appreciate it, Argie."

"Absolutely. Don't worry about her, Rosie. I have several officers watching her carefully."

"Oh, before we hang up, I have one more question. Do you know Lisa Turner? I was surprised to hear she is a chaplain at the prison on week-ends."

"Yes. She is simply a lovely person. She has a servant's heart. During the week, she provides support and encouragement to victims of crime and on weekends she does the same for criminals."

"Do you have a contact number for her?"

"I do. How about if I text you her e-mail and phone number? This weekend she holds an AA group on Sunday afternoon for defendants struggling with addictions."

"Thanks, Argie. Let's talk about lunch next Friday. Maybe Lisa will join us."

"Okay. Bye, Rosie. It was nice to finally connect. I have heard so much about you through the years and look forward to meeting you in person."

***

Just as Rosie was wondering if Bucky and the team got back safely from last night's away game. Her cell phone rang.

"Hi Rosie. I've been thinking about you all day."

"Fine minds think alike. You've crossed my mind a time or two, too. I was hoping to hear from you," Rosie said.

"You haven't forgotten our date for the Willie Nelson concert tonight, have you?"

"Are you kidding, Bucky? That's like asking if I've forgotten our trip to St. Maarten in November. You do remember we're getting married in St. Maarten, don't you?"

"Oh, yeah . . . now I remember," Bucky joked. "Actually, I can't wait. But as for tonight, you never know how long old Willie will be around, so it's good that's coming first. Although, Rosie, getting married on the sands of the Caribbean this fall is right up there with seeing Willie tonight. I'll pick you up before 6. . . See you later!"

CHAPTER 35

UNCLE TY

Dr. Rosie pulled up to the front doors of her Summerhill office, she noticed a truck pulling in beside her. She was forty-five minutes early for her Saturday morning group and wondered who would be arriving that soon. She grabbed her briefcase, stepped out of the car, and opened the back door for Jocko to hop out beside her.

"Hi, Dr. Rosie. It is me, Ty. I brought you my niece's Bible, more journals, and a letter. My mom thought the sooner you had them, the better. She thinks they might provide you important information. As for the Bible, she wants Hannah to have as much comfort as possible."

"Well, thank you Ty. Since you came all this way, do you care for a cup of coffee?" Rosie unlocked the door. "I'm about to brew a pot for my women's group."

"I'll take a cup to go, if you don't mind. There are a few details I'd like to share with you if you have a few minutes. I also have some letters from me and Mom to Hannah. Would you give these to her, too?"

"Absolutely. Why don't you just tell me your details while I get the coffee ready?" Ty placed the letters, journals, and Bible with Hannah's name inscribed on it on the office manager's desk in the foyer.

"Remember Carly? Well, I bumped into her recently at a Dollar General store. She just graduated from law school at Ohio Northern University. When I explained what happening to Hannah, she cried. She told me Hannah had tried to call when they returned from Alaska, and left a message asking her to be Hope's godmother. Unfortunately, Carly was in Ada, Ohio, and didn't get the message from her parents. Once Hannah and Jerry moved to the base near Toledo, Carly lost touch with her."

Rosie stopped moving. "You have her number?"

"Yes, she desperately wants to speak to you. As a matter of fact, I gave her your card and told her I'd let you know. She's married now, to her high school boyfriend, Brett, and her name is Carly Pendleton."

"That's really good news. I have some questions for her." Ty handed Rosie his Tervis to-go mug and Rosie filled it with coffee. "Cream or sugar?"

"No. Black is great. I'm glad to help. Let me know if I can do anything else. You know how to reach me."

"Thank you, Ty. I will definitely stay in touch."

***

After the group members left the building, Rosie decided to read through what appeared to be the first of Hannah's journals. She began highlighting entries that were particularly significant in terms of Hannah's experiences of abuse. The first entry went back to her fifth-grade graduation. It was in pencil, but still legible. Rosie noted one entry per week the entire summer before entering middle school. The entries sounded like typical eleven-year-old thoughts. She was staying with her maternal grandparents and enjoying the undivided attention from her grandmother. She recorded how she and her grandmother purchased her first bra, 32AAA, and stated she really needed it.

In late summer, Hannah wrote in red ink that she had her first period. This resulted in an alarming entry: "I am so afraid to go back home when school starts. Now that I am a real woman, I could get pregnant. My grandmother tried to prepare me for this step, but little does she know how scared it makes me. Maybe if I make him think I am bleeding he won't mess with me. How long can I bleed each month?"

On the last Saturday in September, Hannah had recorded this entry: "Well, my plan kind of works. When he thinks I am bleeding, he goes somewhere else to have his needs met. He has always tried to convince me that 'a man has needs, ya know.' I am sitting in the back seat of our car on the way to the grocery store. He has stopped at Mrs. Jones' house again. She is his private secretary. He says it is to pick up some papers for work. Funny, he needs those papers every time I have my period and he never asks me to go inside with him. It gets stuffy in this car, but it sure beats how difficult it is to breathe when he's on top of me."

Rosie closed the journal and collected all the

materials Ty had brought her. She realized how much time and energy it was going to take to read through seven years of journals.

I need a break from this tragic, hopeless story. She decided to head home for some animal therapy with Jocko. Walking him was always a perfect stress reducer. Hopefully, Bucky would be available to spend some quality time together after the ball game this evening.

Hannah must have been desperate to have no one to turn to with no way out of her private hell. Did she try to tell her grandmother? If not, why not? These questions were some Rosie would ask Hannah in their interview on Monday.

As Rosie entered her condo, a deep sense of gratitude overwhelmed her. Jocko isn't my only respite, it's my blessed life. Here I am with no regrets, no long-lasting trauma other than the death of my husband, and no major concerns for my health or stability. Not like the terrible life an eleven-year-old Hannah was made to endure with an uninvited grown-up world thrust upon her. The phone rang.

"Hi Rosie," Bucky said. She loved the sound of his voice. It elevated her mood and reminded her she had a personal life beyond her career.

"My Bucky," Rosie smiled into the phone. "Last night was delightful. Didn't you think the full moon was gorgeous with its fleeting cloud cover? I loved the warm breeze, it just set the stage for an outdoor concert."

"I'd like to say I noticed the warm breeze, Rosie, but to tell the truth, all I noticed was how breathtakingly beautiful you looked in the light full moonlight."

"Bucky Walker, you are so sweet. Thank you, again, for the Willie Nelson CD. I played it on the way to the office this morning. His hit, Always on My Mind, reminded me of our first outdoor concert together. I can't believe you took my hand and made me dance in the aisle with you."

"That was my right brain operating. By the way, how has your morning been?"

"Let me tell you about it this evening after your four o'clock game at Bowling Green. I plan to be there."

"Good, glad to hear it. I want you to go to dinner with the team. We're going to the Wooden Indian, you know . . . for Betty's homemade salad?"

"I've heard about it. Will Sean be pitching?"

"Yes. I've heard there'll be scouts from a couple of professional ball clubs there looking at him. I think Cincinnati, Detroit, and Cleveland. Funny you should ask. His parents will be with us for dinner, too."

"Great news, I enjoy them. I need to get ready, How about we talk later?"

"Yep. Looking forward to it."

What a sweet man, she thought, hanging up. I am so blessed to have him in my life. It's imperative to compartmentalize my stress and leave the 'nine to five' behind sometimes. Otherwise, the tragic lives I deal with could overwhelm me. Each day brings its own challenges. But I can't help anyone if I don't take care of myself first. I trust that God is present in every aspect of my life. And

that includes bringing Bucky Walker into mine . . .
Thank you, God.

CHAPTER 36

HANNAH: THIRD INTERVIEW

Rosie listened to her Willie Nelson CD while she pondered the line of questioning she would take with Hannah. Leaving her keys in the ignition, she stepped out of the car. "Good morning, Dr. Klein," Geoff greeted her as he slid into the driver's seat. Rosie smiled, and waved over her shoulder.

"Good morning, Kremer, how was your weekend?" She asked, once inside the building, as Kremer pushed the button to release the visitation room door.

"Lots of studying. Thank you for asking. Hannah will be with you shortly."

Hannah came shuffling down the corridor with her head lowered and arms hanging at her sides. She looked up to acknowledge Dr. Rosie as she entered the room and positioned herself with her back to the windows.

"Good morning, Hannah," Rosie said as she removed the journals from her briefcase, sliding them across the table to Hannah. Her eyes opened wide at the sight of them and she grasped them to her chest.

"Thank you, Dr. Klein," she said with emotion. "I don't know what to say."

"Your Uncle Ty brought them to my office along with your Bible and some letters he and your grandmother wrote to you. I thought we would start with the journals. Is that okay with you."

"Sure. Have you read them?"

"I began to read them, Hannah. It looks like you told the truth about your childhood, right up to the time you met Jerry Fields. My first question is: why didn't you confide in your grandmother?" Hannah remained quietly looking at Rosie.

"For a couple of reasons, I guess. She was such a gentle, Christian woman, I didn't think she would believe such ugliness could be true. Secondly, I was afraid for my little sister. My father threatened me never to tell anyone. I figured there were two bad things that could happen. He could seriously hurt me, or he could turn to my little sister and put her through what I had experienced."

"That explains it well. I totally understand."

"Dr. Klein, why do you say the journals prove I told the truth 'through my childhood.' Do you think I lied about other things, once I grew up?"

"You tell me, Hannah. Did you? You said there was a man who attacked you in the basement of the church. Right?"

"Well . . . yes. Some of that was true. I did see a man in the basement the week before, and wanted the lower doors secured. The daycare was housed down there and I was afraid for the children."

"I was told, Hannah, those doors were already being worked on to be locked from the outside."

"I swear I didn't know that. I would not have cut myself and lied if I had known the kids were going to be safe."

"Let's move on to another issue, okay? What did your friend, Carly, know about your relationship with Jerry? Did you ever confide details of Jerry's treatment of you to her? Just so you know, I'm planning on speaking to her soon. Your Uncle Ty gave her my card."

"To tell the truth, I did confide in her. I asked her to be my bridesmaid, and she agreed. She questioned me on why I needed to marry him so soon after graduation when I had just talked to her about breaking up with him."

"You were thinking of breaking up with Jerry at that point?"

"I was second guessing whether I really wanted to move so far away from my grandparents, and put my education on hold. I also realized his attention was kind of suffocating, you know. . . it didn't really make me feel loved."

"What changed your mind?"

"I found out I was pregnant. So, what choice did I have then? I thought once we had a baby, he wouldn't hit me again."

"Are you saying that Jerry physically abused you, Hannah?"

"Sometimes. But only after he made me feel like everything was my fault, like the pregnancy, and my fault that he had to get angry. He said I had a 'big mouth,' and he wouldn't tolerate me talking back to him. He said I was lucky he would marry me at all and make an 'honest woman' out of me."

"Oh, Hannah, I am so sorry. It's never a man's right to hit a woman for any reason, you do realize that don't you? And marrying you because you were pregnant was not a favor on his part. It takes two to make a baby."

"I guess I understand more now."

"Did his behavior change for the better once you moved to Alaska, and had Amy?"

"In some ways, yes. And in other ways, no. He turned most of his attention to Amy which kinda made me feel like a third wheel. But he only played with her in daytime; he never got up for a night feeding or helped me in any other way. He said he was the one going to work and supporting the family and needed his rest."

"How did that make you feel?"

"Like I said: I started to think he was molesting her when he changed her diaper. So, I tried to always do it. I figured at least that way, I was protecting her as much as possible and during the night."

"Did you suspect him of doing anything else?"

"One time, I asked him why he had to talk on the phone to his secretary on the weekends. She's my friend, Sandy, who lost her husband. Jerry gave her a job in his office to help her earn some money. He said he felt sorry for her and that I was being paranoid. After that, I figured he was right. I knew I suspected a lot of men at that time. Besides, Sandy had become my first friend when we were stationed in Ohio."

"It must have been difficult to be suspicious of things all the time."

"It was draining me a lot. Sandy and I went to the gym after Amy was born. I figured I needed to get back in shape so my husband would stop insulting me about my body."

"I imagine that was very hard for you, Hannah. Last time we talked, you told me about what happened to Amy. Now, I'd like to move on to another time. Could we talk a little about Hope, and how she died? Can you tell me what happened?"

"I will try, Dr. Klein. I hate to say it, but she was prettier than Amy. These thoughts kept swirling around in my head about what boys . . . or men . . . or even her own father could do to her."

"Do you think these thoughts were triggered by any words or actions?"

"Funny you should say that. It seemed to me that men kept wanting to pick her up, toss her in the air, and tell her what a pretty little thing she was. I kept thinking she is not a "thing". She is a living, breathing, human being. If they saw her as a 'thing,' it would be easier to abuse her, right?"

"I understand, Hannah. What else triggered your fears?"

"I thought I saw blood spots on the changing

table pad, one day. It made me wonder if Jerry was hurting her."

"What did you do?"

"I took her to the pediatrician for an exam."

"What did the results show?"

"She was fine. The doctor said not to worry, that it was just a urinary tract infection. But I couldn't stop thinking about how she had gotten it. Was he touching her and giving her this infection? I began thinking that I couldn't protect her. That's when I started to develop a plan to protect her. . . for eternity."

"So, what was your plan?"

"On the day, I was ready, I told her I loved her, that I was sorry I had brought her into a world where someone could hurt her, Then, I put her on her tummy like I did to Amy and put the blanket tight around her nose. I turned my head away until she stopped moving."

Dr. Rosie could see the recollection was affecting Hannah but wasn't sure if it was the memory of her daughter, or remorse for her own actions. Did Hannah understand what she had done was wrong, that it was actually murder? She needed to understand if Hannah could make the connection between her actions, no matter what her reasons, as something not legally acceptable anywhere.

"Do you need a glass of water, Hannah?"

The young woman kept her head down and quietly sobbed.

"No," she said when she finally looked up. "I'm just glad that she is out of harm's way."

That answers my question, Rosie thought to herself. "Are you okay to continue?"

"I think so."

"Ty was your son. Yet, you almost took his life, too. What happened?"

"Someone thought he looked like a girl which upset me. I don't know what I was thinking, but one day, I put a pillow over his face. Then something distracted me and when I looked back, I realized what I was doing. So, I took Ty to the emergency room at the base hospital, because I wanted him to live. I realized it didn't matter what strangers said about him. He was not a pretty little girl. He was a strong, husky, baby boy."

Hannah's breathing became heavy and she hung her head down to avoid eye contact. Rosie determined it was best to change subjects.

"Hannah, you have overcome a lot, and I appreciate how helpful you have been in supporting those of us who are working on your case. Have you told your story to anyone else?"

"Thank you, Dr. Klein. I confessed to three people: the special agent at the Air Force Base, Mr. Kelly, and I told Mr. Chickalette, and now I've told you. Dr. Dyer and Chaplain Turner know some, but not all the details. Should I be honest with them?"

"At this time, I think your attorney would tell you not to say anything to anybody about your case or personal life. You can tell them how you are feeling, physically, mentally, and emotionally. But don't provide any more details surrounding the charges against you."

"Before you go, Dr. Klein, I brought you my homework. I finished the sentences the best I could." Hannah slid paperwork across the desk, face down. Rosie tucked them in Hannah's folder to read later.

"Thank you, Hannah. We can discuss them next time." Then, she handed Hannah the Bible engraved with her name, sent by her grandmother.

"Oh, my gosh. I'm so grateful to have my Bible. Did you look inside? I've written in margins and highlighted passages for years."

"No, I haven't read anything in it, Hannah. I certainly understand how your journal has ended up at your grandmother's, but how did she come to have your Bible?"

"To tell you the truth, when she came to Hope's christening, I told her to take it with her and put it with my other personal things. I had a new Bible with Hope's name inscribed, and I planned to read it to Hope and Ty as they grew older."

They were both silent a moment, simply feeling the emotions in the air.

"I wrote my grandparents a letter. Could you please hand deliver it to them?" Hannah asked. "I want to apologize for the pain I've caused them and thank them for redeeming me from the pit of hell. If they hadn't allowed me to live with them, I would not have made it through high school. I was beginning to cut my arms and wear long sleeves to cover the wounds . . . sometimes cutting helped me feel something. Even pain is better than going through life numb every day."

"So, you think the cutting resulted from how you felt after the abuse by your father?"

"Mostly, it resulted from hopelessness, memories of my abortion and the shame I felt afterwards. I felt so hopeless. It was a deep, dark hole I couldn't get out of."

Dr. Rosie noticed Kremer looking in her direction. She gave a small nod of her head and heard the click that signified the door was unlocked. She stood and Hannah followed her movement.

"I'll be back on Friday, Hannah. Meanwhile, I can't emphasize enough the importance of you not discussing your case with anyone other than your lawyer, Dr. Dyer, or Lisa Turner."

"I understand, Dr. Klein. It is just that so many thoughts keep going round in my head almost like they did before my baby girls went to heaven."

"The Prosecutor will ask if you thought about and planned to suffocate the babies or if it was impulsive," Rosie said.

"The truth is, I would have to say I planned it. I could see they were doomed to a painful childhood like I had. What kind of mother would wish that on her daughters?"

"Did you feel you could protect them if your husband, Jerry, was out of the picture?"

"In some ways, yes. But they would still be going to school and church and to their friends' and relatives' houses. You just never know who is capable of abusing little girls."

"I want you to think extremely hard, and let me

know when I come back, if there was anyone at all who you confided in about your fears, okay?"

"I will, Dr. Klein. Thank you for understanding and not judging my motives." Hannah began to weep. She put one hand across her heart and wiped her eyes with the other.

Officer Poole stood outside the room to escort Hannah back to her restricted area. Rosie had not seen her recently and made a mental note to inquire how she thought Hannah was doing mentally. Hannah and Dr. Rosie parted in the corridor with a hug, and Rosie waved good-bye to Kremer.

As the elevator doors opened, Dr. Rosie saw Prosecutor Matthew Murphy about to step off the elevator as she was about to enter. Why would a prosecutor be visiting a defendant without an attorney present? Sounds like a deal in the making, she thought. This elevator is an express elevator going between the fourth floor and the secured area behind the visitation officer's desk. The defendant's attorney is probably with his client just waiting for the arrival of this prosecutor.

"Well, hello Dr. Klein. What a pleasure to almost bump into you," he smiled.

"The pleasure is all mine, Matt. We should stop meeting this way. It was nice seeing you and your wife, Nanci at Marion's after the last home baseball game."

"Yes, it was, and I learned something personal about you, Rosie. I knew you were evaluating Hannah Fields, relative to her competency and sanity. What I didn't know, was that you and Bucky Walker are engaged. Congratulations! He's a talented baseball manager and deserves a bright, beautiful woman like you. You've got a good man there."

"Again, the pleasure is all mine," Rosie said as the elevator doors closed while she was still smiling at him. Yes, indeed.

CHAPTER 37

ATTORNEY CONSULTATION

Rosie sipped her unsweetened iced tea and began reading Hannah's responses to the incomplete sentences. How would she have completed these sentences in past years, Rosie wondered.

The ringing phone jarred her thoughts. It was Attorney Chickalette.

"Hi Rosie. Have a few minutes to talk? I'm sorry I missed you at the jail earlier. I was meeting with Matt Murphy who said he bumped into you on the elevator. He didn't tell you he had a meeting with Hannah and me. Unfortunately, Hannah begged off at the last minute saying her stomach was hurting and she needed to lie down."

"I wondered what a prosecutor was doing there. What was the purpose of the meeting?"

"He has a lot of trust in you and wanted to know how best to proceed with this tragic case: Do we go to trial, or accept her confessions and skip the penalty stage completely? As you know, that would mean we go right to the sentencing phase, and present our evidence to the Judge and jury, or to a panel of three Judges."

"Why would he consider doing that, Big John?"

"He's a decent, fair man and having reviewed her case, is no longer considering the death penalty. The remaining questions have to do with her state of mind immediately prior and at the specific time of the two alleged offenses. Those questions will be answered in part by you once you have made a professional determination. He said he has such respect for you that he will not be requesting a second opinion from another psychologist or psychiatrist."

"That's unbelievable, given this is such a high-profile case. I figured it would become the battle of the experts and there would even be a third doctor to break a tie."

"Not going to happen, Rosie. Matthew is not running for county prosecutor after all. This means politics have been removed from the case. The Governor is appointing him to the Ohio Appellate Court at the end of this term. Great news for Murphy, Hannah and us."

"I have a lot of respect for him," Rosie said. "As you know, some prosecutors, and particularly appointed defense attorneys, don't want to take a case to trial because they're lazy, or it doesn't warrant their time while it hurts their budget. Let me understand, you're saying, Matthew Murphy, is leaving office and looking at the merits of the case as to whether Hannah poses a threat to society, right?"

"Correct. I would say we should meet to plan

our strategy in terms of convincing a three-judge panel to view her as a mentally ill woman and impose justice for all parties."

"You prefer a three-judge panel to a single judge and jury? Help me understand your logic."

"It's not as if the State Prosecutor will be attempting to convince twelve people that Hannah willfully planned to kill two babies. Her confessions stand on their own and provide ample evidence that she's mentally ill with a demented state of mind prior to, and at the time of, these murders. Technically, her confession is not admissible because she wasn't mirandized before she told the officers she committed the crimes. But let's not go there. No good reason."

"I have one more meeting with her, Big John. Then I'm speaking with her high school friend, Carly, as well as our jail medic, Dr. Dyer, and Chaplain Lisa Turner on Friday. That should wrap up my investigation of the mitigating circumstances factoring into Hannah's motives."

"How would you feel about getting together next Saturday, Rosie? I can come to you, or you can come to me."

"Saturday morning at ten will work simply fine. How about if you come to my Summerhill office. You've never seen it, right?"

"It'll be my pleasure. I don't expect you to have a report completed after those final interviews the day before. But I would like to pick your brain as to possible treatment facility options for Hannah, in lieu of federal or state prison?"

Rosie went back to her reading of Hannah's sentence completions. Her mind was more at ease having received the news from Big John. Her research would now take a different direction. Where in the world could Hannah receive the medication and therapy she needed to survive and deserved to receive?

She decided to call her landlord, Dr. Seifer. He was a deeply knowledgeable psychiatrist with vast experience in the forensic arena. Rosie credited him for recommending her services to the lawyers and judges in the greater Lucas County area. She thought it was likely he would know where a reputable hospital for the criminally insane might be located. She, also, hoped there would be a campus setting where Hannah might be able to have visitations with her son, Ty.

Jocko positioned himself beside her chair and resigned himself to the idea that his walk wouldn't be for a while.

***

Rosie was carefully applying her mascara and thinking about meeting with Big John to recommend three judges for Hannah's sentencing trial. Judge Kate Brown and Judge DP Tucker were her two favorites. The presiding judge had, in fact, approved Judge Tucker despite the relationship between his wife and Rosie. She was relieved and expected Big John to make a third recommendation. Judge Lincoln was strictly assigned to family or domestic cases, so he was not in contention.

The phone rang and Rosie quickly answered.

"Hi, Rosie. What are you doing after class today?" Bucky sounded cheerful. "Our game has been cancelled because a number of visiting team members have come down with the flu. The good news is, they were one game ahead of us in the standings so this forfeit at the end of the season ties us in the league."

"Hi Bucky, glad you called. Otherwise, I would have walked over to the baseball diamond and explained I couldn't stay. I have an important meeting today. Do you have something else in mind?"

"Well, it's Judge Lincoln's birthday. He and Darlene would like us to join them for dinner. They want to drive up to a quaint, little seafood restaurant on Lake Erie. It's perched at the top of a lighthouse. Sounds neat, doesn't it?"

"Absolutely. Right after class I have a brief meeting downtown with John Chickalette. Then I'll quickly scoot home and let Jocko out. Can you pick me up?"

"I can . . . and I will. The three of us will get you at five o'clock if that okay."

"I can make that work. See you soon."

Rosie hung up, slipped on her shoes, grabbed her briefcase, and hustled out to her car. Jocko looked forlorn. Again, she enjoyed her Willie Nelson CD as she drove to Big John's office. The purpose of John calling this urgent meeting was simply to discuss the selection of judges.

She sat in the waiting area of Big John's office until his junior associate, Dee Wakefield, came through the double doors to greet her.

"Hi, Dr. Klein, Attorney Chickalette has been held up in a deposition. He asked me to meet with you and discuss the selection of Judges."

"Nice to meet you. That would be fine." Rosie stood and Attorney Wakefield led her to a small, well-organized office, just inside the doors.

"Would you care for a beverage, Dr. Klein?"

"I'm fine. Please, just call me Rosie. I understand Hannah was more comfortable with you than with John. What was your opinion of her, Dee?"

"Well, Rosie, she was quiet and polite. She answered questions but offered no thoughts or conversation. Eye contact was limited, and we weren't with her long. Oh, she did mention you. I could tell she trusts you and your motives. I wasn't sure she trusted John, though, maybe because he is a man."

"Understandable, under the circumstances. Sadly, her belief system is totally influenced by her childhood trauma. She sees potential sex abuse coming out of the woodwork."

"As you know, we have two judges approved for our sentencing trial. I'm not familiar with the judges around here. I graduated from the University of Toledo law school in January, and prior to law school, lived in Cincinnati. So, I still must get familiar with the players in town. How about you, Rosie? Any preference in this selection?"

"Since we already have one woman and one man, probably not a significant preference. In my opinion, we need a judge who is familiar with mental illness, either personally or professionally."

"I'll research some backgrounds. I'm sure John will find your opinion valuable."

"Did I hear you take my name in vain?" John Chickalette said, as he walked in the office with Attorney Bart Meyer.

"Absolutely not! We were hoping you could join us with your great insight and deep wisdom," Dee said with a smile.

"Sorry, for being delayed, Rosie. I do have a great name to offer up: Judge Joyce King. She's spent seven years as a magistrate in domestic relations court prior to being appointed as a probate judge. In probate court, she is knowledgeable about mandated hospitalizations. Nothing about our client will surprise her. If you're not opposed, I'll contact her and see if she's available. With her seniority on the bench, it's likely she will act as presiding Judge."

"I recall testifying in her court before, John. In a case in family court, I made a recommendation for the more suitable parent, a parent who could identify the needs of the child, provide for them, while still fostering a positive relationship with the other parent. Another time, in probate court, I rendered an opinion for an elderly person's competency to take care of his own medical and financial decisions. Personally, and professionally, I like Judge King. Oh, and she has a sense of humor. She doesn't act threatening to the expert witnesses or to client representatives. She would be fine."

"Great, I'll contact her later this afternoon. I believe we can have a trial beginning in two weeks. That should give the judges enough time to clear their dockets."

"Okay, I'm wrapping up with Hannah and my collateral contacts on Friday. I'll send a report with my findings and recommendation a week from then. Does that work for you?"

"Perfectly, Rosie," Chickalette turned to his assistant. "See Dee, I told you she was competent, cooperative . . . and adorable."

Rosie was blushed and had nothing to say as the three lawyers laughed good-naturedly.

CHAPTER 38

LUNCH WITH COLLEAGUES

Dinner with Bucky, Charlie, and Darlene was surreal. The restaurant at the top of the lighthouse rotated. It took an hour for one circle completion which could hardly be felt by any diners. The brilliant colors of the setting sun on the lake's horizon were gorgeous in warm shades of orange and yellow fading into deep russet, as dessert was served.

The foursome had decided to share Bananas Foster. It's warm, caramel liqueur flowing down the side of the vanilla ice cream was a second most delectable sight, this one being delicious, too. On the drive home, they made a pact to go somewhere out of the ordinary each month. Needless, to say the evening ended on a high note.

The following morning, Rosie drove to her Summerhill office to eliminate distractions. She needed to review diagnostic materials of mental disorders without the telephone ringing, the dryer buzzing, or Jocko making demands on her time. She spread all materials out on a sturdy, conference table which was usually used to draw or play games with children. The office copy of the book of diagnosable mental disorders, DSM-IV, was tattered and torn from repeated use over the years finding the difference between schizophrenia and delusional disorders.

Hmmmm, "...outside of delusions or false beliefs, a person's behavior is not markedly impaired. Daily behavior is not obviously odd or bizarre. Inappropriate behavior arises directly from the delusional beliefs. If the beliefs are of a persecutory type, it is usually a result of a person being malevolently treated in some way. A person may have been exposed to a traumatic event. This can mean the person experienced, witnessed, or confronted the event..." Rosie made notes as she read.

"...A child who, on one occasion or repeated ones, experiences sexually traumatic events may demonstrate self-destructive and impulsive behavior. The child feels shame or a sense of being permanently damaged. Physical symptoms may include e stomach aches and/or headaches..."

Rosie stood and stretched. Taking a breath, she walked down the hall and peered out the front door. Thinking on her feet sometimes helped her process thoughts more clearly. She decided to review the long- range effects of posttraumatic stress disorder (PTSD).

"...According to the DSM-IV,"most symptoms begin to manifest within three months of the triggering event known as the sudden event occurring outside the realm of human expectations". This could be an act of nature like lightning striking a person or a tornado *devastating a town. It might be an accident viewed or in which the person is directly involved. It could even be a violent crime perpetrated on the person or others...'*

Although Rosie believed Hannah suffers from PTSD, Hannah didn't fit the usual mold. From a previous case, Rosie remembered a woman who suffered from a condition known as the sleeper effect This occurs when PTSD shows its ugly head many years after the traumatic event. The person usually appeared normal. Then, something triggers specific memories of a past trauma. It could arise from a similar event, an odor, a sound, a nightmare, or flashback. That is also when delusional beliefs can kick in. These false beliefs can cause the person to act irrationally to try to eliminate the terrifying thoughts or perceived threat from the perpetrator.

Rosie looked at her watch and quickly put her materials back in her briefcase. Locking up the office, she drove downtown to meet her colleagues, Lisa Turner and Argie Dyer, for lunch. They had chosen the Toledo Club, a popular restaurant on the second floor of an old, refurbished office building. She saw both waiting for her as she exited the elevator.

"Hi Rosie. I don't believe we have ever had a casual, social time together. Seems like our lives are just passing in the night," Lisa said in greeting.

"Well, if you call the corridors of the courthouse 'passages of the night,' I have to agree. Those halls are dismal with dark, tragic stories," Rosie responded.

"If you girls think the courthouse corridors are

bleak, you should spend your days and nights in prison cells or visitation rooms," Argie added. "I know from what I speak."

The young, tall and handsome server approached their table and asked for beverage orders.

"We'd like ice water with lemon, right girls?" Lisa asked. Everyone nodded.

"If we weren't working women, we could go for something stronger," Argie said.

The server smiled at the ladies and walked away to fill their order.

"Listen to your friendly medic, dark red wine is excellent . . . for medicinal purposes after five o'clock," Argie said.

"Isn't it five o'clock somewhere?" Lisa smiled.

After sharing small talk, a large veggie pizza, and Greek salads, the trio got down to the reason for their meeting.

"I just found that Hannah Fields will not be going to trial. Prosecutor Murphy accepted her insanity plea and decided to move forward to the sentencing phase." Rosie began.

"What a relief, Rosie. That protects Hannah from grueling cross examination that she isn't emotionally or physically capable of enduring," Dr. Argie said.

"And her spiritual beliefs are totally out of the realm of any religious or even a non-religious person's understanding. As you both know, her delusions led her to think little girls are better off in heaven rather than succumbing to the attentions of boys or men," Chaplain

Turner added.

"If you don't mind my asking, why would Murphy agree not to try her? This is a high-profile case, and it's public knowledge that Matt plans to run for Lucas County Prosecutor this November. My colleagues in the Victim-Witness division are endorsing him," Lisa Turner said.

"I guess it's not been announced, but John Chickalette told me that the Governor is appointing Matthew Murphy to the Appellate Court of Ohio and Bart Meyer will be taking his place," Rosie said.

"Let me say, your interpretations of Hannah's mental state are in total agreement with my own conclusions. We've decided to utilize a three-judge panel rather than to put all our eggs in one basket with a judge and jury."

"Makes sense to me, Rosie. I've sat through jury trials and several three-judge panel trials. For one thing, it's a crapshoot with a jury of twelve local citizens. No matter how the selection goes, a juror found acceptable by the defense attorney or prosecutor can change his or her position mid-stream. The defendant or a witness testimony might touch a personal chord nobody could see coming. Even one of the attorneys may say or do something a juror finds aggressive or repulsive. I think the three-judge panel is more objective in most instances," Lisa explained.

"What medication is she on, Argie? I know you've prescribed Zoloft, which the FDA has approved to reduce anxiety and depression. Is she on any antipsychotic meds?" Rosie asked.

"No, and the purpose of Zoloft is not only to lessen anxiety and depression but to stop thoughts of her own victimizations so she can go to sleep without fear of nightmares. Basically, delusional disorder is difficult to treat. Medication coupled with individual and group therapy is found to be the most therapeutic. The problem I have is that my patients, known as defendants, are simply passing through. Therapy and therapeutic relationships between myself and someone like Hannah, take time. Time not allotted to me in my position as jail medic."

"I agree. Her dual-diagnosis of PTSD coupled with Delusional Disorder magnifies her need for long-term therapy, in my opinion. Lisa, are you familiar with facilities for the criminally insane that don't simply lock them up but actually provide treatment?" Rosie asked.

"I believe Dayton State Hospital does that. It's a lockdown facility, but has a campus with green lawns and large oak trees. It also has gazebos and picnic tables and benches for patients and families. There's a stream and a pond with ducks, fish, turtles, and frogs. I once transported a teen-aged girl to visit her mother who was serving time there," Lisa said.

"When I submit my report, I hope you both don't mind my inclusion of your professional opinions," Rosie said.

"Not at all, glad I could help, Rosie," Argie said. "I hate it when defendants are transported to prison if I haven't had an opportunity to provide closure.

Sometimes, I don't even have a chance to wish them well, or say good-bye. When possible, I follow up to inform the prison medics of any medication I started the defendant on, but it doesn't guarantee they'll be able to continue the prescription even when it may have finally taken effect and reduced their symptoms. Believe me, that has been extremely frustrating."

"I'll bet," Rosie said, "I understand how you must feel. How about you, Lisa?"

"Okay with me, Rosie. I don't know the type of relationship you have established with Hannah, but if she ends up at Dayton State, and you want to drive her little boy to visit, I would be glad to arrange it through Victim-Witness, even go with you." Lisa offered.

"Today has been so helpful. Let's get together again. I've enjoyed getting to know you. If either of you want to sit in on my post-abortion group or women's support group in Summerhill sometime, just let me know," Rosie said.

As the last person left her office, Rosie sat to reflect on a productive gathering.

After that meeting, I somehow feel refreshed; like we exchanged a kind of positive energy among ourselves. Working together with like-minded people must be good for the soul.

CHAPTER 39

HANNAH: FINAL VISIT

Ruth wasn't sure if Rosie would call in time. She looked at the clock just as her desk phone rang.

"Boss! Am I glad you called. I just reached Carly Pendleton and am waiting for a call back from Jerry Fields' parents. Carly wants to see you late this afternoon in your LaSalle Tower office. Can you meet her? The Fields couple want to cancel their Monday appointment. Would you want to try for a telephone conference call with them? Like, maybe in the morning?" Ruth was trying hard to juggle things for Rosie's schedule.

"I'm heading to jail now to see Hannah, so, yes, I can meet Carly at the LaSalle Tower after four o'clock. Also, a conference call with Jerry Field's parents at nine or eleven-thirty tomorrow morning would work, if that time is good for them. John Chickalette wants to meet me at the Summerhill office in the morning at ten. He's secured the third judge and wants to run things by me ASAP, and needs to know what my testimony will be."

While walking and talking, Rosie showed her ID to a new weekend sheriff's deputy and signed the visitor's log. After she and Ruth hung up, she noticed in the log that Chickalette and Dee Wakefield had spent an hour with Hannah the previous day. Slinging her briefcase onto the conveyer belt, she stepped through the metal detector. Nothing beeped, as she expected.

All this security because years ago, bad people did bad things which changed the way we have to live these days, she thought, grabbing her briefcase and heading toward the double doors. The first door beeped, allowing her to open it. A deputy behind a desk noticed her approaching and released the lock on the second door.

Testerman stood just inside.

"We've sent for Fields, Dr. Klein. Go ahead and take the elevator to Visitation and get comfortable."

"Golf on your itinerary this week-end?" Rosie asked, making small talk.

"Yup. Weather permitting. It's a member/guest two-day tournament and it won't surprise you to know my partner in crime will be Ambrose, right?"

"Nope. What surprises me is that you both have the entire weekend off," she laughed. He smiled.

"Hi Kremer," Rosie greeted the guard as she stepped off the elevator.

"Hi, Dr. Klein. Hannah will be here in a minute. She was napping, I guess."

"It's later than I usually come. Does she nap every afternoon?"

"I don't know. The medic would know. I've heard she doesn't sleep well at night so that could be why she naps mid-afternoon until dinner."

"I'll ask her. Thanks for the information. It could be relevant." Rosie turned as Hannah came down the corridor accompanied by Officer Poole. She noticed the state of Hannah's appearance: stringy hair in need of washing, eyes downcast, facial expression devoid of any smile. Classic depression.

"Hi Hannah, how are you feeling? Heard you were napping."

"I'm okay. Been reading my Bible. It's given me some peace to know God has a plan for my life. The women talk all day in the common area. Guess I tend to doze off in my cell."

.   "I heard you haven't been sleeping well at night. I was wondering if that was causing you to nap a lot during the day," Dr. Rosie said.

"It's a lot noisier at night around here. Some of the new, younger inmates are rowdy. It disrupts my thoughts, my prayers, and, yes, my sleep."

"Oh, sorry to hear that, Hannah. I imagine it's not your nature to complain."

"Nothing would come of it. Freedom of speech, you know. I spend time alone writing in my journal until lights in the common area go out at ten p.m. Then, on my bunk I use my pen light to read my treasured Bible. It comforts me."

"Well, I have some good news. In preparation for your sentencing trial, I've met with your attorney, Dr. Dyer, and Chaplain Turner. It looks as if you won't be required to testify. So, if that's what's caused you to worry, you don't have to think about it anymore. I'll be testifying before a panel of three judges on your behalf. How do you feel about that, Hannah?"

"That's good. That's a relief. That actually answers my prayers. I know you have my best interests at heart, Dr. Rosie. Mr. Chickalette isn't too bad either . . . for a man. Maybe I can trust him . . . a little, anyway."

"That's good, Hannah. How are you doing with the Zoloft? Dr. Dyer said by now it's probably working. Do you feel any better?"

"I guess I feel as well as I can, considering my circumstances. I don't have crying jags like I used to. When I do sleep, I don't seem to have nightmares anymore. I think being anxious is normal, don't you? I mean, being in jail and everything, right?"

"I agree. But I've heard you had a panic attack recently. How did that happen?"

"I overheard some inmates talking to some male officers. Sounded like they were going to trade sex favors for cigarettes. That really upset me. It reminded me how helpless I am. I'm glad I don't smoke so I'd need to . . . do things."

"Sounds like information that should be forwarded to a sergeant."

"Please, Dr. Klein, don't do anything. I'm not sure whose involved. It could even be a sergeant. I could get in trouble just for telling you."

"Okay, Hannah. I won't say anything until you're no longer here. Given that we aren't going to trial, I don't need to ask you any more questions. Do you have anything else you want to talk about?"

"No. But I would like to tell you how much I appreciate all you're doing for me and my son. I believe I'll see my little girls again . . .in heaven. Do you think Jerry will let Ty visit me? Little Ty needs to know his mother is not some kind of monster. I probably won't be free for years, right?"

"I won't lie to you, Hannah. You're probably right," Rosie hesitated a moment. "Hannah . . . there is something important, we need to talk about. You know, we want you to be in the best possible environment. There's a semi-locked down hospital that has a park outside where you could enjoy nature and have family and friend visits. You would be able to roam the grounds with an ankle bracelet, as long as they can trust you to return for therapy and meal- times."

"That sounds nice. I know I need counseling, not just medication. When will all of this happen? How far away is this place?"

"Well, It's two hours from Toledo, and your hearing should happen within a few weeks. But what we must talk about are the charges. I know you're glad that your little girls are safe in heaven, but have you come to understand that it was not your place to put them there?"

Hannah was silent. She looked down at her fingernails, examining them like they had something to do with what Rosie was saying. Finally, she spoke.

"I should have let God decide about it, is that what you mean?"

"Well, Hannah, just as God has a plan for each of us, there was a plan in place for each of your girls, too. Do you realize that in your fear for their safety, you actually took that decision away from God, and imposed your will on their lives?" Hannah was silent. Then, very quietly, she said something to make Rosie believe she was on the road to recovery.

"Yes, Dr. Rosie, I've been thinking about those fears, lately, and what I did to my girls. I'm realizing that what I did was not something God wanted me to do. I'm starting to understand that I cheated them from having their own lives. Maybe what happened to me wouldn't have happened to them . . . and I find myself crying at night."

"The reason I'm having this conversation with you, Hannah, is that for us to get you to the place where you can have visits and get better, you need to accept the fact that you were not thinking clearly all those times, that your mind was sick with worry. Do you understand how that made you not think straight about what the right thing to do was for you?"

"Yes, I'm beginning to understand that now. That I'm not crazy anymore, but I was then. But if I think about it too much, I WILL go crazy."

"I know, but that's where you will start working on forgiving yourself. . . you know God has already forgiven you, don't you?" She waited a few moments before continuing. "So, you will understand why your attorney will submit a plea of Not Guilty by Reason of Insanity for you? Do you know what that means?"

"It means that when I did what I did to Amy, and then to Hope, that I wasn't thinking with a good mind." She lifted a tear-streaked face to Rosie and waited to hear her answer.

"Yes, it means that at the time you were doing those things, your mind was sick . . . extremely sick. There was another way, but you couldn't find it. You didn't know what to do to get help, so you decided, on your own, what to do. The problem was that you weren't in your right mind."

"If I think about it, with the medicine helping me, I can hardly stand knowing what I did to them. Only reading my bible and knowing God will help me, do I not want to kill myself," she said.

"Don't think about harming yourself ever, Hannah, that would truly be another wrong thing to do. As we continue to talk, and you continue to get help, you will see that making peace with yourself about what happened will begin to make your mind healthy. There is always a brighter future . . . and you will begin to see it."

Hannah was very still. Rosie let her think a few minutes and watched her facial expressions.

"For now, I suggest you keep journaling to keep your thoughts from going round and round in your head. Second best thing is to talk to someone. Do you understand?"

"I understand, Dr. Klein, and agree with you. Thank you for caring to help me."

"My next recommendation is when you wake

up every morning, plan to be a blessing to someone each day. It takes your mind off yourself and makes you find God's purpose for your life. Some women who are serving long sentences in state penitentiaries told me that's what helps them. What do you think? Can you do that, Hannah?"

"I'll do what you say, Dr. Klein. I see women here who could use prayer and encouragement, especially some who are really angry and addicted. Do you think I'll be better soon?"

"Absolutely, Hannah. I'm sorry, but I need to go now. I'm meeting your friend, Carly, in my office this afternoon. Is there anything you want me to tell her for you?"

"Tell her I love her and have never had another friend as caring and trustworthy as her. Ask her to please write me once I'm settled with my new address." Hannah's voice wavered as she realized the visit was over. She liked Dr. Rosie and felt safe in her presence.

Rosie stood and gave Hannah a hug. She waited for Kremer to help her exit and unlock the elevator. As she left the building, Rosie felt hopeful for Hannah's future for the first time since this case began.

CHAPTER 40

THE CHILDHOOD FRIEND

At exactly four o'clock, Rosie unlocked the door of Dr. Seifer's suite. She helped herself to a bottle of water from the refrigerator and grabbed a second bottle to offer Carly when she arrived. Dropping her belongings behind her desk, she looked up to see Carly Pendleton entering the waiting area.

"Hello. Are you Carly?"

"Yes, Hi, Dr. Klein." Carly extended her hand and smiled. She was a pleasant looking young woman, late-twenties, mid-height, dirty-blond hair, nicely dressed.

"Please come in; have a seat. Would you care for a bottle of water?" Rosie pointed to the sweating cold bottle sitting on her desktop.

"That would be great. I hustled over here from a parking meter about four blocks away," Carly explained.

"And I just returned from visiting Hannah. She asked me to tell you that you are the best friend she has ever had. She's sorry to have lost touch and wonders if you could be pen pals."

"Awe. That is so sweet. She is the nicest person,

Dr. Klein. Of course, I will be happy to write to her. Do you know where is she going to be located?"

"We're uncertain at this time. Rest assured, though, it will not be a state prison. It appears to those of us who have been spending time with Hannah that she suffers from a delusional disorder and post-traumatic stress disorder. Are you familiar with those conditions?"

"As a matter of fact, I am familiar with PTSD because my brother suffers with flashbacks and nightmares from his experiences in the military. But I admit I'm not knowledgeable when it comes to delusional disorders or severe mental illness."

"Carly, I wanted to speak with you about the time you spent with Hannah, and your impression of Jerry Fields. Is that okay? I will keep anything you say confidential."

"We met on the cheerleading squad during our junior year. I was strong and muscular, and she was petite. So, we were assigned to work together. We worked on routines involving a cheerleader being thrown into the air and caught by someone. Of course, I'm proud to say, I always caught her."

"Sounds like fun. Did she seem to enjoy high school activities and friendships? She was new at your school, right?"

"Yes, Hannah was new, a bit shy, but ambitious enough to try out for cheerleading. It's pretty competitive, you know. Even though we went to a small high school, she didn't attempt to make many friendships. Ours just grew out of common interests and proximity. I lived three blocks from her grandparents. We rode the same bus to school and her grandmother, or my mother, picked us up after practice."

"How did she meet Jerry Fields?"

"He was a popular guy. He was quarterback of the football team. He noticed her and pursued her. Eventually, at a bonfire for the football players and cheerleaders, she spent time getting to know him. They sat off from the rest of us and talked while the rest of us sang and laughed and carried on."

"What happened next?"

"Jerry graduated and when we returned from cheerleading camp they began to go steady. He worked in his dad's hardware store, but didn't get along with the manager, his older brother. It wasn't long before he joined the Air Force, around Christmas. That's when he gave her an engagement ring."

"Was she happy?"

"Well, we had planned on going to a Columbus junior college, Owens Community College, where we could pursue something in a medical, dental, or the legal field. But her engagement changed everything. When he left for basic training, she told me she thought she was pregnant. I never saw her get big enough for it to be noticeable.

"How did she feel about that?"

"Jerry had been extremely possessive in the fall and during the holidays. I think he really prevented her from enjoying her senior year, you might say. Instead of being happy that she was Homecoming Queen, he accused her of getting votes by sleeping around. Can you imagine that!"

"I almost never saw her that fall until he went off for basic training early the next year, and at that point it was too late. She was pregnant and planning to follow him wherever he was stationed. He did ask her to marry him, but it was as if he wasn't sure the baby was his."

"Who knew about their plans?"

"Hannah was so ashamed she didn't want to tell her grandfather. She asked her grandmother not to tell him, or her Uncle Ty. She had no choice but to tell Grandma Michaels since she needed prenatal medical care. I was the only other person she told."

"So, her own mother didn't know?"

"That's a joke. Her mother spent zero time with Hannah. It was like she dropped off the face of the earth. I guess she divorced Hannah's father and moved out of state with her other two kids."

"Interesting. Here Hannah was living with her mother's parents and her mother left the entire family unit behind. I understand from Ty that you both stood up for Hannah and Jerry at their wedding. Was it held at a church? Who gave her away?"

"It was held at the Church on The Square. As you know, we lived in a small town and there were not many church denominations. People drove to larger, surrounding towns for their Sunday worship. But since the Church on The Square was in town, it was used for weddings, baptisms, high school band performances, and other celebrations. Her grandfather Michaels walked her down the aisle. I held her bouquet and Ty had the wedding band. I suppose Ty told you he was best man because once Jerry left high school, he had no real friends, not even his older brother. Kind of sad if you ask me."

"Is there anything else you would like to tell me? Hannah said you don't need to keep anything secret anymore. She told me to ask you to tell the truth as you see it."

"Okay then, I believe you. She was thinking of breaking up with Jerry. I guess, she was starting to see the handwriting on the wall. There was a senior guy in our class who was a friend of hers, almost like a brother. He watched out for her and they secretly studied together. It wasn't because there was anything romantic going on between them. It was just that Jerry would have had a cow if he had known. This guy, Fritz, was what we called a 'nerd.' He was great in math which Hannah struggled with. I wasn't in advanced math like he was, so, it wasn't an option for me to help her."

"What happened to Fritz after high school?"

"He went on to medical school and is a pediatrician in Worthington, Ohio. He hasn't married yet, as far as I know. But he did purchase a nice home for his parents, in Dublin, Ohio, where they relocated just a few miles down the road from Fritz' practice."

"Last thing, Carly, did you know that when Hannah was about 12 or 13, she was impregnated by her natural father and was forced to have an abortion?"

"No! I knew he was abusive, or she wouldn't

have been living with her grandparents. I guess she didn't trust me as much as I thought she did. I told her every sordid detail of my life, but she never told me that."

"I can't thank you enough for taking the time to meet with me. Can I pay for your parking meter?"

"No, thanks, I paid in advance and it won't be expired. I'm happy to help Hannah in any way. She's always been such a kind person. I'm sorry for the road her life has taken, Dr. Klein."

"Here is my business card, Carly. If you think you remember any more that would be useful to the professionals handling Hannah's case, please feel free to call me. Okay?"

"Definitely will do that. Thank you for helping her to receive the treatment she needs to be rid of her terrible thoughts and beliefs. I had no idea. I heard she had lost a child to SIDS and knew she would be grieving that death forever, probably. I know I would."

Rosie watched her depart. If she only knew the truth about that SIDS death, she would never believe it.

Not long afterwards, Rosie headed for home.

***

The following morning, Saturday at 9 a.m., Rosie reached the office, sat down in Ruth's chair, and dialed the Field's information into her computer for their teleconference call. She was pleased to hear Mrs. Fields say they were expecting her call as they came onscreen.

"I hope this time is convenient for you and Mr. Fields. I'm hoping you'll share your thoughts about your daughter-in-law's circumstances."

"Yes, Dr. Klein. We're more than happy to help in any way we can. The loss of our granddaughters saddens our hearts so deeply. We're so grieved by Hannah's actions and mindset. We had no idea she suffered from childhood abuse. But her actions certainly do speak of mental illness."

"You met Hannah when she was just a teen-ager, is that right?"

"Yes. That is correct. She was a junior in high school, and a lovely girl. She was polite and thoughtful. Our son fell instantly in love with her. He graduated from high school and worked briefly in our business before joining the service."

"What was your understanding as to why she was living with her grandparents?"

"We understood that Hannah's parents were experiencing marriage problems. Hannah was extremely bonded to Mr. and Mrs. Michaels, so moving in with them lessened her mother's responsibilities," Mrs. Fields said. "It actually seemed a logical move."

"You would think under normal circumstances, that Hannah's mother would have appreciated her help with the younger siblings. Why would she pose more responsibilities for her mother?" Dr. Rosie suggested. It was a way to help people think.

"I am unsure. I guess you are right, Dr. Klein. I never thought of that," Mrs. Fields responded. "Jerry and Hannah lived with us for a few months when they were transferred back from Alaska, you know. Little

Hope was precious. We never got to know Amy. That all happened in Alaska. But Hannah and Jerry seemed like devoted parents. Once they moved to the Toledo area, they got involved in a church and we went up for Hope's christening."

"Well, that's what I needed to know, Mrs. Fields, I want to thank you for your time. What you have told me is, you did not see evidence of mental illness on the part of Hannah Fields while she was dating your son, when they lived with you, or when you went to Toledo for Hope's christening. After Ty was born, you did not see her as a threat to her baby son or her daughter. Is that all correct?"

"Yes, Dr. Klein, that about sums it up. We believed that Amy died from SIDS, and when it happened to Hope . . . well, I can only say, my suspicions were raised then. That is just not natural to happen twice. Then, when Hannah was arrested for attempting to murder Ty, it was hard to believe. But that's when we knew something was very wrong. Our son was devastated by the loss of his daughters, I can tell you. Now, that he's losing his wife, too, he sees his mission as protecting his son."

"Again, Mr. and Mrs. Fields, I appreciate your input. I won't keep you any longer. You've been more helpful than you know. I hope you both have a good week-end."

"Thank you, Dr. Klein. We are sorry we were unable to be there to support our son and grandson, but with our age and the distance between us, it has been difficult," Mr. Fields said, speaking up for the first time. He was obviously a man of few words.

Rosie looked at the couple on her screen. They were peaceful, their faces were mature and kind, the way people who have lived a good life seem to be.

Man of few words, or not, he seems to be a very caring one, she thought.

CHAPTER 41

TRIAL PREPARATION

After closing off with the Fields, she had a few minutes to write notes before 10 a.m. Exactly on time, Big John walked through the double doors and stood in the lobby. Rosie, still at the receptionist's desk, welcomed him to her Summerhill office. Briefly shaking hands, they walked down the narrow hall toward her private office. He took a seat in the large, wing back chair.

"Would you like a cup of Rosie's brewed coffee? I'm going to have a mug, myself," she said.

"You drive a hard bargain. Black suits me fine, Rosie." She handed him a sturdy mug, steaming hot.

"You should be impressed. Since last I saw you, I've interviewed Hannah one more time, met with Carly, her best friend, and just hung up from a conference call with Mr. and Mrs. Fields, her husband's parents."

"Impressive! Well done, So, let's get down to work on your very relevant testimony."

"Will Matthew Murphy provide the three judges with an opening statement?"

"Yes. You know the drill, Rosie. Although, when

three judges conduct a sentencing hearing, it may not be what you're accustomed to. Would you say?"

"I've only testified before a three-judge panel on a couple of death-penalty cases. We've never jumped the gun and gone straight to a sentencing hearing before," she said.

"Following Matt's opening statement, I will render my opening statement. At my table will be Hannah Fields and Dee Wakefield. Hannah will be in street clothes. If she doesn't have anything appropriate to wear, Dee will purchase something conservative for her."

"Interesting. I hadn't thought of that. With Matt Murphy's position on Hannah's culpability, or lack thereof, what kind of an opening will he provide?"

"He will apprise the Court that the State wishes to dismiss the charges of murder and attempted murder. Having reviewed the evidence, the State believes that Hannah Fields does, in fact, suffer from PTSD and Delusional Disorder with Paranoid Ideation. He will explain that, in his opinion, these conditions warrant placement in a facility for the criminally insane."

"It won't surprise you to hear she's a survivor of an incestual childhood, culminating in an abortion. I think it was her natural father's child."

"Well, there you go. That was probably what sent her down this path. If parents only realized how devastating sexual abuse, especially incestual abuse is, and that it changes a child forever, they would watch them more closely. It's forever, you know, the changes that are made."

"I know. I wish I could tell it to the world. By the way, that will simplify my testimony, right? Matt is basically accepting the 'not-guilty by reason of insanity' plea and going as far as making a placement recommendation with which you and I concur. I would like to bring out that Delusional Disorder differs from Schizophrenia in that a person's life may appear normal. Their mental illness only appears relative to the nature of their false beliefs. That's why it's extremely difficult for their family and friends to identify this extremely, dangerous, profoundly serious condition."

"Absolutely correct, Rosie. Educating these judges won't hurt a bit. It may assist them on other cases in the future. It may even set a precedent in Ohio. Maybe other attorneys will view your testimony in Courts of Appeal for years to come."

"When I couple her delusional beliefs with her chronic, pervasive post-traumatic stress disorder, they will understand how deadly a combination that can be," Rosie said.

"Well, that about wraps it up. Just go enjoy the rest of your weekend, Rosie, Doctor's orders. By the way, I happened to hear that the University of Toledo baseball team is playing the last home baseball game this afternoon. Don't think about submitting a report until you receive notice of a hearing date."

"I might take you up on that prescription. First, let me show you around before you leave."

"I would like that since I drove all the way out here," Big John said.

"This is my group room where we recline in easy chairs or on the carpet around this low table. You know you can refer clients to me. Most of my practice is not of a forensic nature."

"Yes, of course, I realize that and to tell the truth, I heard from other lawyers that you helped some of their sons, daughters, and even wives suffering from situational depression or fear and anxiety."

"I do what I can. It's nice to know it's appreciated. Thanks for letting me know."

Proceeding down the hall, Rosie showed Big John her art and family therapy room having shelves lined with board games, art materials, and chalk. In the far corner sat a huge roll of banner paper.

"I frequently have families draw pictures of themselves having fun together. They can take the banner home and hang it on a wall," she said. "Their decision-making and dialogue tell me so much about their family dynamics."

They stepped out the building together and wished one another a good week. Rosie headed home to sweep up Jocko for a quick, brisk walk. She listened to praise music on the radio and felt blessed beyond belief. The rest of her day would be filled with baseball and after-game pizza, win, or lose, at Marion's. She looked forward to seeing Bucky soon.

***

Big John, on the other hand, was thinking whether it would be inappropriate for Rosie to counsel his own teen-age son, John Jr., who seemed to be withdrawn and less interested in high school friends or activities of late. He planned to take this up with his wife as soon as they found an afternoon without work-related responsibilities. John's wife, a high school librarian, was more in-tune to kids of their son's generation. She often tried to show him how to remain alert to John Jr.'s moods and school performance. She might think having their son see Dr. Rosie as a good idea.

***

Later, when Rosie arrived at the ballfield wearing her University of Toledo blue and gold jersey, and her baseball cap, Julie Matthews, wife of assistant coach, Luke Matthews, quickly took her aside. Rosie followed her behind the bleachers where the spectators and fans could not hear their conversation.

"Just want you to know, there's going to be a special celebration honoring Bucky's years of commitment to the athletic program and his teams," Julie told her. "It will be held at Marion's, but in a private room. The President of the University as well as the Athletic Director will be presenting him with some handsome plaques. I believe the teams have also purchased gifts with their autographs on it."

"Oh, Julie, that's so nice! He will really be touched and appreciate it. He has such mixed emotions about leaving his role as varsity baseball coach and taking on the new position as University Athletic Director. It eases his mind knowing your husband will be a great coach and mentor for these young men."

"Good, so now you're forewarned. I didn't want

it to take you by surprise. Let's take our seats in the first row beside Sean Simmons' parents, and cheer our team on to victory." Julie gave Rosie a pat on the shoulder and a happy smile as they walked to their seats.

The game went into extra innings after Sean's base hit in the bottom of the ninth brought in the tying run from third base. The crowd cheered and the home team came running out of the dugout to swamp Sean and give each other high fives. After two more scoreless innings, the Toledo Rocket's shortstop hit a walk-off home run to end the game with a 3-2 win for Toledo, his team. Before Bucky could move, the team captains dumped a large, bucket of cold water over his head, the traditional way to end a season.

Most of the fans knew about the surprise party to be held for Bucky Walker, their esteemed coach. Bucky, drenching wet, showered and changed his shirt and pants in the locker room. By the time Bucky and Rosie arrived at Marion's, the parking lot was at capacity. Julie had suggested that Rosie tell Bucky some of their close friends were in the back of the restaurant holding seats for them.

"Geez," Bucky said, as he spotted the large crowd standing with bottles and glasses held high in the private room. He turned around just as the team was about to encircle him and lift him on their shoulders.

Pizza, drinks, and cake were served before the celebration began. Luke Matthews spoke on behalf of the team and presented Bucky with a plaque and a gift card to Dicks Sporting Goods. Sean Simmons gave a speech about all Bucky meant to the guys on the team and presented him a team jersey with a large number "1" on the back. Each team member had autographed the front and shoulders of the jersey.

"Aww, you guys. . . I'll wear this forever," Bucky laughed and joked in deep appreciation and camaraderie. He was loving it. Co-captains of other years were there and presented Bucky with team pictures and autographs on the back.

Finally, John Lazarus, the retiring Athletic Director, shared his hopes for the future of the University's athletics under the new leadership of Bucky Walker. Lastly, the President of the University of Toledo, Richard Hunt, explained how proud the University was to have such an honorable, committed, knowledgeable man coming on the faculty. He handed Bucky an engraved, solid oak name plate to place in front of his desk in his new office.

"Just so we don't forget your name, somehow," he said, trying for a little levity.

Bucky was speechless. He was left standing up front, alone. He began by thanking everyone, especially his staff, his teams, the honored guests and spouses, and the fans and families of the players.

"I am so honored to have been head coach of this team and all preceding teams through my years here at the University of Toledo. I will always be your number one fan. I will wear this jersey with great pride, unless I frame it first! Remember, my door will always be open to you . . . each, and every one of you. . . anytime! Stop by and know I am there for you, guys, if you need me. For all you returning players next season, enjoy the journey with Coach Matthews. He is one of the best, and you will learn great things from him. Thank you. . . thank you all, very much."

Rosie could see tears in his eyes.

CHAPTER 42

DR. KLEIN TESTIFIES

*The day of Hannah Field's sentencing tria*l was finally at hand. Dr. Rosie Klein, in a navy suit with cream-colored silk blouse, pearl earrings, and navy pumps, took a seat in the third row on the left of the courtroom. In the first row, sat Hannah between Dee Wakefield and attorney John Chickalette. As planned, Hannah wore a simple, button down, long sleeved, white blouse tucked into a pair of black trousers. Her hair was pulled back into a ponytail secured by a black elastic band.

Across the aisle, to the right of them, sat Matthew Murphy along with just one other prosecutor. Rosie recognized Bart Meyer. Unbeknownst to the public Bart would soon be stepping into Matt's role as the senior assistant Lucas County prosecutor.

Just prior to the official beginning of the hearing, Jerry Fields slipped into an aisle seat in the last row behind Dr. Rosie. Lisa Turner accompanied by Hannah's grandparents, Mr. and Mrs. Michaels, and her uncle, Ty Michaels, took seats directly across from Mr. Fields. They all acknowledged one another with quiet nods.

As Rosie glanced over her shoulder, she recognized a professionally-dressed young woman with an unknown, well-groomed man taking seats beside the Michaels family. Only Lisa Turner and Dr. Rosie knew the gentleman was Dr. Fritz Messing, Hannah's nerdy friend from long ago. The woman with him was Carly Pendleton from Clifton, Ohio, and they were present to lend support to Hannah Fields. Carly had contacted Lisa Turner for permission to attend and requested specifics in terms of date and time.

The bailiff, Bill Gorman, stood barring the door to the judge's chambers and Officer Poole, who had escorted Hannah from the jail, stood beside him against the wall. As the judge opened his chambers door, two judges could be seen behind him. The bailiff announced their entrance.

"All rise."

Everyone stood as the three judges came through the doorway and took their seats behind a high, wooden platform. Presiding Judge Joyce King took a seat between Judge D.P Tucker, and Judge Kate Brown. Judge King spoke to the courtroom.

"You may be seated."

The three officials looked striking dressed in black judicial robes, with serious looks upon their faces mixed with a soft kindness.

"Is the State ready to make their opening statement at this time?"

"Yes, your honor," Matthew Murphy said.

"If it pleases the court, I would like to inform the

court that the State is dropping the charge of Murder One and the Attempted Murder charge. Given the evidence, we are willing to accept a plea of Not Guilty by Reason of Insanity on both counts. We are deferring to the professional opinion of the expert witness, Dr. Rosie Klein, whose testimony the court will hear momentarily."

"Let me understand you Mr. Murphy," Judge King responded. "This defendant was indicted on one count of Murder of her minor daughter, Hope Fields, and one count of Attempted Murder of her minor son, Ty Fields. You are now willing to accept her pleas of Not Guilty and the expert witness for the defense is going to present testimony to validate Not Guilty by Reason of Insanity. Is that correct? Speak loud and distinctly so our court reporter can get this down accurately, please."

Sally Jacobs, the court reporter was seated at a small desk below the judges' bench. She stopped momentarily to hear Judge King's instructions which she decided to put into the record.

"Yes, your honor. You have correctly interpreted the State's position at this time," Matt answered in a deep, clear voice.

"Attorney Chickalette, do you have an opening statement, sir?" Judge King asked.

"Yes, your Honor, I do. With the court's permission, I will proceed."

"Please do."

Chickalette began: "Hannah Fields is not a murderer, by nature. Through her childhood, she, herself, was the helpless victim of numerous heinous crimes which Dr. Klein will identify for the court. Her commission of the crimes for which she has been charged came as a direct result of the serious mental illness to which she succumbed following the abuses inflicted upon herself. Her mental illness was never diagnosed and, therefore, she never received treatment."

Chickalette continued presenting to the court, his version of Hannah's fragile condition. He ended his opening statement by appealing to the court to hear the facts and honor the recommendations made collectively by Matthew Murphy, himself, and Dr. Rosie Klein, court-appointed forensic psychologist.

At this point, Judge King turned and spoke quietly to Judges Tucker and Brown. Then, she addressed the lawyers.

"We would like to adjourn to our chambers to discuss this serious matter off the record. Attorneys Murphy and Chickalette, please follow us. Your co-counsels may remain seated here until we return. Is that understood?"

"Of course, your Honor," Chickalette answered.

"Absolutely," Matthew Murphy responded as he rose from his seat to follow.

The bailiff requested the courtroom rise as the judges stood to leave the room. People spoke quietly amongst themselves for the next fifteen minutes. Then the bailiff, again, requested everyone to rise as the judges and attorneys returned to the courtroom.

"You may all be seated," Judge King said. "Please

call your first witness, Mr. Chickalette."

John Chickalette called Dr. Rosie Klein to the witness stand. The court reporter rose from her chair and placed a Bible on the ledge in front of where Rosie stood.

"Do you swear to tell the truth, the whole truth, and nothing but the truth, so help you God?" Sally Jacobs asked.

Dr. Rosie placed her left hand on the Bible, lifted her right hand, and said, "I do."

"You may be seated Dr. Klein."

Attorney Chickalette ran through Rosie's credentials just for purpose of the record while every professional in the courtroom including the attending Press waited expectantly to hear what she would say. Wes Hall, investigative reporter for The Toledo Blade, quietly took a seat just inside the doors. He had produced evidence for Rosie in previous cases that often helped shape the outcomes one way or another. Sometimes, evidence that he had produced surprised her, and had changed Rosie's point of view. Other times, his information had confirmed the position she held from materials read and interviews she had personally conducted. Most assuredly, Wes Hall was an asset to Dr. Rosie.

Now, Chickalette allowed Dr. Rosie to "run with it" as they said in legal circles. Rather than to ask question after question about Hannah Fields' personal, social, mental history, or her state of mind at the time of the offenses, he posed one simple question. In that manner, Dr. Klein could answer it in paragraphs rather than two or four word responses, such as "Yes, Sir," "No, Sir," or "I don't know, Sir."

Attorney Murphy voiced no objections to anything brought forward by the defense attorney regarding the Court-Appointed Expert Witness. He politely listened to the surprise of many attendees. He also took notes and, without facial expression, made frequent eye contact with Dr. Klein.

Previously, Dr. Klein had submitted a detailed report to the court and now without cross-examination, basically deferred to its contents. She discussed Hannah's childhood abuse, the impregnation and abortion at the hands of her father, the completion of high school in the custody of her maternal grandparents, and her quick marriage to Jerry Fields.

Dr. Klein went on to explain the delayed onset of Post-Traumatic Stress Disorder triggered by the birth of a baby girl. She told of Hannah's delusions of severe harm being rendered to her daughter and coupled with flashbacks and nightmares of her own abuse, how Hannah had transposed her own suffering to a possible abuse of her baby.

"Hannah believed she had no choice but to prevent an abuse of her second baby girl, by sending Amy 'into the arms of Jesus', as she told me on several occasions," Dr. Rosie said.

Inside the Judges' Chambers, it had previously been determined by the panel of judges that there would be no mention on record of the prior murder charge in Alaska, since Alaskan authorities had agreed to dismiss their case. Therefore, it was not to be considered in regard to sentencing for the crimes she committed in Ohio.

"Is there anything the State would like to ask, Prosecutor Murphy?" Judge King. Inquired.

"No, your honor," Attorney Murphy answered respectfully.

"And you, Attorney Chickalette?"

"Nothing, your Honor," Chickalette said.

"You may step down, Dr. Klein," the judge said. Dr. Rosie gathered her materials and returned to her seat.

Thank God, that's over, Rosie thought.

Prosecutor Murphy stood to address the Court.

"With permission," he said, "The State rests its case with the completion of Dr. Klein's testimony. The State wishes to thank Dr. Klein for her thorough evaluation. Your Honor, and Judges Tucker and Brown, the State would like to recommend Hannah Fields be placed at Dayton State Hospital until such time as the medical personnel treating her determine she should be released. The release, of course, would require a hearing and would be conditional upon her remaining compliant with medication and mental health treatment recommendations."

Attorney Chickalette stood and spoke. "The Defense is in total agreement with the mandate of the State and recommendations of Dr. Rosie Klein. We would also like the opportunity for Hannah to have visitation with her family."

"Before we conclude this hearing," Judge King said, "the Judges would like a thirty- minute recess for private consultation to consider these recommendations.

"Attorney Chickalette, please confer with your client as whether she has a statement she would like to make to the Court. If so, we will hear her remarks after the break." She hit her gavel and simultaneously rose with the other judges to retire to her chambers.

Neither the Prosecutor nor Defense Attorney were anticipating this action. Keeping their heads down, they glanced at one another and shrugged their shoulders. Bailiff Gorman, in a deep, loud voice announced. "Court is now in recess for thirty minutes. You may exit or remain seated, as you wish."

Chickalette turned to Hannah and beckoned Dr. Rosie to take a seat beside them.   "You don't need to say anything, Hannah. If you decide to speak, you will step to the podium where the Prosecutor and I stood and speak clearly into the microphone."

"Is it okay if I apologize for the heartache, I have caused my family, my husband, and my little son? I won't go so far as to ask for their forgiveness. That would require they understand my dilemma and I know they can't do that."

"Yes, Hannah, that would be very appropriate. Why not also thank the Court for the opportunity to be heard. Do you have any other suggestions, Dr. Klein?"

"I just want to say how brave you are, Hannah, to want to do that. The judge might ask you a question or two. You need to be prepared, and simply answer honestly."

"I've been preparing to speak, in case I had a chance," Hannah said. "I guess I didn't think about the fact that the Judges could ask me anything . . .but, I will take a chance. God is in control, now, and I will live with the outcome."

CHAPTER 43

THE SENTENCING

E*xactly thirty minutes later,* all three judges entered the courtroom, again, and took their seats.

"Attorney Chickalette, does Mrs. Fields have anything she would like to say to the Court?" Judge King inquired.

"Yes, your Honor. She would like to address the court at this time."

"You may step to the podium, Mrs. Fields," Judge King said removing her glasses and looking directly at the young woman now standing in front of her.

"Thank you, Judges, for permitting me to share my feelings," Hannah spoke clearly although softly while looking at the judges before her. "First, I want to apologize to my husband, Jerry Fields, for the pain I have caused him, and for now giving him the sole responsibility for raising our son, Ty. I would like to tell my family how sorry I am to have disappointed them. I thank them for taking me in years ago and giving me the two best years of my life. I am not asking for forgiveness.

I can't expect that from my loved ones and friends. Only God can provide that, and I will pray for that every day. Lastly, thank you to the professionals who have spent time with me while I waited in jail for this day. Without your support, I would not be standing here today." Tears glistened in her eyes as she looked downward.

When no one spoke, she looked up at her attorney, and he nodded approval. She returned to her seat between her attorneys.

"The court unanimously approves both the State's and Defense Counsel's positions," Judge King intoned. "Court is now adjourned. Mrs. Field's family may step forward to say good-bye to her." She tapped her gavel lightly. It was over.

Once all three judges left the courtroom, the attorneys walked out the back doors into the corridor. Bailiff Gorman and Officer Poole remained at the door to the judges' chambers. Lisa Turner escorted the Michaels family to where Hannah stood. Behind them was Jerry Fields. They stepped aside to allow Jerry to be the first to embrace his wife. Jerry hugged her warmly.

"You look good, Hannah. Everything will be okay. Don't worry about Ty or me. Just work on getting well. We love you."

"Your love means a lot, Jerry. Take good care of our little guy. I'll be fine. I hope you both can visit me soon. They say it isn't too far away." She spoke softly. Jerry walked away while wiping his eyes. He never noticed Carly and Fritz standing to the side waiting their turn.

Hannah huddled together and hugged her grandparents and her uncle, Ty. "We will keep you in our prayers, Hannah. God has a purpose for your life, Sweetie," her grandmother said. They kissed her cheeks and stepped back.

"Hello, Hannah."

Carly encircled her friend with both arms. "Now that we're near each other again, you can trust me to stay in close contact. Look who I brought with me." She pointed to the young doctor who had been Hannah's tutor and friend.

"Oh, my goodness, Fritz! How great to see you. How awful it's under these circumstances. I can't tell you how often I've thought of you and our times together." Hannah reached her hands out and took his hands in hers.

"I feel the same way, Hannah. If you would like to stay in touch, we can write back and forth. I'll come see you on weekends if I'm not on call," he said and smiled.

"You must be kidding, Fritz. You would drive all that way to visit?"

"Absolutely. I'll go the distance with you. I'm in this for the duration and will be here as long as you want to keep me in your life," Fritz said.

"I am sorry to break up this gathering," Office Poole said, "but it's time to return to jail, now, Hannah."

Everyone said their final good-byes and left the courtroom. Only Dr. Rosie remained.

"As soon as you are settled, Lisa Turner and I

plan to drive down for a visit. If there is anything you want us to bring, just drop me a line. Okay?"

"Okay, Dr. Klein. I can't thank you enough for what you have done to mend the bridges in my family. And now I have my two best friends back, Carly and Fritz." Hannah reached out and hugged Dr. Rosie then exited through the back door with Officer Poole.

There will be no contact with the press today. Thank God, Rosie thought.

As Rosie stepped into the main lobby on the ground floor, she spotted Bucky and Wes. "What are you two doing here together?"

"Remember, we're ball players. After you introduced us, we immediately started talking ballgames. You didn't see us in the courtroom for the hearing?"

"No, do you mean you sat through the entire morning?" Rosie asked.

"We did, and Rosie, you were great. You summed it all up in a nutshell. If you thought my article about sex trafficking on Mother's Day was good, wait till you see this bombshell article," Wes said. "It's quite a story."

As they exited through the front doors, they saw the prosecutors and defense attorneys confronted by cameras and reporters with microphones. Rosie felt relieved she had dodged that bullet. Wes would produce the most accurate, objective story and her words would not be twisted or distorted.

"How about lunch at Mancy's? Bucky said. "Wes, you're welcome to join us. But, Rosie, I must admit, Wes knows about a surprise I have for you."

"Thanks, but no thanks. Have a great weekend. Read the Toledo Blade on Sunday," Wes waved as he left.

Rosie turned to Bucky with a look of happiness.

"What surprise?"

"You'll see soon," he said with a mischievous smile, taking her hand and kissing it.

"I have a feeling the rest of my life is going to be full of surprises with you, Bucky Walker."

"I hope so, Rosie, I certainly hope so."

HOTLINE NUMBERS FOR
HUMAN TRAFFICKING / DOMESTIC VIOLENCE

Human Trafficking Hotline

1-888-373-7888

National Domestic Violence Hotline

1-800-799-7233 (SAFE)

Sexual Assault Hotline

1-800-656-4673 (HOPE)

TO COMBAT HUMAN TRAFFICKING CONTACT
THE FOLLOWING ORGANIZATIONS:

Stop the Traffick	https://www.stopthetraffik.org
Polaris Project	https://polarisproject.org
Free the Slaves:	https://www.freetheslaves.net

HOTLINE NUMBERS FOR

SUBSTANCE ABUSE AND/OR MENTAL HEALTH

Mental Health Hotline (Depression)
1-877-435-3741

National Helpline Referral Service for (SAMHSA)
Substance Abuse and/or Mental Health
1-800-662-4357 (HELP)

Suicide Prevention Hotline
1-800-273-8255

DISCUSSION QUESTIONS

1. Has your understanding of sex trafficking changed after seeing Sophie as a victim?

2. Does it surprise you that a woman is the key to luring and abducting girls for trafficking?

3. Is there anything Doris Simpson or Sophie's counselor could have said or done to prevent Sophie's drastic actions toward Farid?

4. What did Sophie's counselor, Maria Gomez, recommend or encourage Sophie to do rather than to remain in the abusive situation? Did she recommend anything at all?

5. Could rape charges have been filed against Hannah's father at this time?

6. During Hannah's life with Jerry, where was any fault? What could have made a difference?

7. What is your opinion of Jerry Fields, and why?

8. Should Bucky accept the promotion as Athletic Director? Why or why not?

9. How would you describe Rosie's relationships with her friends, colleagues, and mother?

10. Name some personality differences and similarities between Rosie and Bucky.

ABOUT THE AUTHOR

About Phyllis Kuehnl-Walters Ph. D.

A retired clinical psychologist from Ohio, I live at The Villages, Florida, and write inspirational self-help books meant to encourage the reader to joyfully finish the race set forth by God.

On December 1, 2019, I began another genre writing on cases I cannot forget. My first novel *The Christmas Slayings* was inspired by an evaluation I completed on a young woman charged with murder. It will touch your heart! *Wives Who Kill,* is my second novel in the series based on two women I can't forget.

In addition to a career in private practice, I have had the privilege of teaching at The University of Dayton and other Dayton area colleges. Most recently, I taught the subject matter of my books to retirees at The Enrichment Academy in The Villages, Florida. I continue to lead Bible studies at church and am the Academic Dean and instructor at Casa Hope, a Christian transitional living house for young men who have struggled with addictions and/or served time for drug-related offenses. I develop courses that are relevant to their success and teach classes implementing the books I have written. My former students have encouraged me to write the inspirational books.

Recently, I have written a Christian book based on my keynote presentation at the North Lake Presbyterian Church 2020 retreat. *Become a Beacon of Light: Develop the Fruit of the Spirit and reflect God's love.* This book takes you through the Divine Fruits of Love, Joy, Peace, Patience, Kindness, Goodness, Faithfulness, Gentleness, and Self-Control and provides a three-week Action Plans to further cultivate the Fruit of your spirit. In the paperback edition, there is a twenty-one day Gratitude Journal section as well as an index of Bible verses or Books used in the contents of the book. (May, 2020)

I am a member of the Florida Writers Association, Word Weavers International, and Writers League of The Villages. Professionally I maintain memberships in Ohio Women In Psychology, Ohio Psychological Association (Emeritus), and the American Psychological Association (Emeritus).

Personally, I have been blessed with a balanced life as a mother, wife, grandmother, aunt, friend, beloved daughter and more recently, sister. I don't believe we were meant to simply retire, but to re-fire our passion in a new direction. Writing is now my passion. My hope is to inspire others to understand their purpose in life and believe they are equipped to achieve it.

I look forward to sharing that Good News with you.

MORE BOOKS BY PHYLLIS K. WALTERS

One Week . Six Murders. Based on a True Story. On her 21st birthday, Angel Morgan steps out of Juvenile Detention after serving five years for grand theft auto. The next 12 hours will change the course of her life forever. About to purchase a bus ticket to live on the beaches of Florida, she meets Sam and April. Never having any real friends before, these two offer Angel comfort such as she's never known before. Little does she suspect their dark path will turn her world upside down. Soon, angel is sitting in prison awaiting sentencing for six murders committed by her new "friends" in the week before Christmas.

Then, Dr. Rosie Klein, enters Angel's life. A court-appointed forensic psychologist, Dr. Klein looks at all the mitigating factors of Angel's childhood that could influence the Judge in sentencing this young woman, including abuse suffered at the hands of her mother and the men who used her.Angel takes Dr. Klein on a journey depicting the slayings of six innocent people the week before Christmas and to which Angel becomes guilty by association. In her 35-year career as a forensic psychologist, Dr. Phyllis Kuehnl-Walters has written this book inspired by this one case she will never forget.

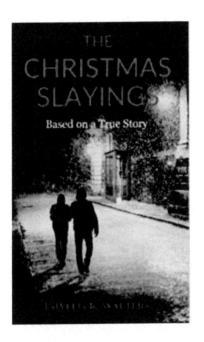

THE CHRISTMAS SLAYINGS

Available now on amazon.com and

www.thewritersmall.com

Worry,
Fret, and
Fear...
No More!

Covid-19 Edition

Phyllis Kuehnl-Walters, Ph.D.

Worry, Fret, and
Fear... No More!

Study Guide &
Gratitude Journal

Phyllis Kuehnl-Walters, Ph.D.

WORRY, FRET, AND FEAR... NO MORE!
Covid-19 Edition

This is a six-week challenge for you to stop worrying and build faith and confidence.

learn to face your fears while moving forward toward a life filled with hope and a sense of purpose. Read, write, pray, and plan your next six weeks to be followed by the rest of your life!

Completing this challenge will put your concerns in perspective. It will foster confidence as you will remember who you are; a child of a merciful, loving God. Know that He loves you and that with the direction of the Holy Spirit all things will work out for your own good.

ALSO AVAILABLE!

A companion workbook to Worry, Fret, and Fear... No More!

This workbookhelps you write out your thoughts and feelings as you go through your six-week challenge as suggested in the primary book.

AVAILABLE ON AMAZON.COM AND THROUGH HTTPS://WWW.THEWRITERSMALL.COM

Become a Beacon of Light

Develop the Fruit of the Spirit
and Reflect God's Love

Phyllis Kuehnl-Walters, Ph.D.

Creating Balance & Purpose in Life

Finding Meaning in All Seasons &
Stages of Life

Phyllis Kuehnl-Walters, Ph.D.

BECOME A BEACON OF LIGHT:
DEVELOP THE FRUIT OF THE SPIRIT AND REFLECT GOD'S LOVE

Dr. Phyllis Kuehnl-Walters guides the reader in becoming more like Jesus by developing the gifts of the Fruit of the Spirit. Her personal story, scripture and other supportive information provides a sound, enlightening and thought provoking read. Action plans and Group Discussion Questions promote personal growth and/or group study.

CREATING BALANCE & PURPOSE IN LIFE

In Creating Balance & Purpose in Life, the reader will be led to create balance in this season of life: physical, mental, emotional, social, and spiritual. The emphasis will be on learning to deal effectively with life transitions and unforeseen challenges. The reader will develop strategies for planning and implementing purposeful goals to experience joy, peace, dignity.

Available on **Amazon.com** and at

www.**TheWritersMall.com**

Made in the USA
Middletown, DE
30 March 2021